China's Global Rebalancing and the New Silk Road

B.R. Deepak
Editor

China's Global Rebalancing and the New Silk Road

Springer

Editor
B.R. Deepak
Jawaharlal Nehru University
New Delhi
India

ISBN 978-981-10-5971-1 ISBN 978-981-10-5972-8 (eBook)
https://doi.org/10.1007/978-981-10-5972-8

Library of Congress Control Number: 2017947838

Printed on acid-free paper

This Springer imprint is published by Springer Nature
The registered company is Springer Nature Singapore Pte Ltd.
The registered company address is: 152 Beach Road, #21-01/04 Gateway East, Singapore 189721, Singapore

Preface

In 2015 between 26 and 29 March, China convened its 14th annual event, the Boao Forum for Asia. The theme of the forum was "Asia's New Future: Towards a Community of Common Destiny." The 'community of common destiny' in Asia and beyond was to be realized through the 'project of the century'—the 'Belt and Road' Initiative (BRI), and it was during this forum that the National Development and Reform Commission, Ministry of Foreign Affairs, and the Ministry of Commerce of the People's Republic of China, with State Council authorization issued the 'Vision and Actions on Jointly Building Silk Road Economic Belt and 21st-Century Maritime Silk Road' which for the first time clarified the framework, principles, cooperation priorities and mechanisms of the initiative.

Coinciding with the Boao Forum for Asia, I convened an international conference in Jawaharlal Nehru University (JNU) titled "Silk Road Economic Belt and the 21st Century Maritime Silk Route: Opportunities and Challenges", perhaps the first of its kind in India on 26–27 March 2015. Over two dozen papers were presented by scholars expounding civilizational, geopolitical and geo-economic paradigms of the New Silk Road, as well as the rivalry between the established hegemon and the challenger. With the passage of time, there is an increasing level of clarity about the 'Belt and Road.' The identification of the pivot cities and ports within China and connecting these to the six economic corridors has lifted the veil from China's intended foreign policy goals. This undoubtedly has invited a much fury from some countries, but also nearly 70 countries across Asia, Europe and Africa have expressed their support for the Chinese initiative. The institutionalization of the 'Belt and Road' Forum, after it was first convened in Beijing in May 2017, demonstrates China's seriousness about the initiative.

It was with this background that I requested scholars from China, India, Uzbekistan, Pakistan, Germany and ASEAN etc. countries to organize their thoughts and contribute to this volume. The topics they covered are vide ranging—from India–China and the ancient silk route spirit; Bangladesh, China, India, Myanmar Economic Corridor (BCIM), China–Pakistan Economic Corridor (CPEC), China–Mongolia–Russia Economic Corridor, China–Central Asia Economic Corridor, China–Indochina Peninsula Economic Corridor, the US and the BRI, dealing with the risks of BRI, and the role China perceives for itself in the emerging international order, etc. The papers delve into various facets of the BRI, including economic integration, regional development, and strategic considerations of respective countries, as well as building common security, cultural, and economic communities at regional and trans-regional levels.

I would like to record my thanks to all the contributors for their cooperation at various levels, because without their support it would have been impossible to imagine the publication of this volume. Besides them, there are numerous other people who helped me in this endeavour. I wish particularly to thank Prof. Girijesh Pant, the then Dean of School of International Studies, Jawaharlal Nehru University, Shri Tarun Vijay, the then Rajya Sabha (upper house) Member of Parliament, Ambassador Le Yucheng, the then Ambassador Extraordinary and Plenipotentiary of the P.R.C to the Republic of India for supporting my initiative at that time, and thus initiating public policy debate on the issue in India.

New Delhi, India B.R. Deepak

Contents

Editors and Contributors

About the Editor

Prof. B.R. Deepak (狄伯杰) was trained in Chinese history and India–China relations at the Peking University and Chinese Academy of Social Sciences, Beijing, at Jawaharlal Nehru University, New Delhi, and University of Edinburgh, UK. He has been the Nehru and Asia Fellow at the Chinese Academy of Social Sciences, Beijing. Dr. Deepak's publications include *India and China: Foreign Policy Approaches and Responses* (2016), *India and China 1904–2004: A Century of Peace and Conflict* (2005); *India–China Relations in first half of the Twentieth Century* (2001); *India–China Relations: Future Perspectives* (co ed. 2012); *India–China Relations: Civilizational Perspective* (2012) *China: Agriculture, Countryside and Peasants* (2010); and *Confucius Sukti Sangrah* (The Analects of Confucius) (2016). The author has been a visiting professor at the Chinese Academy of Social Sciences, Tianjin Foreign Studies University, Beijing Language University, China, Doon University, Dehradun, India, and Teaching Fellow at the Scottish Centre for Chinese Studies in the University of Edinburgh, UK.

Contributors

Bruno Jetin Institute of Asian Studies, University of Brunei, Gadong, Brunei Darussalam

Jingkui Jiang Centre for South Asian Studies, Peking University, Beijing, China

Jianxue Lan China Institute of International Studies (CIIS), Beijing, China

Chintamani Mahapatra Centre for Canadian, US and Latin American Studies, Jawaharlal Nehru University, New Delhi, India

Ahmad Rashid Malik Institute of Strategic Studies, Islamabad, Pakistan

Reena Marwah Indian Council of Social Science Research, New Delhi, India

Guoxing Ouyang Hainan Institute for World Watch, Hainan, China

Ajay Patnaik Centre for Russian and Central Asian Studies, Jawaharlal Nehru University, New Delhi, India

Williams Lawrence S. Prabhakar Madras Christian College, Chennai, India

Mirzokhid Rakhimov Institute of History, Academy of Sciences, Tashkent, Uzbekistan

Sharad K. Soni Centre for Inner Asian Studies, Jawaharlal Nehru University, New Delhi, India

Honggang Wang Institute of World Politics, CICIR, Beijing, China

Yiwei Wang Chongyang Institute for Financial Studies, Renmin University, Beijing, China

Siegfried O. Wolf South Asia Democratic Forum, Brussels, Belgium

Xiaoping Yang National Institute of International Strategy, Chinese Academy of Social Sciences, Beijing, China

Abbreviations

ADB	Asian Development Bank
ADIZ	Air Defence Identification Zone
ADMM	ASEAN Defence Minister's Meeting
AEC	ASEAN Economic Community
AEP	Act East Policy
AIF	ASEAN Infrastructure Fund
AIIB	Asian Infrastructure Investment Bank
AIIF	Asian Infrastructure Investment Fund
AMPC	ASEAN Master Plan for Connectivity
AMS	ASEAN Member State
APEC	Asia Pacific Economic Cooperation
APTA	Asia Pacific Trade Agreement
ARN	ASEAN Roll-On Roll-Off Network
ASEAN	Association of South East Asian Nations
BCIM EC	Bangladesh, China, India Myanmar Economic Corridor
BIMP-EAGA	Brunei Darussalam-Indonesia-Malaysia-Philippines East ASEAN Growth Area
BIMST-EC	Bangladesh-India-Myanmar Sri Lanka-Thailand Economic Cooperation
BRI	Belt and Road Initiative
CACO	Central Asian Cooperation Organizations
CAICF	China-ASEAN Investment Cooperation Fund
CECA	Comprehensive Economic Cooperation Agreement
CEPA	Comprehensive Economic Partnership Agreement
CES	Common Economic Space
CIMC	China International Marine Containers (Group) Ltd.
CIS	Commonwealth of Independent States
CLGFEA	Central Leading Group on Financial and Economic Affairs
CNSC	Central National Security Commission
COMECON	Council for Mutual Economic Assistance

CPEC	China–Pakistan Economic Corridor
CSTO	Collective Security Treaty Organization
EAEC	East Asia Economic Caucus
EAEU	Eurasian Economic Union
ECO	Organization of Economic Cooperation
ECS	East China Sea
EDCA	Enhanced Defence Cooperation Agreement
EEC	Eurasian Economic Community
EEU	Eurasian Economic Union
EEZ	Exclusive Economic Zone
EHP	Early Harvest Programme
FATA	Federal Administered Tribal Areas
GCA	Greater Central Asia
GCC	Gulf Cooperation Council
GMI	Ganga-Mekong Initiative
GMS	Grand Mekong Subregion
GVC	Global Value Chain
IMT-GT	Indonesia-Malaysia-Thailand Growth Triangle
INSTC	International North-South Transport Corridor
IONS	Indian Ocean Naval Symposium
IOR	Indian Ocean Region
IPP	Independent Power Projects
ISIS	Islamic State of Iraq and Syria
JETRO	Japan External Trade Organization
JMSDF	Japanese Maritime Self-Defence Force
KKH	Karakoram Highway
KPK	Khyber-Pakhtunkhwa
LEP	Look East Policy
MSR	Maritime Silk Road
NATO	North Atlantic Treaty Organization
NDB	BRICS New Development Bank
NDRC	National Development and Reform Commission
NPIWC	National Propaganda and Ideology Work Conference
NSA	National Security Advisor
NSP	Net Security Provider
NTC	Non-tariff comprehensive Trade Costs
OBOR	One Belt One Road
OIC	Organizations of Islamic Cooperation
PCPCCC	Politburo of the Communist Party of China Central Committee
PLA-N	People's Liberation Army Navy
PTA	Preferential Trade Agreement
RCEP	Regional Comprehensive Economic Partnership
RETRACK	Reorganization of Transport Network by Advancing Rail Freight Concepts
RTA	Regional Trade Area

SAFTA	South Asian Free Trade Area
SCO	Shanghai Cooperation Organization
SCS	South China Sea
SKRL	Singapore-Kunming Rail Link
SLF	Silk Road Fund
SLOC	Sea Line of Communication
SR	Special Representative
SREB	Silk Road Economic Belt
TPP	Trans-Pacific Partnership
TRACECA	Transport Corridor of Europe-Caucasus-Asia
TTIP	Transatlantic Trade and Investment Partnership
UIC	International Union of Railways
UNCLOS	United Nations Convention on the Law of the Sea

Chapter 1
China's Global Rebalancing: Will It Reshape the International Political and Economic Order?

B.R. Deepak

Ever since being elected as the General Secretary of the Communist Party of China (CPC) in November 2012 and subsequently the President of China in March 2013, Xi Jinping has put forth grandiose ideas like the 'Chinese Dream', the 'Belt and Road Initiative' (BRI), or the 'One Belt One Road' (OBOR), the literal translation of *yidai yilu*. The former aims to 'realize the great rejuvenation of the Chinese nation', by realizing the two centenary goals, i.e., to double the 2010 GDP per-capita income and build a moderately prosperous society by 2021 when the Communist Party of China marks its 100th anniversary; and second goal is to turn China into an all-around modern and socially advanced country by 2049 when the People's Republic marks its centenary. The BRI refers to setting up of a geopolitical and geo-economic Silk Road Economic Belt (SREB) and the 21st Century Maritime Silk Road (MSR) connecting China to Arica and Europe by land and sea.

These grandiose initiatives, especially the BRI, have raised hopes as well as suspicions as to what China is up to, and that, even if silk routes existed in ancient times, what is the relevance of such initiatives in modern times? Also, whether such initiatives are in sync with China's foreign-policy goals, such as multi-polarity, not seeking hegemony, common security, etc., or an antidote to the US foreign-policy goals like 'pivot to Asia' or 'Trans Pacific Partnership' (TPP), albeit the context may change as Donald Trump abrogated the TPP immediately after assuming the office. Or, is China challenging the US hegemony and rewriting the rules of global political and economic order?

These are some of the questions which have been debated ever since the idea was floated, and more specifically, since May 2017, when China convened the Belt and Road Forum in Beijing, attended by 1,500 delegates from across the world and

B.R. Deepak (✉)
Centre for Chinese and Southeast Asian Studies, Jawaharlal Nehru University, New Delhi, India
e-mail: bdeepak@mail.jnu.ac.in

B.R. Deepak (ed.), *China's Global Rebalancing and the New Silk Road*,
https://doi.org/10.1007/978-981-10-5972-8_1

which had 29 heads of the states and officials, entrepreneurs, financiers, academicians and journalists from over 130 countries, including figures such as Vladimir Putin, UN Secretary-General António Guterres, World Bank President Jim Yong Kim, and Managing Director of the International Monetary Fund Christine Lagarde, etc. In order to bulldoze the $1.4 trillion 'project of the century', Xi Jinping pledged $14.49 billion more to the existing $40 billion Silk Road Fund founded in late 2014. The Development Bank of China and the Export-Import Bank of China pledged to inject $124 billion into the Belt and Road Initiative to support infrastructure, financing, and industrial capacity (Deepak 2017a).[1] On the occasion, China also signed 76 megaprojects with Belt and Road countries, signed trade cooperation deals with 30 countries, and signed agreements related to unimpeded trade with 60 countries. What exactly is the BRI? Why at all China has initiated this strategy? Furthermore, the geographical boundary of the BRI was further extended to Latin America, thus bringing the entire globe into the ambit of the New Silk Road.

1 Intent, Content and Aim of the BRI

Well, the concept was first proposed by Xi Jinping during a speech at Nazarbayev University, Kazakhstan, on 7 September 2013 when he said that "To forge closer economic ties, deepen cooperation and expand development in the Euro-Asia region, we should take an innovative approach and jointly build an 'economic belt' along the silk road. This will be a great undertaking benefitting the people of all countries along the route". Xi (2014) proposed that traffic connectivity needs to be improved so as to open the strategic regional thoroughfare from the Pacific Ocean to the Baltic Sea and gradually move toward creating a network of transportation that connects Eastern, Western, and Southern Asia. The Chinese president also urged the regional members to promote local-currency settlement so as to improve their immunity to financial risks and their global competitiveness.[2] In October, he visited Indonesia and floated the idea of building a twenty first-century MSR with the aim to deepen China's economic and maritime links with the MSR countries and regions. The MSR begins in Fuzhou's Quanzhou in southeast China's Fujian province and extends south into the ASEAN nations, crosses the Malacca Strait, and turns west to countries along the Indian Ocean before meeting the land-based Silk Road in Venice via the Red Sea and Mediterranean. Under the ambit of MSR, China plans to build hard and soft infrastructure from Indo-Pacific to Africa, including transport, energy, water management, communication, earth monitoring, economic, and social infrastructure.

[1] Deepak (2017a).

[2] Xi (2014).

During the Boao Forum for Asia convened in Sanya, Hainan, 26–29 March 2015, China's National Development and Reform Commission (NDRC), Ministry of Foreign Affairs, and Ministry of Commerce issued an action plan on the Belt and Road initiative on 28 March. The document points out that economic connectivity is the heart of the matter for which Xi Jinping also announced the establishment of a Silk Road Fund with US$40-billion to support infrastructure investments in the countries involved and have also linked the establishment of Asia Infrastructure Investment Bank (AIIB) and BRICS New Development Bank (NDB) to the initiative. The document talks about a 'Silk Road Spirit', interpreted as "peace and cooperation, openness and inclusiveness, mutual learning, and mutual benefits." It states that the initiative is in line with the purposes and principles of the UN Charter. Since the initiative is open and inclusive, former Chinese ambassador to India, Le Yucheng, does not subscribe it as a Chinese solo but 'a symphony performed by various countries.'[3] The document identifies five major goals of the initiative in terms of promoting policy coordination, facilitating connectivity, uninterrupted trade, financial integration, and people-to-people exchanges. Professor Wang Yiwei of Renmin University, Beijing, recommends yet another element to it, i.e., the interconnected network, the Internet Silk Road.[4] Thus the idea may be turned into 'one belt, two roads' in the future.

In order to facilitate these 'five connectivity goals,' China has identified six major economic corridors along the BRI for a new type of regional development model. These are: the Bangladesh, China, India, Myanmar Economic Corridor (BCIM); the China Pakistan Economic Corridor (CPEC); the New Eurasia Land Bridge; the China, Mongolia, Russia Economic Corridor; the China Central Asia economic corridor; and the China Indochina Peninsula Economic Corridor. China has committed US$46 billion to the CPEC, which has been selected as the pilot project. If the recent reports are to be believed, China's investment in its CPEC has already reached US$62 billion, increasing more than 34% from its initial investment of US$46 billion.[5] CPEC will link the Pakistani city of Gwadar to China's Xinjiang via a vast network of highways, railways, and oil and gas pipelines. The above six corridors have connected more than 10 Chinese provinces with Asia, Africa, and Europe. For example, Yunnan has become a hub connecting China to Southeast Asia and South Asia. Kunming, the capital city of Yunnan, would be connected to various transport corridors, the most ambitious of these—the Trans-Asia Railway (TAR)—to be completed by 2020, connecting Kunming to Singapore. In the same vein, Xinjiang is turning into a hub for connecting China with Central Asia, South Asia, and Fujian as a fulcrum for the twenty first century MSR. It has been reported that, by 2020, China will build 172 major water-conservancy projects with an investment of US$87.6 billion, and by 2030,

[3]Deepak (2016).

[4]Wang, Yiwei. *The Belt and Road Initiative: What will China offer the world in its Rise?* 12. Beijing: New World Press. 2016.

[5]Live Mint (2017).

1,600 airports with an investment of US$23.3 billion.[6] Therefore, there is a new wave of competition amongst the regional provinces for the BRI projects, inside, as well as outside, China.

2 Regional Responses to the BRI

China has sought the participation of countries and regions touching the 'Belt and Road' zone. There are 32 littoral countries that touch the MSR. The combined population of these countries is around 4 billion people, with a combined GDP of around $16 trillion. These are the countries with huge potentials and have achieved rapid economic growth recently. From 2007 to 2012, the lowest annual growth rate was 5.27% (that of Sudan), and the highest average annual growth rate was 22.83% (that of Myanmar).[7] In view of these figures, China believes that the 'twenty first century MSR' is going to be an important driver of regional, as well as global, economic growth. And, given the overall capacities and structural adjustments being carried out in China, also pronounced as the 'New Normal', China sees an opportunity for sustaining its domestic economy, on the one hand, and strengthening strategic partnerships with various countries, on the other. So far, more than 65 countries have joined the Chinese initiative. This is understandable because China's trade volume and investment with the Belt and Road countries, in 2016, exceeded $3 trillion and $50 billion respectively (Deepak 2017b). Asia remains the bulwark of Chinese economic engagement, as almost 50% of Chinese exports made their way to various Asian countries.

Most of the ASEAN countries, with whom China has a trade volume of over $400 billion, though wary of China's rise, have nonetheless welcomed the idea. So much so that the Philippines, which dragged China to the International Court of Justice over the South China Sea issue, has also leaned towards China against the backdrop of Rodrigo Duterte being elected as the president. As far as South Asia is concerned except India, most of the smaller nations have also welcomed the idea because they perceive the initiative as a great opportunity to comprehensively deepen economic and people-to people relations. Russia, Central Asia, and many of East European countries have also joined the Chinese bandwagon. It should not be surprising, for China, since 2009, has upstaged Russia in Central Asia (CA) in terms of trade and investment; today, it controls one-third of Kazakhstan's oil production. China's downstream investment, especially in refineries in Central Asian Republics (CARs), will further reduce their dependence on Russian-refined fuel, and hence the overall trade. If China has invested over $60 billion in energy-related projects in the CARs, it has also secured huge energy-security guarantees from Russia, for example, it signed a 30-year (2018–2047), US$400 billion deal with Russia in

---

[6]Liu (2015).

[7]Deepak (2016).

May 2014.[8] Russia, though wary of China's presence in its backyard, nonetheless has collaborated with China in the face of Western sanctions on it led by the US during the Obama regime. It is believed, however, that this equation may change with Trump in the White House. However, at the Trump–Xi summit in April 2017, it appears that both have reached a certain consensus on the issue of North Korea and trade, therefore, one may not witness the kind of turbulence the world speculated in China–US relations when Trump had a telephonic conversation with Tsai Ing-wen, the newly elected leader of Taiwan. Japan and the US, who had been holding out so far, also gave in and participated in the Belt and Road Forum for International Cooperation held 14–15 May 2017 in Beijing, implying that both, while reserving their differences, are not averse to do business with China.

As regards Africa, China is nurturing its relationship from a futuristic perspective, as is evident from Chinese Premier Li Keqiang's visits to Ethiopia, Nigeria, Angola, and Kenya in 2014. During these visits, he underlined that Africa is an important force in the democratization of international relations, the world's fastest growing economic region, and a new pole of global economic growth. A resource-rich Africa already has US$200 billion annual trade with China, which, the Chinese premier said, would be doubled by the year 2020. China has heavily invested in Africa's energy resources, infrastructure development, telecommunications, and mining sectors. Irrespective of the fact that over a million Chinese have settled in Africa and that China has increasingly been criticized as a neo-colonialist power in Africa, China has been sought more intensely by Africa than anyone else in the entire phase of African history. On 31 May 2017, Kenya opened a US$4 billion Chinese-built railway, the largest infrastructure project ever undertaken since Kenya's independence.

3 Responses from the Strategic Community

The strategic community has formulated various opinions on the BRI. Shennon Tiezzi, associate editor of the *Diplomat,* and Chen Dingding have drawn parallels between the 'BRI' and 'Marshall Plan', which established the US as a 'bona fide super power' at the end of World War II.[9] Chinese scholars, including Prof. Ze (2014) of the China Institute of International Studies, however, have denounced Western criticism of the initiative, and have maintained that the policy of 'Three Nos, that, is non-interference in the internal affairs of other nations, not seeking the so-called 'spheres of influence', and not striving for hegemony or dominance, equally applies to the "Belt and Road" policy.[10] They argue that the Marshall Plan had a political agenda, which resulted in the formation of NATO and ultimately

[8]Deepak (2013).
[9]Chen (2014).
[10]Ze (2014).

lead to the Cold War with the Soviet Union. The initiative indeed is larger than the Marshall Plan as it attempts to encompass the entire world, the economic value of which could reach a whopping US$21 trillion.[11] China's projected investment in the BRI project is expected to reach around US$1.4 trillion.[12] Will this grandiose concept succeed and realize not only the Chinese dream but the dreams of various other countries and people around the world? Will it sink the poor nations into a Chinese debt trap? Or will it give rise to geostrategic rivalries around the world and a cold or hot war with the sole and declining superpower of the world?

There are various arguments put forth by the analysts as far as the historicity, geo-economics, and geopolitics of the new Silk Road is concerned. As far as the question of claiming the ancient routes of communication is concerned, people have hinted about the 'Sinosphere' and China's imperial 'tributary system.' If the Silk Road has been portrayed as the route of peace and cooperation, nonetheless, there have been instances of mass killings and regime changes, too. For example, it is mentioned in the *Old Tang Annals. Biography of Tian Shengong* 《旧唐书.田神功传》 that, when Tang general Tian Shengong entered Yangzhou, which was controlled by a renegade Liu Zhan, Tian ransacked the city and slaughtered thousands of Persian and other foreign merchants (JTS; Ji 1991: 92).[13] Similarly, the motive of Admiral Zheng He's voyages between 1404 and 1433 could not have been entirely peaceful. The intention behind these visits, contrary to the Chinese claim that they were peaceful and non-expansionist, has to be studied carefully. While the economic factor was one of the reasons, other factors such as a quest for the missing emperor Huidi, at least during the first voyage, the showcasing of Chinese cultural and military might, and, also rewriting the geopolitical order in Pacific and Indian Ocean were some of the other factors surrounding Zheng He's voyages. Some of the incidents revealing this aspect of Zheng He's maritime explorations include: China's regime change in Annam (Vietnam); extending Chinese tributary system to Siam (Thailand) and Java prior to Zheng He's voyages; the defeat of Palembang (a Srivijaya principality) ruler, Chen Zuyi and his decapitation in Nanjing during the first voyage (Fei 1996, 53),[14] as well as the dethroning of Alagagkonara (Fei 1996, 64–65), and taking him all the way to China in 1411 during the third voyage albeit he was released and sent back the next year. Therefore, according to Sen (2014), the portrayal of Zheng He as an agent of peace and friendship is problematic; however, he agrees that China's Silk Road initiatives could boost the economies of those in Asia or Europe willing to claim ancient links.[15] It also must be emphasized that,

[11]Tiezzi (2014).

[12]"China's US$1.4 trillion 'One Belt, One Road' set to make bigger impact than US' Marshall Plan to rebuild post-war Europe" South China Morning Post, 8 August 2016. http://www.scmp.com/news/china/policies-politics/article/2000835/chinas-us14-trillion-one-belt-one-road-extends-beijings.

[13]JTS [Old TangAnnals]. Biography of Tian Shengong 《旧唐书.田神功传》. Available at http://so.gushiwen.org/guwen/bookv_7570.aspx.

[14]Fei 费信. (1996).

[15]Sen (2014).

contrary to the Western military expeditions of the eighteenth and nineteenth centuries, Zheng He's voyages were largely peaceful and did not actually claim territories to expand China, despite the fact that Zheng was in a position to do that.

Many view the BRI as China's global rebalancing against the backdrop of the US's 'pivot to Asia' that China believes is essentially devised to contain its rise. Others have interpreted it as a re-globalization in the wake of the financial woes of the West and the latter's increasingly protectionist tendencies of late. Brexit in the UK and the triumphalism of Donald Trump in the US are some of the indicators in which direction the wind is blowing in the Western camp. We have witnessed that China immensely benefitted from the deep globalization of the 1990s and 2000s, thus lifting millions of people from poverty. Various countries, including India, have initiated their own connectivity initiatives, inside and beyond their borders. For example, ever since Prime Minister Modi ascended to power, he has initiated a series of projects, such as 'Make in India', 'Digital India', 'Start Up India', 'Sagarmala', and 'Bharatmala', 'Act East Policy', Mekong-Ganga Cooperation, International North-South Transportation Corridor, etc., with global ramifications. Can India and China align their respective processes and create a new global economic ecosystem with deeper economic and political stakes? Or, should we encourage building spheres of exclusive interests? Should not we move away from the Westphalian paradigm of security? Shouldn't we argue in favor of "security with" as opposed to "security against" the adversary? Should we build a common economic, cultural, and security community in Asia as proposed by the Chinese president?

3.1 India's Responses

As far as the BRI and India is concerned, India has been part of the initiative through its signing of the BCIM in 2013, an important corridor linking the overland and sea routes. India is the founding member of the AIIB and the NDB, which have been announced as important financiers of the BRI projects. However, India has been lukewarm, primarily because it was not consulted by China prior to declaring the BCIM as a part of the BRI and initiating projects like the CPEC. In this development, India holds that China has cared little for its territorial sensitivities, even though the economic corridor runs through the disputed territory claimed by India. Chinese scholars and the diplomats are of the view that India's connectivity and investment projects are in sync with the BRI, however, since India looks at the Chinese initiative through the prism of geopolitics, therefore, its connotations becomes entirely different.[16] Indeed, India's silence, which has been gradually

[16]Lin (2017).

broken of late, arises out of its security dilemma over land as well as sea, together with the issues related to sovereignty as spelled out by India's foreign secretary S. Jaishankar on the sidelines of recently restructured India–China strategic dialogue. Jaishankar (2017) wrote: "The fact that China Pakistan Economic Corridor (CPEC) is part of this particular initiative, CPEC violates Indian sovereignty because it runs through Pakistan-occupied Kashmir (PoK)."[17]

India is also wary of the prospective Trans-Himalayan Economic Zone of Cooperation with Nepal and Bhutan and China's courting of its smaller neighbors in the vicinity. India has been slow at operationalizing the BCIM as well, for it fears China's interference in the insurgency-infested northeastern region of India. Is New Delhi ready to forgo its sensitivities in the Northeast in turn for economic development of the region? Can the massive trade between China-ASEAN and India-ASEAN percolate to northeast India and northwest China? The answer to all these questions is yes, provided we start looking at boundaries as gateways rather than as barriers.

As regards the issue of sovereignty, the constructivists uphold that India must draw lessons from other nations as far as the issue of sovereignty is concerned. They have pointed to an agreement between Russia and Japan as regards economic cooperation in the disputed Kuril Islands. The agreement was reached in November 2016, during Russian President Putin's Japan visit. "The agreement sets out the beginning of bilateral consultations for collaboration in fishing and other forms of marine agriculture, tourism, ecology and other matters on the archipelago," according to the EBL News (2017).[18] As regards the BCIM, the constructivists posit that the cooperation will essentially alleviate poverty in the landlocked region and give a fillip to the 'Act East Policy' of India and aggressively engage it with the ASEAN and China's southwest region. Moreover, they also argue that, since India has stakes in Afghanistan, Iran and Central Asia, joining or negotiating various nodes of connectivity with the CPEC to these regions should be explored.

In the same vein, India and China could think of developing similar corridors along the northwest regions of China, primarily Xinjiang and Tibet, with India's Jammu and Kashmir, and the plains of Bihar and Uttar Pradesh intersecting Nepal. The BRI Action Plan defines Xinjiang as a core area both politically and geographically. China considers Xinjiang as a 'window to the west and Central, South and West Asia'. Both medium- and long-term goals have been in place to realize the BRI. The medium-term goals are aimed at completing railway and road connectivity between China and Pakistan within 5–10 years, whereas the long-term goals are set to be achieved by the year 2049; these goals are Three Channels, Three Bases, and Five Centres in Xinjiang. Three Channels include North-Central-Southern Channels; Three Bases comprise oil and gas, coal, and wind-power bases; and Five Centres are

[17]Jaishankar (2017).

[18]"Russia, Japan agree to economic cooperation on disputed Kuril Islands" EBL News 31 March 2017. https://eblnews.com/news/world/russia-japan-agree-economic-cooperation-disputed-kuril-islands-48563.

finance, healthcare, logistics, culture, and education etc. Will these channels and bases heighten the existing rivalry in the India, China, and Pakistan triangle or pave the way for soft borders and reconciliations? Could India's Gwadar dilemma be rendered irrelevant by extending some of the nodes from the CPEC into the Chinese investment in Gujarat? Will the idea of a Trans-Himalayan railway cutting across Nepal and connecting India's prospective line in Nepal become another battle ground for competition and rivalry? These are some of the questions that will determine the future course of India–China relations.

The 21st Century Maritime Silk Route (MSR) has also been viewed with much scepticism in India. India's response so far has been to deepen maritime partnerships with the US, Japan, Vietnam, Australia, etc. on the one hand and a layered engagement with the ASEAN on the other. Trump's ascendancy to power, visible fissures in the US–Europe alliance, and apprehensions about the US security umbrella with in US's Asia-Pacific allies have made the possibility of a loose alliance amongst these countries more realistic. Nevertheless this will also depend on China's malevolent or benevolent engagement with these countries. Besides, there are new initiatives such as 'Project Mausam' initiated by the Ministry of Culture in tandem with the Archaeological Society of India (ASI) as the nodal agency and the Indira Gandhi National Centre for the Arts (IGNCA), both in New Delhi, as its Research Unit. Since the area covered under the project extends throughout East Africa, the Arabian Peninsula, the Indian subcontinent, Sri Lanka, and Southeast Asia, and has been termed as the Indian Ocean "world", analysts and the media have considered it as India's response to China's MSR. In fact, this is so noticeable that Chinese scholars have termed it as a "threatening and competing" initiative that will pose a major challenge for China's Belt and Road plans, and the competing initiatives could turn into a major tussle between the world's two biggest rising powers."[19] However, there are other narratives in China, for example, ambassador Le Yucheng holds that "Belt and Road initiatives can also be docked to India's 'Spice Route', 'Act East Policy, and 'Mausam' projects, thus forming a new starting point and a new bright spot in China–India cooperation."[20] I believe, 'Mausam' is a pure cultural construct and doesn't pose any challenge whatsoever to the BRI. Even if the 'project' sounds ambitious, the kind of economic muscle that is required to materialize it simply does not exist. Contrary to this 'project', the ambitious 'Sagarmala' by way of which India desires to lay a network of deep-sea ports, rails, roads, smart cities, industrial parks, and hi-speed railways along the east and west coasts of India is the area where Indian and Chinese initiative could be aligned.

---

[19]WCT (Want China Times) (2015).

[20]DH (Daccan Herald) (2015).

4 India's Options

Should security analysts and skeptics see these initiatives as part of 'strategic encirclement' of India? It would be unfortunate if India remains outside the value chain of such an initiative; however, it may decide for itself what kind of project it could carry out with China on a case-to-case basis. These could form a realm of a variety of infrastructure-related projects including energy, transport, power, e-commerce, and projects that integrate investment and trade. Perhaps, China will also frame its own responses and priorities towards countries along the Belt and Road. For example, it will likely assume different strategy when dealing with smaller- and medium-sized countries, with the conflicting parties in the South China Sea, 'pivot' countries like Pakistan, and large countries like India. Secondly, as India faces uncertainties, as well as opportunities, it must capitalize on the invaluable geopolitical strategic space it has in the Indo-Pacific. If the US is attempting to offset China's geopolitical pull by way of India confronting China or in tandem with the US and its allies on the sea and land, it would be disastrous for all the stakeholders. From an Indian point of view, if the US is looking for a strong economic partnership with India, the case is similar for India's economic engagement with China and the US alike. It would be naïve to say that the US would dump its interests in China for India. Imagine the US$529-billion trade between China and the US, and compare it with India's trade with China and the US combined! Therefore, if at all India would like to be is a so-called 'swing power' between China and the US, it ought to be a swing power as far as cooperation and healthy competition and India's national interests are concerned, not the confrontation and conflict, which is neither in India's interest nor in the interest of China and the US.

5 Conclusion

It appears that, if grandiose initiatives such as Asia Infrastructural Development Bank (AIDB), Silk Road Fund, MSR and most recent Free Trade Area of the Asia Pacific (FTAAP) have put China at the centre of the global geopolitics and geo-economics, they have forced the US to scramble for a leadership role at least in the region, if not the globe; the same have challenged the US hegemony in the region, including the US notions of 'pivot to Asia' and Trans Pacific Partnership. Though there are strategic temptations to fall into the Thucydides' trap, however, China has consciously avoided the trap so far by advocating the 'peaceful rise' which was modified into 'peaceful development' in 2006, and more recently the notion of a 'new type of major power relationship' that seeks 'mutual respect, no conflict and mutual benefits.' So far, the US has remained reluctant to endorse the

Chinese notion, but it remains to be seen if the US would also be able to avoid the Thucydides trap.[21]

Finally, the BRI is indeed an instrument by way of which China is initiating a global rebalancing, civilizational rebalancing, and globalization 2.0. The aims and goals of the BRI have been defined in various ways by the strategic community and economists. Many have also cast doubt about the success of the strategy, for the risks—political, economic, security, legal, and moral—are huge, given the geographic and security boundary of the BRI. Some of the Chinese projects in Asia and Africa have faced hurdles, and many countries are heading into the Chinese debt trap. Conversely, if successful, China through the BRI will indeed alter the existing regional and global political architecture and pose a big challenge to the established hegemon. It remains to be seen how India approaches both camps, because for now it is out of the ambit of the US, as well as the Chinese initiatives. The Chinese have realized that the US would not be supportive of Beijing's renewed drive as it was during the formative years of reforms and open-door policy in the late 1970s. The US sees China as the only potentially qualified rival to its own hegemony. China also believes that, if there are any countries that restrict China's maritime ambitions, these are the US, Japan, and India.[22] Under such circumstances, will India maintain its strategic autonomy or lean to one side? The choice would be difficult to make.

References

Chen, Dingding. 2014. China's 'Marshall Plan' is much more. *The Diplomat*, November 10, 2014. http://thediplomat.com/2014/11/chinas-marshall-plan-is-much-more/.

Deepak, B.R. 2013. China in Central Asia: Is there any room for India? Chennai Centre for China Studies Paper No. 0140/ 2015, July 13, 2015. http://www.c3sindia.org/china/5114.

Deepak, B.R. 2016. *India and China: Foreign Policy Approaches and Responses*, 17. New Delhi: Vij Books.

Deepak, B.R. 2017a. China's Belt and Road Forum: Should India get back on board? *The Dialogue*. May 16, 2017. http://www.thedialogue.co/chinas-belt-road-forum-india-get-back-board/.

Deepak, B.R. 2017b. Trump-Xi Summit in Florida: Can the US avoid Thucydides trap?. *The Dialogue,* March 28, 2017. http://www.thedialogue.co/trump-xi-summit-florida-can-us-avoid-thucydides-trap/.

DH [Daccan Herald]. 2015. *China says 'Mausam' can be linked to 'One Belt One Road'*, March 4, 2015. http://www.deccanherald.com/content/463755/china-says-mausam-can-linked.html.

Fei, Hsin 费信 1996. 《星槎胜览》*The Overall Survey of the Star Raft*. Translated by R. Ptak JVG Mills, Revised, Annotated. Germany: Harrassowitz Verlag.

Jaishankar, S. 2017. CPEC violates sovereignty. *Indian Express,* February 22, 2017.

Lin, Minwang. 2017. "一带一路",印度为何迟迟不愿加入?" *Belt and Road: Why India is reluctant to join?* http://chuansong.me/n/1730509752418.

[21]Deepak (2017b).

[22]Zhang (2009).

Liu, Jinsong. 2015. "一带一路"将给工商界带来八大机遇 Belt and Road will bring eight major opportunities to the business world, *Dagong Bao*, May 19, 2015. http://news.takungpao.com/mainland/focus/2015-05/3003993.html.

Live Mint. 2017. China's CPEC investment in Pakistan reaches $62 billion. *Live Mint*, April 24, 2017. http://www.livemint.com/Politics/dB5tQKISoKNrvl7EwDPFbP/Chinas-CPEC-investment-in-Pakistan-reaches-62-billion.html.

Sen, Tansen. 2014. Silk Road Diplomacy—Twists, Turns and Distorted History. *Yale Global*, September 23, 2014. http://yaleglobal.yale.edu/content/silk-road-diplomacy-%E2%80%93-twists-turns-and-distorted-history.

Shi, Ze. 2014. One Road & One Belt New Thinking With Regard to Concepts and Practice. In *Lecture delivered at the 30th anniversary of Conference of the Schiller Institute*, on October 14, 2014. Germany. http://newparadigm.schillerinstitute.com/media/one-road-and-one-belt-and-new-thinking-with-regard-to-concepts-and-practice/.

Tiezzi, Shennon. 2014. The New Silk Road: China's Marshall Plan? *The Diplomat*, November 6, 2014. http://thediplomat.com/2014/11/the-new-silk-road-chinas-marshall-plan/.

WCT [Want China Times]. 2015. India counters Xi's 'belt and road' with competing project, March 1, 2015. http://www.wantchinatimes.com/news-subclass-cnt.aspx?id=20150301000123&cid=1101. Accessed on 14 Mar 2015.

Zhang, Shiping. 2009. 《中国海权》*China's Sea Rights*, 331. Beijing: People's Daily Publication.

Xi, Jinping. 2014. *The Governance of China*, 317–318. Beijing: Foreign Language Press.

Part I
Civilizational Moorings

Chapter 2
Silk Road Cultures and the Silk Road Economic Belt

Jingkui Jiang

1 Introduction

Generally speaking, the Silk Road mainly consists of two routes, i.e., the overland Silk Route and the maritime Silk Route. In the present article, however, the concept of Silk Road will be used only in the sense of the overland Silk Route.

The Silk Road began to take shape around the second century BCE, owing to the groundbreaking travels of the Chinese imperial envoy Zhang Qian during the Han Dynasty. The road started at Xi'an in China and extended all the way to West Africa and southern Europe. It was one of the main cross- and transcontinental routes in ancient times that connected Asia, Europe, and Africa. The Silk Road travelled over the Longshan Mountain, followed the Hexi Corridor, passed Yumenguan Pass and Yangguan Pass, reached Xinjiang, stretched along the oasis and the Pamir Plateau, crossed Central Asia, West Asia, and South Asia, and then led to Africa and southern Europe. The countries and regions linked by the Silk Road included China, Afghanistan, India, Central Asia, Iran, Iraq, Syria, Turkey, Saudi Arabia, Egypt, Italy, etc. The people traversing this route included busy traders and merchants, independent travelers, diplomatic envoys, and pious pilgrims heading to their sacred places. From the second century BCE to the fifteenth century CE, the Silk Road not only served as a bridge connecting China, India, Mesopotamia, Egypt, Greece, and Rome, but also acted as one of the most important channels for trade, political, and cultural exchanges between the East and the West. Such dynamic exchanges of commodities, religions, and cultures between the East and the West marked this period of more than a thousand years, a truly glorious chapter in human history.

The concept of the Silk Road Economic Belt was put forward by Chinese President Xi Jinping in 2013 in order to reinforce regional collaboration and to

J. Jiang (✉)
Centre for South Asian Studies, Peking University, Beijing, China
e-mail: jiangjk@pku.edu.cn

B.R. Deepak (ed.), *China's Global Rebalancing and the New Silk Road*,
https://doi.org/10.1007/978-981-10-5972-8_2

produce a win-win situation among the regional countries. On 7 September 2013, President Xi Jinping delivered a speech titled "Promote People-to-People Friendship and Create a Better Future" at Nazarbayev University, Kazakhstan. He proposed to join hands in building a Silk Road Economic Belt with an innovative cooperation mode and to make it a grand project benefiting people in regional countries along the route. On 22 June 2014, "Silk Roads: the Routes Network of Chang'an-Tianshan Corridor" jointly proposed by China, Kazakhstan, and Kyrgyzstan was successfully added to the World Heritage list. The decision was announced at the 38th session of UNESCO's World Heritage committee in Doha, Qatar. As the first successful World Cultural Heritage application that was jointly proposed in a transnational manner, this project will surely provide a wider arena and more opportunities for the development of the Silk Road Economic Belt in the future. Later, on 1 February 2015, the Chinese government held a conference to promote the implementation of "One Belt One Road" scheme by outlining a series of major issues and follow-up points. As a result, the idea of Silk Road Economic Belt took a step to further and more concrete action.

In his speech in Kazakhstan, Xi Jinping expressed that, more than 2,100 years ago, during China's Western Han Dynasty, the imperial envoy Zhang Qian was sent to Central Asia twice to open the doors to friendly contacts between China and the Central Asian countries, as well as along the transcontinental Silk Road linking the East and the West, i.e., Asia and Europe. It is thus safe to say that the spirit of the Silk Road Economic Belt is essentially in line with that of the Silk Road (Xi 2014). In other words, the Silk Road Economic Belt, stemming from the concept of the ancient Silk Road, has in turn advanced the scale, function, and significance of the Silk Road. Connecting the European, Asian-Pacific, and North African economic circles at the same time, the Silk Road Economic Belt is the longest and the most promising economic corridor in the world.

2 Silk Road Cultures

The Silk Road is to some extent a geographical concept that involves a number of states and ethnic groups, although these states and ethnic groups have been constantly moving, merging, transforming, and even disappearing over the centuries. This vast area has been playing a crucial role in human history, not only because it is home to many civilizations of the world, but also because it encompasses the four major ancient civilizations in the world, i.e., the Egyptian, Mesopotamian, Indian, and Chinese civilizations. After the second century BCE, when the Silk Road officially began, the civilizational context in this area underwent some changes as new cultures entered the arena. At this stage, the various cultures of Europe (Greece and Rome), Arabia and Persia, Central Asia, India, China, and Mongolia were constantly evolving, expanding, and encountering one another, shaping a new cultural landscape. Meanwhile, some cultures gradually vanished and merged into another culture, for example Arabia, Persia, and Mongolia came under the domination of Islamic culture, while some absorbed other cultures and gained new momentum as happened between Chinese culture and Indian Buddhism. Moreover, the Jewish culture also was resuscitated during this period. In this way, the diversified Silk Road cultures came into being. Though the Silk Road served initially as a route mainly for trade and merchandise, it later became a larger platform on which the travel of people, the spread of religions, and exchanges of arts continuously took place. Undoubtedly, the states and residents along the Silk Road benefited greatly from these active cultural contacts.

The major actors in the arena of cultural contacts along the Silk Road included the civilizations of China, India, Mongolian, Islam, Europe (Greek and Christian civilizations), etc. The civilizations of Central Asia and Persia during the early Islamic period should also be given due attention. In terms of activeness and vitality, however, the Chinese, Indian, Islamic, and European civilizations definitely played a more important part because they each remained long-lasting and thriving until now, while those of Mongolia, Central Asian, and Persia, during the early Islamic period, were eventually assimilated into Islamic culture.

3 Silk Road and the Cross-Cultural Interface

Chinese civilization has long been a time-honored and highly influential one. Under the reign of Emperor Wu during the Western Han dynasty, Confucianism was officially elevated to an orthodox status that was to shape the subsequent Chinese civilization. After a thousand years' interaction and metamorphosis with other cultures along the Silk Road, Chinese civilization developed into a civilization with great diversity in unity. In this context, "unity" refers to Confucianism and "diversity" refers to foreign cultures along the Silk Road, such as the Buddhist culture of Indian civilization and the Christian/Catholic culture of European civilization, as well as the Islamic culture of Arab civilization. Buddhism, originating on the Indian subcontinent, was brought into China around the first century CE. During the subsequent period, it was enthusiastically embraced by Chinese culture and developed rapidly in China due to both official and non-official patronage, as well as the remarkable efforts made by official missions and Buddhist monks travelling back and forth on the Silk Road. Although Buddhism died out in India in the early thirteenth century, it flourished rapidly and widely in China. Consequently, Buddhism became not only one of China's major religions, but also an indispensable part of Chinese culture. It is noteworthy that China now has the largest Buddhist population in the world. In my point of view, China should be grateful to India for creating and sharing Buddhism and Buddhist culture; similarly, India also owes China for generously accepting and developing Buddhism and Buddhist culture. Drawing support from foreign missionaries and local followers, the Christian/Catholic and Islamic cultures also took root in the land of China. In addition, the Manichean/Zoroastrian culture from Persia and the Mongolian culture from the Northern Desert also had dramatic clashes and then amalgamation with

Chinese civilization, and later became a part of Chinese culture that cannot be neglected.

Indian civilization derives from the Indus valley civilization around 3000 BCE. Its essential elements are Hinduism, Buddhism, Jainism, and Sikhism, which all have their own salient characteristics and special effects. Hinduism and Jainism have lasted for a very long time, with continuing vitality, even after suffering from serious attacks by invading cultures. As a religion with strong international awareness, Indian Buddhism spread far and wide and had profound influence on the neighboring regions. Being an independent school between Hinduism and Islam, Indian Sikhism has been evolving steadily with great flexibility. Coming with the *Quran* and sword in their hands, the Muslims also found their place on the subcontinent. At present, among the eight South Asian countries, four are Muslim countries (i.e., Afghanistan, Pakistan, Bangladesh, and the Maldives), and the population of Indian Muslims is the second largest in the Islamic world. It is thus true that the Islamic culture has played a significant role in shaping today's Indian culture. In addition, there is evidence that China's Taoism and Confucianism were also brought to India and further enriched Indian civilization.[1]

Islam and Islamic culture, on the contrary, have been inclined toward violence ever since its genesis, and their preference for expansion is greater than that of any other major religion. During the centuries since medieval times, the Muslims on the Silk Road played an extremely active role in proselytizing people to Islam amidst their conquests, which led to the fact that almost the entire middle part of the Silk Road, including North Africa, West Asia, Central Asia, and South Asia, came under Islamic rule. Islam was so dominant at that time that even such mighty cultures as those of Europe and Mongol could not escape its effects. In spite of this, there is no denying that the Islamic culture of Egypt, Mesopotamia, Iran, and South Asia still respectively intermingled with the cultural elements of ancient Egypt, Babylon, Persia, and India. The various minor differences between Islam in these regions and that of its cradle in Saudi Arabia clearly demonstrates that Islamic culture also to some extent blended with the local cultures. In other words, the Islam in Egypt, Mesopotamia, Iran, and South Asia was the outcome of the metamorphosis between Islam and Egyptian, Babylonian, Persian, and Indian civilizations. Therefore, it was in these fruitful interactions where the cultural elements became embedded.

Situated at the western end of the Silk Road, European civilization was literally the terminal point of this route. Prior to the Silk Road completely connecting from the East to the West, the Mediterranean civilization (Aegean Sea civilization/Greek civilization) had already reached West Asia, Central Asia, and South Asia. When the powerful Macedonian Empire was at its zenith (circa the first half of the fourth century BCE), its vast territory stretched across much of the European, African, and Asian continents, reaching the Fergana Valley and the Indus River Valley in the

[1]It is believed that Xuanzang translated *Daodejing* at the request of the Kamarupa king Bhaskara Varman, whom Xuanzang mentions as "Kumara Raja". His translation of *Daodejing* was a highly intentional endeavor to introduce Chinese philosophy and culture to the Indians. But alas, this translated text in Sanskrit is lost to us (Ray 1998).

East, Balkan Peninsula in the West, Central Asia, the Caspian Sea and the Black Sea in the North, and the Indian Ocean and North Africa in the South. This area almost covered the entire west and middle parts of the later Silk Road. The Roman Empire was another influential empire which spanned Europe, Africa, and parts of Asia. It bordered Spain and Britain in the West, the upper reaches of the Euphrates River in the East, the northern part of Africa in the South, and the Rhine and Danube rivers in the North, making the Mediterranean an enclosed central sea of the empire. The Eastern Roman Empire, which endured until the fifteenth century, was the most long-lived empire of ancient and medieval Europe. While its core area was located on the Balkan Peninsula in southeast Europe, its peripheral area once covered West Asia and North Africa. When the empire reached its greatest extent, its territory also included Italy, Syria, Palestine, Egypt, the Caucasus, and the Mediterranean coast of North Africa. It is hence evident that the civilizations along the Silk Road were greatly influenced by the Greek civilization (Mediterranean/Aegean Sea civilization) and Christian/Catholic civilization, as well as the Eastern Orthodox Church. It is natural to find some European elements in Islamic culture, because Islam and Christianity to some extent shared the same origin. The Christian/Catholic cultural elements in Indian and Chinese civilizations were largely attributed to the contribution that the European civilization had made through the Silk Road. On the other hand, the European civilization can also attribute its cultural elements from the East to the existence of the Silk Road. Judaism, from which Christianity and Catholicism were derived, was also rooted in the regions along the Silk Road. Moreover, the commodities from China and India, Chinese silk and porcelain in particular, as well as the folk tales circulated from India via Arabia, also had enormous effects on European culture and lifestyle. In fact, the ancient Persian Empire, centered on the Iran Plateau in West Asia, also extended far into parts of Asia, Africa, and Europe. During the period of its greatest power and prosperity, the Persian Empire reached the Indus Valley and the Pamir Plateau in the East, Egypt and Libya in the South, Asia Minor and the Balkan Peninsula in the West, and the Caucasus Mountains and Aral Sea in the North. After being conquered by Alexander the Great, the vast territory of the Persian Empire fell under the domain of the Macedonian Empire. There was obviously a relationship of interaction and continuity between these two empires.

Besides the dynamic interplay between the just-mentioned four major civilizations along the Silk Road, other civilizations in this area, such as the Judaic, Mongolian, and Russian civilizations, were also to various degrees involved in the interaction and exchanges with alien cultures via the Silk Road. In a nutshell, the Silk Road provided the space in which various civilizations in this area encountered, clashed, and metamorphosed with each other. In this context, a new kind of Silk Road civilization with its own unique characteristics was created.

4 Silk Road Cultures and the Silk Road Economic Belt

Taking the past and the present into consideration, we can now argue that the Silk Road and the Silk Road Economic Belt closely correspond to one another. The major difference between them is that the former belongs to the past, while the latter has just come into being. Only by drawing experiences and learning lessons from the past and working hard at the present can we build a better future together.

Reviewing the formation of Silk Road cultures in history, we have memories of harmony, like the cultural contacts between China and India, as well as recollections of bitterness like the conflicts between Islamic, Christian, and Indian cultures. The eastward dissemination of Buddhism was a harmonious symphony jointly composed by the Chinese and Indian civilizations. This happened in a time when Indian Buddhism was internationally oriented, and Chinese civilization was open to absorb foreign cultures. As a result, the eastern part of the Silk Road was crowded with Buddhists coming from both sides. Despite the arduous journey and the difficulties in translating and preaching, they interacted actively and together contributed to the harmonious exchanges between the two great civilizations that further shaped the destiny of China and India. On the contrary, the Islamization of West Asia, Central Asia, and South Asia appeared to be less peaceful as the whole process was full of wars, brutal killings, and even genocide. The cruelty of this process was further reflected in the Crusades which took place between the Catholic Church and the Islamic civilization, the Islamic conquest in South Asia, plus the Mongolian invasion of Central Asia.

While advocating and building the Silk Road Economic Belt, we shall always adopt the right attitude, which is continuing to learn critically from the history. We are supposed to build the Silk Road in a new manner by maintaining the peaceful and benevolent elements of the Silk Road cultures and discarding the opposite.

Having carried out a general review of the major civilizations on the Silk Road Economic Belt (i.e., the Chinese, Indian, Islamic, and European civilizations), I believe that fraternity, tolerance, equality, peace, and cooperation are some common and universal spirits shared by these civilizations and are also favored by all peoples living in the area of the Belt.

In China, "Wu Chang" which means five constant virtues in Confucianism, including *Ren, Yi, Li, Zhi, and Xin*, has been the core of the Chinese civilization and Chinese value system throughout history, where *Ren* is benevolence, *Yi* righteousness, *Li* propriety, *Zhi* wisdom, and *Xin* is honesty. Being in line with the concept of "Wu Chang", fraternity, tolerance, equality, peace, and cooperation are not only embedded in Confucianism, which plays a central role in Chinese culture, but also are widely seen in subcultures like Buddhism and Taoism. Thus, it could be said that these five spirits are the common traits and main characteristics of the Chinese civilization.

Similar spirits could also be found in the Indian civilization, for example, the Five Cordial Virtues in Hinduism and the Five Precepts in Buddhism and Jainism, as well as the sayings of Sikh *gurus*. The Five Cordial Virtues in Hinduism are loyalty, non-violence, asceticism, self-control, and purity with non-violence as the core. The Five Percepts of Buddhism are non-violence, and abstinence from theft, lust, lying, and drinking, while those in Jainism are non-violence, and abstinence from theft, lust, lying, and the possession of wealth. The God in Sikhism is love and truth. All these principles and disciplines contain the spirits of fraternity, tolerance, equality, peace, and cooperation, which constitute the inherent nature of Indian civilization.

According to the *Quran*, *Hadith* and other Islamic classics, Muslims should have such virtues as peace-loving, working in unity and helping each other, showing respect for knowledge, doing business honestly, paying attention to hygiene and exercise, being charitable, loyal, tolerant and forgiving, etc. It is not hard to notice that fraternity, tolerance, equality, peace and cooperation are also intrinsic characteristics of Islamic civilization, and common moral codes binding all Muslims.

As the heart of European civilization, Christianity holds that equality and fraternity are universal truths that all human beings should accept. Faith, hope, and love are the three virtues of Christianity. Specifically, faith means being trustful and reliable; hope means having expectations and wishes; and love is the essence of God, which is the most important thing in God-human and inter-human relationships. In addition, humility, gentleness, charity, chastity, modesty, zeal, and generosity are also some virtues that should be followed by Christians. Tolerance and forgiveness play an equally important role. In short, fraternity, tolerance, equality, peace, and cooperation are also the spirits residing in and emphasized by European civilization.

Therefore, while building the Silk Road Economic Belt, all civilizations, countries, and peoples along the Belt should uphold the virtues like fraternity, tolerance, equality, peace, and cooperation. All civilizations should discard their habitual thinking inherited from the past, for example, China should not take itself as the center of power, waiting for tributes presented by other countries; India should not cultivate an excessive sense of nationalism or hold hegemony over South Asia; the Islamic world should not embrace the idea that only Muslims are brothers; and the Europeans should not consider themselves always right. While mutual economic benefit is the main aim of the Silk Road Economic Belt, political and cultural aspects should not be ignored. This is because they are the preconditions and backups of economic exchanges, and, together with spirits and virtues like fraternity, tolerance, equality, peace, and cooperation, they will ensure the success of the Belt.

5 Conclusion

The Silk Road Economic Belt, spanning a vast territory and possessing abundant natural, mineral, energy, and land resources and precious tourism resources, is a strategic base for energy and resources in the twenty first century. However, we also face many problems, such as the considerable regional difference, inconvenient transportation, rugged natural environment, unbalanced economic development, and so on. Only when all the countries in this area critically learn from the history and regard fraternity, tolerance, equality, peace, and cooperation as common principles, can the ultimate goal of building a Silk Road Economic Belt be finally achieved, and all participants truly benefit from a win-win situation.

References

Ray, H.P. 1998. Understanding Xuanzang and the Xuanzang Spirit. In *Across the Himalayan Gap: An Indian Quest for Understanding China*, ed. Tan Chung. New Delhi: Gyan Publishing House. http://ignca.nic.in/ks_41020.htm.

Xi, Jinping. 2014. "共同建设'丝绸之路经济带" (Work together to build the 'Silk Road Economic Belt') 《习近平谈治国理政》 *Xi Jinping: The Governance of China*, 287–289. Beijing: Foreign Language Press.

Chapter 3
Silk Road and Civilizational Connections Between India and China: Role of the Buddhist Scholar Monks

B.R. Deepak

India and China are two of the most ancient civilizations with extremely rich cultural and literary traditions. There has been an uninterrupted civilizational dialogue between the two for two millennia. The dialogue sprawls across various fields, but could be broadly classified into two categories—material and cultural domains. The literary dialogue, which could be categorized under the latter, was an important part of the civilizational dialogue. The Chinese historical records stand testimony to these interactions and have been referred to by various eminent researchers, such as Ji Xianlin, Xue Keqiao, and Geng Yinzeng on the Chinese side and scholars like P.C. Bagchi, H.P. Ray, Tan Chung, Tansen Sen, and many others on the Indian side. Most of the Chinese, as well as Indian scholarship, has tried to explain how the Chinese literary scene was influenced by the Indian literature and how the Indian content became absorbed into the Chinese. Even though the dialogue has to be two-way traffic, the findings reveal that the ancient Chinese literature was more influenced by the Indian literature than the other way round, for the simple reason that Buddhism acted as a catalyst for this influence.

Buddhism was the world's earliest missionary religion, missionary in the context of austerity and not present day luxuries, and, for that matter, it was also different from the missionary zeal of the Western church that acted upon its own need for spreading gospels. This was contrary to Buddhism, which was sought out by kings and paupers for alternative routes of spiritual emancipation and for restoring peace in the society, albeit there was an element of exaggeration in the accounts and diaries of the Chinese and Indian travelers about India's divinity, civility and sophistication (Sen 2004, 9). It was perhaps natural that the missionary zeal of Buddhism would take it to the territories beyond India; equally important to its success was the Chinese response, which revolutionized the movement altogether.

B.R. Deepak (✉)
Centre for Chinese and Southeast Asian Studies, Jawaharlal Nehru University, New Delhi, India
e-mail: bdeepak@mail.jnu.ac.in

B.R. Deepak (ed.), *China's Global Rebalancing and the New Silk Road*,
https://doi.org/10.1007/978-981-10-5972-8_3

Both the missionary nature of Buddhism, as well as the Chinese response, resulted in the number of waves of Indian scholar monks going to China and Chinese monks coming to India.

The earliest wave perhaps started with Kashyapa Matanga and Dharamraksha reaching Luoyang in the first century CE and continued till the end of the third century. Some of the leading personalities of this missionary zeal were Dharamkala (reached China 249–50 CE) and Kangsenghui, Weizhinan, and Zhuluyan (reached Wuhan in 224 CE). The second wave stretched between fourth and the fifth centuries. Personalities such as Sangabhadra and Sanghadipa (reached Chang'an in 381 CE), and Kumarajiva (reached Chang'an in 401) reigned supreme in the Buddhist horizon. Two years before the arrival of Kumarajiva in China, Faxian started off for India in search of *Vinaya* texts. The third major wave occurred during the sixth and seventh 7th centuries, and the most prominent figures of the times were Bodhidharma, Paramartha,Amoghvajra, and Vajrabodhi. Xuan Zang's journey to India was in response to this Indian wave to China. Though each and every Indian and Chinese scholar monk made extremely valuable contribution to the spread of Buddhism in China, nevertheless, the kind of feats accomplished by Kumarajiva, Parmartha, Xuan Zang, and Yijing in the field of sutra translation were remarkable.

1 Sutra Translation in Ancient China

Translation of sutras started in the reign of emperor Wu (156–87 BC) of the Han Dynasty (206 BC–220 CE). Initially, sutra translation was not done straight from the Sanskrit or Pali languages but through Central Asian and ancient languages of Xinjiang that are extinct now, for example, the Tokharian languages (Ji 1985, 2). This may have been due to the fact that Buddhist missionary activities in China were primarily led by scholars from Iran and other Central Asian countries. At the same time, it is interesting to note that Christian missionaries, unlike their Buddhist counterparts, resorted to the translation of Chinese classics into English thus giving birth to the school of Orientalism in the West.

The first two Indian scholars who travelled to China were Kasyapa Matanga and Dharamraksa during the reign of the Han emperor Ming (28–75 CE) in 68 CE. The duo translated into Chinese five Buddhist texts related to the "resumes of the legends of the birth and childhood of Buddha, a resume of his prediction, a short treatise on the main principles of Buddhism, a sutra on the purity of monastic life, and a sutra on the principles of ascetic life of those who wanted to follow the way of spiritual perfection. Of these, the 'Sutra of 42 sections', which has been preserved up till now, is clearly a catechism for the use of missionaries intending to preach the Buddhism in foreign countries" according to professor Bagchi (Wang et al. 2011, 13).

During the second century, Parthian scholar monk An Shigao (148–180 CE) founded a school of translation in Luoyang upon his arrival in 144 CE. As

Buddhism was still not popular among the Chinese people, rather than presenting faithful translations of the entire sutra, he extracted texts from sutras belonging to four principal Agamas of the Sutrapitika. One hundred and seventy nine translations of Buddhist texts are ascribed to An Shigao. His team included an Indo Scythian monk named Lokaksema and three Indians, Buddhadeva (?), Mahabala (?) and Dharmasatya (?) (Wang et al. 2011, 14). As the religion started to attract the attention and interest of the Chinese people, Chinese monks started to invite more scholar monks from far and wide. In the middle of the third century, Dharamkala, Sanghavarman, and Dharamsatya were invited to Luoyang. The three Indian monks translated a number of Vinaya texts to spread the Buddhist monastic discipline in China (Wang et al. 2011, 14).

The appetite for Buddhist doctrine among the people then multiplied, especially after the accession of Fu Jian of the Yaoqin dynasty in 350 CE. He invited erudite scholar monks like Dao An (312–385) to Chang'an, who critically examined the Buddhist text rendered previously into Chinese. He composed a series of commentaries and perhaps the first-ever catalogue of the translations. It has been said about Dao An (Wang et al. 2011: 18) that "Before his times, many Buddhist texts have been translated. But the ancient scholars paid attention to the general sense of the texts. But Dao An examined the sutras closely and brought out their inner meaning." It was he who invited scholars like Gautama Sanghadeva, Dharamanandi, Sanghabhuti, and Kumarajiva to Chang'an. Unfortunately, Dao An died in 385 and never met Kumarajiva who reached Chang'an in 401. It was under such circumstances that the translation of sutras gradually grew into a mammoth project that involved hundreds of scholar monks, foreign as well as local. In fact, the number of locals reached into the thousands as they assisted the foreign monks. Consider the words of Parmartha and Kai Hui, his Chinese counterpart (Martha et al. 2006, 128–9):

> I was lucky to have met you [Kaihui]…now that we have translated the two sutras [摄大乘论Mahayanasamparigraha Sastra] 阿毗达磨俱舍释论 Abhidharmakosa Sastra] so well, in terms of both language and accuracy of content, I have no regret in my life." …every sentence, every chapter would be carefully studied until the meaning was thoroughly debated and elucidated, and then the rendition was recorded in writing.

This was also the time when Faxian travelled to India in search of Buddhist sutras, especially the *Vinaya* texts or the texts related to monastic rules. He started off from Chang'an to India, in 399 CE via the central Asian route. After returning to China via the sea route in 412 CE, he completed his monumental work *Foguoji* (*Accounts of a Buddhist Country*). The perilous journey across the Taklimakan desert (in present Xinjiang) emerges vividly in his account. The treacherous journey over the Taklimakan has been described by Faxian in the following words (Hui 1994, 68):

> "There is neither a bird in the sky, nor an animal on the ground. I looked around the vast emptiness, and had no idea of whither to proceed. The only thing we could do was to use the sun to get our bearings of the east and west, and to take the human skeletons as our road."

When he left Chang'an (present-day Xi'an), he had more than ten companions; however, when he reached Sri Lanka on his way back to China, he was the only survivor.

According to the *Kaiyuan Era Catalogue of Buddhist Canons* (开元释教录) and *Zhenyuan, New Buddhist Catalogue* (贞元新定释教目录), in a span of 734 years starting from tenth year of the Yongping Era in Han Dynasty (67 CE) to the 16th year of Zhenyuan Era in th Tang Dynasty (800 CE), in all 185 prominent translators translated 2,412 sutras that ran into 7,352 fascicles (Jiang 2014, 208–09). Of these translators, 16 translated more than 50 sutras or 100 fascicles. The 'The Five Great Chinese Buddhist Sutra Translators' namely Kumarajiva, Paramartha, Xuan Zang, Yi Jing, and Amoghavajra were outstanding and could have been responsible for the entire repository of the Buddhist literary heritage of East Asia (Table 1).

The style of literal translation took a definite change after the arrival of Kumarajiva in China. Once in Hou Qin, Yao Xing treated Kumarajiva with respect and appointed him as his *Rajyaguru*. Both deepened and nurtured this relationship of priest and patron with great care, and they established a translation bureau headed by Kumarajiva, who in turn was assisted by over 800 scholar monks (Hui 1994, 56). The king himself sometimes participated in the work as well. According to another account (Martha et al. 2006, 229).

Table 1 Translators translating more than 50 sutras or 100 volumes

Period	Dynasty	Name	Number of sutras translated	Number of fascicles
Three Kingdoms and Western Jin	Sun Wu	Zhi Qian	88	118
	Western Jin	Dharmaraksa 竺法护	175	354
Eastern Jin and Sixteen Kingdoms	Eastern Jin	Dharmaraksa 竺昙无兰	61	63
		Gautama Sanghadeva	5	118
		Buddhabhadra	13	125
	Northern Liang	Dharmaksema	19	131
	Yao Qin	Kumārajīva	74	384
Northern and Southern Dynasties	Liu Song	Gunabhadra	52	134
	Wei	Bodhiruci	30	101
	Chen	Paramārtha	38	118
Sui and Tang	Sui	Jñānagupta	39	192
	Tang	Xuan Zang	76	1347
		Siksananda	19	107
		Yi Jing	68	239
		Bodhiruci	53	110
		Amoghavajra	111	143

Source Jiang 2014, 210

> In the summer of the 8th year of Hongshi reign of the king of Later Qin (406 CE) Kumarajiva gathered together over 2000 learned monks from different parts of the land and assembled them in the great monastery of Chang'an. Here he studied this sutra [Lotus Sutra] with them in detail, then bring forth [出] a new translation. Holding a Hu version of the Sutra in his hand he straightway translated it orally into Chinese. He was able to use the language of this land to convey a meaning that did not distort the source [乖本]. The merits in style were also a significant gain. It was magnificent feet; not even the clearing away of darkest clouds or the splendour of the morning Sun could compare with it.

Thus, started the biggest ever project of translation in the history of mankind. Between the second and the thirteenth centuries, some 6,000–7,000 fascicles of the sutras were disseminated to China and translated into Chinese, primarily from Sanskrit. Among the translators, Kumarajiva undoubtedly was the most prominent. He was perhaps rivaled only by Xuan Zang. Hui Jiao tells us that over 300 Buddhist scriptures were translated from Sanskrit to Chinese under Kumarajiva's leadership. The quality and clarity of Kumarajiva's translation surpassed the quality of previous translations. Much of Kumarajiva's translation have survived the vagaries of time and are still available in China. Before Kumarajiva died, he proclaimed that, if his translation was in accord with the genuine principles of Buddhism, his tongue would remain intact and not turn into ash. As prophesized, Hui Jiao says that, after cremation of his mortal remains, the tongue remained intact and was not damaged (Hui, 58). The story, even though it cannot be deemed to have actually happened, however, reflects the rigor, faith, and devotion this iconic translator.

When Kumarajiva reigned supreme in China, Faxian lived 14 precious years in India; by the time he returned to China at the age of 74, Kumarajiva was no more. With the help of Budhhabhdra and Baoyun, Faxian also initiated sutra translation. In all, they translated 6 sutras with 63 fascicles, including the Mahasangha Vinaya (《摩诃僧祇律》) and Mahaparinirvana Sutra (《大泥洹经》).

Xuan Zang and Yijing had certain advantages over Faxian because the Tang Emperor Taizong (626–649) and Empress Wu Zetian (690–704) patronized both, respectively. Xuan Zang set out for western regions in 628 CE at the young age of 29. He crossed many lands and through many cities, including Xinjiang, the former Soviet Union, Afghanistan, and Pakistan and finally reached Kashmir. He studied at Nalanda for a few years (632–636) and became proficient in Sanskrit. Xuan Zang arrived back in Chang'an in 645 at the age of 46 and engaged himself in the work of translating sutras. When he had returned to China, he installed all his collection in the Hongfu monastery. His collection included numerous images and paintings, 150 pieces of relics, 550 scrolls of Buddhist sutras, totaling 657 texts in total number (Fan 2007, 199). For the next 19 years, Xuan Zang devoted himself to sutra translation. The project commenced in the Hongfu monastery and subsequently shifted to Cien and Ximing monasteries. In 657 CE, Xuan Zang moved to Yuhua Palace and turned it into a monastery; he lived there until his death in 664 CE.

It was in these monasteries that Xuan Zang and his team systematically translated 73 Buddhist scriptures, 1,335 volumes in all, from Sanskrit to Chinese. These translations contributed greatly to the rise of Buddhism in China and were probably his greatest achievements of all. During this time, he also wrote the Chengwei Shilun, a commentary on the translated texts. *Wei Shi* means *consciousness-only*, which is the basic philosophy of the Yogacara School. Based on this school of thought, Xuan Zang also founded the Fa Xiang School, which gained popularity during his lifetime and his disciple's, but faded away into obscurity after their deaths.

1.1 Translation of Non-Buddhist Classics

Under the Buddhist umbrella, other Indian classics were also rendered into Chinese. Professor Jiang (2014, 210–11) argues that translation of non-Buddhist classics could be classified into two categories—one, unconscious translation of Indian folk literature embedded in the Buddhist literature, and two, conscious translation of Indian philosophy, astronomy, classics on traditional Indian medicine, etc. Even though the scale of such translation may not match those of Buddhist sutras, it did enrich Chinese civilization. In Sata Sastra 百疏论, there are notes and commentaries on Vedas, Vedanta, Samkhya, Vaisheshika, yoga, and even descriptions of Indian astronomy, geography, arithmetic, military strategy, music, medicine, and so forth (Jiang 2014, 211).

It was Kumarajiva who introduced the "Three Treatises School" to China. His translations of Nagarjuna's *Madhyamaka Sastra*, *Dwadshanikaya Sastra*, *Sata Sastra* were largely responsible for the Chinese form of Madhyamika School. He was also responsible for Five Lineages of Transmission in China.[1] Paramartha and Xuan Zang respectively translated *Hiranyasaptati* of Samkhya and *Vaiseshikadashapadartha*. P.C. Bagchi (1981, 212), the doyen of Indian Sinology quoted *Sui Annals* records that non-Buddhist classics such as *Brahaman Sutra of Astronomy,Astronomy of Brahaman Rishi Garga*, *Astronomy of Brahaman,* which were rendered into Chinese. Astronomers belonging to the Gautama, Kasyapa and Kumara clans held high positions in the official astronomy institute of the Tang Dynasty. An astronomer identified as Gautama from the Gautama clan translated the Indian astronomical classic *Navagrah-siddhanta*.

[1]These are the lineage of *Vinaya* or discipline; lineage of Tantra; lineage of vast conduct; lineage of profound view; and lineage of quintessential meaning. Paramartha and Xuan Zang respect.

2 Translation Methods and Legacy of Buddhist Scholar Monks

During the initial stages of sutra translation, starting from the late Eastern Han to Western Jin (148–316), scholar monks mostly from India adopted the literal technique. This could be attributed to limited knowledge of the Chinese language, as well as classics of China. The reverence for the sutras may have forced the translators not to fiddle too much with the contents of the text. This practice continued during the second stage too, i.e., between the Eastern Jin and Sui Dynasty (317–617). However, with the arrival of Kumarajiva, the literal translation was replaced with free translation. He advocated that the words and syntax need not be same as long as the meaning and argumentation of the text are maintained. During the third stage (618–907), translation methods were perfected, and an entire set of rules was devised.

In the course of translation, local and foreign translators compiled numerous Sanskrit–Chinese reference books, thus constructing a database of Indian Buddhist and non-Buddhist terminologies. These terms have become part and parcel of the Chinese language and are being used even today. This is an example of culturally conflicting terms, syntax, etc. that pave the way to fusion. Secondly, the translators evolved a complete methodology. The methodology Kumarajiva adopted was first rendering the text into Chinese, followed by debating it with fellow team members, verification of the text while referring to original-locally translated texts, and finally the proofreading.

The translators were supposed to hold high moral status in society, and specific qualifications were established for the translators. For example, Yan Zong (557–610), a translator of Sui Dynasty (581–618) recommends eight qualifications of the translators. These were: one, adherence to the path of Dharma and doing good to people; two, uprightness and sincerity; three, vast knowledge of classics and clarity of thoughts; four, well versed in Chinese history and literature and cannot afford to be negligent; five, broad-minded, humble, and non-obdurate; six, love Dharma and do not seek notice and fame; seven, well-versed in Sanskrit, the methods of translation, and should not overlook the argumentation of the Sanskrit texts; and eight, good at Chinese exegetical studies and must maintain accuracy in the translated text.[2] In essence, Yan Zong was directing that the translators, apart from being good Buddhists, should also possess vast knowledge of the classics and foreign languages, as well as the translation methods.

During the Tang Dynasty, the translation bureau scaled new heights. The positions and duties related to the translation work were clearly defined, for example, some of the portfolios were assigned to the translators such as Yizhu

[2]http://dictionary.buddhistdoor.com/word/33564/%E5%85%AB%E5%82%99%E5%8D%81%E6%A2%9D (accessed on September 16, 2014).

(chief translator), Zhengyi and Zhengwen (proofreaders), Duyu (interpreters), Bishou (written translator), Zhui Wen (essay composers), Canyi (cross-checking), Kanding (proofreader and reviewer,), Runwen (polisher), Fanbai (rituals performers), etc. (Jiang 2014, 213). Xuan Zang must have benefitted immensely from the methods and rules established for the translators by his predecessors, such as Kumarajiva. He advocated the amalgamation of literal, as well as free translation. Besides, Xuan Zang recommended six translation skills[3] (Shi et al. 2013, 46). In addition, Xuan Zang also recommended 'five don'ts' for translation—don't translate when the original is secret, such as incantation; don't translate when there is ambiguity; don't translate when you do not find equivalent vocabulary in target language; don't translate the existing and acceptable transliteration of terms; and don't translate when there are no stylistic equivalents. In the view of these 'don'ts', Xuan Zang used transliteration as the best tool. Dao Xuan (596–667) a historian specializing in scripture history once visited the translation workshop of Xuan Zang and discovered that Xuan Zang at the outset comprehended and analyzed the meaning of original text and then rendered it into Chinese. Rather than taking the text to team members, he simply uttered the translation that was perfect and better than that yielded by practice of literal translation—using Chinese syntax—polishing it for fluency technique (Cheng, 53). In essence, what Xuan Zang practiced was Kumarajiva's free-translation technique.

It was owing to the refinement of the translation processes over the years that the quality and clarity of these monks, especially Kumarajiva and Xuan Zang, surpassed the quality of previous translations, for they abandoned the prevalent method of concept matching[4] for meaning and substance. The translation projects undertaken by these great monks were a mix of oral, collective, and in-depth knowledge of Buddhist doctrine that reached the quality of accuracy, fluency, and elegance, which is obvious from Parmartha's comments on translation.

> But translation is an extremely difficult task. It must not aim at flowery [华] language. The difference of one word can make an argument go astray and become farfetched. If unhewn language [质] can capture the meaning, then one should not allow refined [文] writing to cause the essential message to be lost. Thus the present translation seeks to be at once refined and unhewn, trying to keep the two in balance… (Martha et al. 2006, 128–9)

[3]These are: substantiation; omission; conjugational change; separation-combination; loan words method; and the pronoun-replacement method.

[4]Translators seeking Chinese equivalents for Indian Buddhist technical terms and concepts borrowed heavily from Chinese classics; especially Daoist literature, however, the definition has been refuted by Victor Mair (2012) who wrote that it means more like 'pedantic and categorized concepts'.

3 Conclusion

It could be deduced that the scholar monks laid a solid foundation for India–China civilizational dialogue. Their efforts not only made Buddhism universal in China but also enabled Indian philosophical traits to make inroads or amalgamate with the Chinese philosophical thought. The concept of *narka* (hell) and Chinese literature about ghosts and spirits, especially during northern and southern dynasties, as well as other literary genres such as *bianwen* (narrative literature with alternate prose and rhymed parts for recitation and singing) and *Chuanqi*(short stories or poetic dramas) could be attributed to the synthesis of the Indian and Chinese cultures.

The greatest contribution of these scholar monks is that they were responsible for the core of East Asian Buddhist literature. Without the efforts of these monks, it would have been difficult to imagine the kind of relationship China would have had with its East and South Asian neighbors. They also fostered the material linkages between China and other countries in the vicinity and strengthened people-to- people exchanges. They were also instrumental in laying foundations of a thriving translation industry in the East that enhanced people-to-people interaction and understanding among nations. It could be said that Faxian paved the way for thousands of his countrymen to travel to India and bring back scriptures. Besides, these scholar monks left behind their travelogues and autobiographies, which have enabled various countries to reconstruct their ancient history. Needless to say, the Silk Road connecting these civilizations played an invaluable role. As China has advocated the construction of New Silk Road Economic Belt, I believe there is a lot to learn and claim from the ancient Silk Road that fostered the civilizational dialogue between the nations.

References

Bagchi, P.C. 1981. *India and China: A Thousand Years of Cultural Relations*. Calcutta: Saraswat Library.

Cheng, Mei. 2003. Xuan Zang's Translation Practice. *Studies in Translatologies*, 11 (1): 53–62.

Fan, Jinshi. 2007. Sutras translated by Xuan Zang and Dunhuang Wall Paintings. In *Xuan Zang and the Silk Route*, ed. Lokesh Chandra and Radha Benerjee, New Delhi: Indira Gandhi National Centre for the Arts and Munshiram Manoharlal.

Hui, Jiao 慧皎"鸠摩罗什传. 1994. (Biography of Kumarajiva) produced from Hui Jiao's Biographies of Eminent Monks by Institute of South Asian Studies Peking University (1994) In 中国载籍中南亚史料汇编 (*Collection of South Asian Historical Materials from Chinese sources*) vol. I, Shanghai: Shanghai Guji Publishing House.

Ji, Xianlin. 1985. 《大唐西域记校注》(*Journey to the West with Annotations*) ZhonghuaShuju, Beijing. Annotations based on Xuan Zang's original work.

Jiang, Jingkui. 2014. "试论印度经典的汉译"(*On Indian Classics in Chinese Translation)*, ed. Zeng Qiong and Zeng Qingyan. 认识东方学 (Approaching the East), Beijing: Peking University Press.

Martha Cheung, Pui Yiu, and Lin Wusun. 2006. *An Anthology of Chinese Discourse on Translation: From Earliest Times to the Buddhist Project*. St Jerome Publishing, University of Virginia.

Mair, Victor H. 2012. What is *Geyi*, After All? Reprinted in *China Report*, 48: 29–59, Sage Publications.

Sen, Tansen. 2004. *Buddhism, Diplomacy and Trade: The Realignment of Sino-Indian Relations, 600-1400*. New Delhi: Manohar.

Shi, Xiaomei, and Lu Xiaohong. 2013. 石小梅、路晓红. “玄奘术语翻译理论的创新性及其现代意义” (The innovativeness and relevance of Xuan Zang’s terminology translation theory) 民族翻译 (Nationality Translation) 2013 (2) 46. Xi’an: Foreign Language University.

Wang, Bangwei, and Tansen Sen. 2011. *India and China Interaction through Buddhism and Diplomacy: A Collection of Essays by Professor Prabodh Chandra Bagchi*. Delhi: Anthem Press.

Part II
The 'Belt and Road' Initiative and the Corresponding Economic Corridors

Chapter 4
The 'Belt and Road' Initiative: Fundamental Principles, Content, and Significance for Sino-Indian Relations

Jianxue Lan

The 'Belt and Road' Initiative (BRI), also known as the 'One Belt One Road' (OBOR) was first proposed by the Chinese President Xi Jinping during his visit to Kazakhstan in September, and to Indonesia in October, 2013. China proposed the BRI aiming to connect and bring together the Asia-Pacific economic circles and the European economic circles by promoting policy coordination, facilitating connectivity, uninterrupted trade, financial integration, and people-to-people exchanges. It aims to share China's developmental dividend with the overall development of all people along the 'Belt and Road'; it's like adding on two wings for the entire Asian growth. The BRI has already been proposed for more than three year, and there are already 65 countries that have expressed their positive response and willingness to join the initiative and jointly share the mutual development strategies. BRI will provide an open and inclusive platform for the development and cooperation of all the countries along the 'Belt and the Road' and will greatly boost Sino-foreign cooperation.

1 The 'Belt and Road Initiative': Fundamental Principles and Contents

The 'Belt and Road' Initiative essentially is a strategy generated out of China's opening-up policy in the new century. The BRI is the product of globalization. China has implemented its reform and opening-up policy since 30 years, and the economy has achieved remarkable achievements and become the world's second largest. At present, as China's domestic economy demands transformation and upgrading, the opening-up strategy also needs to be upgraded. The BRI aims to

J. Lan (✉)
China Institute of International Studies (CIIS), Beijing, China
e-mail: lanjianxue@ciis.org.cn

B.R. Deepak (ed.), *China's Global Rebalancing and the New Silk Road*,
https://doi.org/10.1007/978-981-10-5972-8_4

carry forward the spirit of the ancient Silk Road of mutual learning and peaceful coexistence and expand mutually beneficial cooperation in various fields between China and Eurasia. Overall, the BRI proposes promoting foreign cooperation that is open, inclusive, and mutually beneficial for both the sides. More importantly, the initiative is in line with the purposes and principles of the UN Charter, as other institutions of governance created by China in tandem with other countries supplement the existing institutions.

In coming years, the comprehensive promotion of the 'Belt and Road' Initiative will form the core focus of China's domestic and foreign policy. This can be discerned from various pronouncements of the Chinese leadership at various domestic and international forums. For example, the Premier of the State Council of China, Li Keqiang, in the "Government Work Report" delivered at the Third Session of the 12th National People's Congress on March 5, 2015, stated (The State Council 2015):

> ……We will encourage Chinese companies to participate in overseas infrastructure developmental projects and engage in cooperation with their foreign counterparts in building up production capacity. We will work with the relevant countries in developing the Silk Road Economic Belt and the 21st Century Maritime Silk Road. We will move faster to strengthen infrastructure connectivity with China's neighbours, simplify customs clearance procedures, and build international logistics gateways. We will work to build the China-Pakistan Economic Corridor and the Bangladesh-China-India-Myanmar Economic Corridor. We will make China's interior and border areas more open to the outside world, promote the innovation-driven development of economic and technological development zones, and upgrade both border and cross-border economic cooperation areas….

In the same vein, the Chinese Premier reemphasized China's resolve to construct the Belt and Road in his 2016 and 2017 Government Work Report. In his 2016 Work Report, he further linked the initiative with the domestic development strategy of China, when he said (The State Council 2016): "Work continued to promote the coordinated development of the eastern region, the central region, the western region, and the northeast; priority was placed on moving forward with the Three Initiatives-the Belt and Road Initiative, the Beijing-Tianjin-Hebei integration initiative, and the Yangtze Economic Belt Initiative." In the 2017 Report, Li Keqiang wrote that: "Rapid progress was made in pursuing the Belt and Road Initiative, and a number of major projects and industrial-capacity cooperation projects with other countries were launched" (The State Council 2017).

The promotion of the "Belt and Road Initiative" primarily adheres to the following principles:

(a) To focus on achieving common development and common prosperity for all countries along the 'Belt and Road', uphold the spirit and the idea of a common destiny for the entire community, emphasize equality and the mutual benefits of joint consultation, joint construction, and joint sharing. It will be an open and inclusive platform for regional cooperation, taking into full consideration the position, interests, and convenience of every side.

(b) The BRI will be sensitive to the comfort level of other parties, ensure transparency and openness, and create synergy with the existing regional cooperation mechanisms. The initiative is not a "solo performance, but a symphony performed by all relevant countries" according to Wang Yi, China's Foreign Minister (Ministry of Foreign Affairs 2015).

(c) The primary significance of promoting the 'Belt and Road Initiative' is to initiate a new vigor and vitality for the ancient Eurasian continent; it shall add the power of two strong wings to the prosperity of this vast land mass. Through the mutual win-win development strategy, it will facilitate the development of China and the other countries concerned in the direction of regional equilibrium. It shall also be beneficial to eliminate the contradictions and conflicts arising from the cause of development and will help create an environment of peaceful development for the nations that ultimately can lead to common prosperity.

As regards the BRI content, it aims to actualize the "Five Connectivities" in China and countries along the 'Belt and Road' through the land and the sea routes. The connectivities have been identified as: policy coordination; facilitating connectivity; uninterrupted trade; financial integration; and people-to-people exchanges.

2 Significance of the BRI to Sino-India Relations

China considers India as an important country along the 'Belt and Road'. The initiative therefore, undoubtedly, would be a new *platform* and a *window* for India–China trade and economic investments and people-to-people and cultural exchanges. The BRI will bring about huge business opportunities for China and the countries along the Belt and the Road. Under the BRI, China will increase its investments for infrastructure development towards India; this shall in turn boost the modernization process of traffic and communications in India. Under the framework of the initiative, if India and China can strengthen policy communication and coordination, facilitate communication, enable a better flow of trade, accommodate better financing and funding, and establish people-to-people communication, then the entire world population will be more attached to each other. In ancient times, when Xuanzang came to India, travelling along the Silk Road in pursuit of knowledge, this brought about extensive exchanges and mutual learning between China and the Indian subcontinent. In the later part of 2014, the primary founder of the Alibaba Group, Jack Ma, disclosed that Indian businessmen have been partners with Alibaba for 15 years already, about 40 million Chinese customers buy Indian tea and spices, etc., through Alibaba, and about 1.3 million Indian businessmen use the platform of the Alibaba net to expand and make their businesses flourish. Secondly, in light of India's unique geographical location and the age-old history of India–China relations, India stands as an important cooperative partner for China in the actualization of the 'Belt and Road' Initiative.

Strengthening India–China relations in the framework of the 'Belt and Road' Initiative will be conducive to the interface of the two major markets of India and China, for the interface of the national development strategies of both nations, and for the reconciliation of the two great civilisations. It shall also be conducive to the market and the developmental dividend mutually for both India and China. India's entry into China's "Belt and Road Initiative" is also conducive to the Indian market and the development of each other's dividends. If India joins China in the initiative, it shall provide a new impetus to further substantiate India–China strategic cooperation and partnership from several aspects, such as political-trust building, trade and investments, infrastructure building, people-to-people contacts, the tourism industry, and many others. India is an important member of the Asian Infrastructure Investment Bank and the BRICS New Development Bank. The 'Belt and Road' Initiative is destined to create and bring along more developmental opportunities for India. Thirdly, India and China's joint partnership in the 'Belt and Road' Initiative will send out a positive signal to the outside world of the mutual political trust between the two, will increase the mutual interdependence between India and China, and will also be beneficial for their interwoven interests. Looking from the practicalities of transport, communication, and economic and trade exchanges, China's development is inseparable from the Indian Ocean. Among the 39 major foreign air routes of China, 21 routes are via the Indian Ocean region. Ninety percent of China's foreign trade is through maritime transport and around 70% of it is via the Indian Ocean. China's dependence on the import of crude oil has exceeded 60%, more than two-thirds of which is via the Indian Ocean. In the long run, India and China, if they expand their cooperation in the Indian Ocean region, will be in a position to set the general trend in the region. This is also an integral constituent of the 'Belt and Road' Initiative. The Indian government expressed its willingness to be the 'Net Security Provider' in the Indian Ocean region, reflecting that India will be the major player for providing public safety for the goods in the Indian Ocean Region.

2.1 India's Anxieties and Some Recommendations

India's cautious attitude towards the initiative is understandable. On a personal level, I would suggest that China and India must set up a consultation mechanism on the 'Belt and Road' Initiative where India's concerns can be openly discussed, along with mechanisms for linking up the maritime cooperation issues between both countries.

Speaking from the perspective of its national interests, it is very normal and understandable that India will carefully assess and evaluate its benefits of joining the China-led initiative. For the BRI and especially for the 'Maritime Silk Road' (MSR), India indeed has its doubts concerning certain issues. The BRI is a concept that has been proposed as a means to boost regional cooperation. It will maintain adequate openness and transparency, pay attention to the legitimate concerns of all stakeholders, and constantly revise and improve on the basis of recommendations. Currently, various forms of consultative mechanisms have already been established between India and China, such as bilateral dialogues on issues such as energy security, Afghanistan, Central Asia, counter terrorism, and even issues related to Africa. Therefore, why also not devise a dialogue mechanism for India and China to discuss the 'One Belt One Road' or the 'Belt and Road' Initiative? Under this kind of dialogue mechanism, I firmly believe that China will, for certain, gladly communicate with India on action plans, pay attention to the concerns and recommendations of the Indian side, and consider joint projects for maritime cooperation between the two countries. All the concerns and doubts of both sides can be discussed frankly and openly in order to narrow down the differences and further expand cooperation on both sides.

Secondly, India may wait for a period and consider an appropriate and suitable opportunity to join the initiative as this initiative will still be open. But this kind of procrastination and hesitation should not persist for too long because the late entrants may be at a loss compared to the early entrants, and it may not enjoy the same benefits as the early entrants. For example, China announced an investment of US$40 billion for the Silk Road fund[1], i.e., an investment into the countries along the "Belt and Road". Practice indicates that India's strategic judgment on the issue of the Asian Infrastructure Investment Bank (AIIB) is very accurate; it is one of the first founding members. This is clearly conducive for importing foreign investment into India. It reflects India's foresight; it reflects that both China and India have insisted on development and cooperation as a priority. On the issue of the 'Belt and Road', it is believed that the Indian government will resort to similar kinds of wise decision making. Thirdly, the discourse on this subject in the Indian academic community has been positive. For example, Professor Deepak (2014) in an article in People's *Daily* commented that the 'Belt and Road' could be considered as a carrier of hopes and dreams. Citing historical sources, he argued that maritime communications between India and China can be traced back to the Han Dynasty. In Ban Gu's *Former Han Annals*, the history of exchanges between the southern region of India and China were recorded. This maritime communication reached its peak during the Yuan and the Ming Dynasties. Zheng He led entire fleets of ships to the east and west coasts of India. If India joins the initiative, it will help to revamp its domestic infrastructure. Most of the Asian countries still belong to the developing countries; therefore, our path to development is still quite long. Cooperation and common development are the only remedies. From the standpoint of common security and common prosperity, the BRI can be instrumental in resolving problems related to development. India's participation will render the so-called Western notion of China containing India through the 'String of Pearls theory' untenable. Secondly, the 'Maritime Silk Road' shall connect the economic fortune of the

[1]During a keynote address to the Belt and Road Forum on 14 May 2017, Chinese President Xi Jinping pledged a massive funding boost for the Silk Road Fund to the tune of 100 billion Yuan (US$14.50 billion).

countries of Asia and will greatly develop the economic, trade, and people-to-people exchanges among countries. From a constructivists point of view, it would put forth the case of common security in Asia. Senior Indian scholar, Mohan (2014) argued that the Indian anxiety regarding the China-led initiative of the "One Belt One Road" is mainly due to its narrow perspective on geopolitics. In the long run, the Indian government should not continue to have an attitude of procrastination or hesitation for the Chinese initiative. Similar views were expressed by seasoned diplomats like Shyam Saran (2015) and many others. However, there is a constituency in India that believes that India's participation in "One Belt One Road" strategy will cause serious damage to India's sphere of influence. This fear has grown stronger ever since China and Pakistan signed a pact for the China–Pakistan Economic Corridor that runs through Indian-claimed territory in Pakistan-controlled Kashmir. But this fact is groundless for the following reasons:

(a) Indian officials on several occasions have emphasized that they would be happy to see economic, cultural and people-to-people exchanges among the people of the Eurasian continent. India has joined the Asian Infrastructure Investment Bank and the latter will provide an important financial channel for the establishment of the 'One Belt One Road'. The planned Asian Infrastructure Investment Bank (AIIB), which would finance infrastructure construction along the 'Belt and Road, conform to the needs of the region and complement existing financial institutions.
(b) China highly appreciates 'Project Mausam', 'The Spice Route', and India's 'Act East Policy', as well as other maritime cooperation projects proposed by the Indian scholars and academics (in fact, the Spice Route was an ancient route where spices from North Africa, the Middle East, and the South Asia subcontinent were imported into China, and it itself is an example of a cooperation model in the history between India and China). The spirit of these initiatives and China's initiative echo the same vision, so the participation and support could be on mutual basis. This also indicates that India and China as ancient civilizations uphold the tradition of openness, tolerance, and inclusiveness. India has also opened up the gateway to Central Asia and participated in the Bangladesh China India Myanmar (BCIM) Economic Corridor. As an embodiment of its support for China's 'Belt and Road Initiative', if it also recognizes the Silk Road connections, then the road will be accessible from all sides and retain its openness and not impose exclusivity.
(c) Although the Indian Ocean is international waters, due to historical factors and geographical factors, India in the Indian Ocean region can indeed play a unique role that cannot be substituted for either by China, the United States, or any other country. China's 'One Belt One Road' initiative cannot and will not influence or affect India's unique position in that region. On the contrary, it may offer new opportunities for India–China cooperation in the Indian Ocean region.

3 Conclusion

Comrade Deng Xiaoping once said that if the two countries—India and China—are not developed, there shall never be an Asian century. I expect India to take positive action and actively participate in the strategic plan of the 'Belt and Road' Initiative, in order to provide an impetus to the rapid revival of the two large civilizations of the East and also to promote the common prosperity of the two major emerging markets together. We believe that India will take positive action in some form and actively participate in the "Belt and Road Initiative". India could provide a great impetus to the rapid revival of the two great Eastern civilizations, dock the development strategy between the two countries, and promote the common prosperity and the common interests of these two major emerging markets.

References

Deepak, B.R. 狄伯杰 2014. "狄伯杰: 印参与"海上丝路"可破"珍珠链论" (India's participation in Maritime Silk Road will render the 'Strings of Pearl' untenable). *Global Times (Chinese version)*, September 18, 2014. http://opinion.huanqiu.com/opinion_world/2014-09/5141651.html.

Ministry of Foreign Affairs, People's Republic of China. 2015. *Foreign Minister Wang Yi Meets the Press.* http://www.fmprc.gov.cn/mfa_eng/wjb_663304/wjbz_663308/2461_663310/t1243662.shtml.

Mohan, C. Raja. 2014. One Belt One Road. *Indian Express*, August 13, 2015. http://indianexpress.com/article/opinion/columns/chinese-takeaway-one-belt-one-road/.

Saran, Shyam. 2015. India must join China's Silk Route initiative. *Hindustan times*, March 18, 2015. http://www.hindustantimes.com/ht-view/india-must-join-china-s-silk-route-initiative/story-cZJ5kG4ktsvRaRXI9yRkqO.html.

The State Council, People's Republic of China. 2015. *Full Text: Report on the Work of the Government.* http://english.gov.cn/archive/publications/2015/03/05/content_281475066179954.htm.

The State Council, People's Republic of China. 2016. *Full Text: Report on the Work of the Government.* http://english.gov.cn/premier/news/2016/03/17/content_281475309417987.htm.

The State Council, People's Republic of China. 2017. *Full Text: Report on the Work of the Government (2017).* http://english.cctv.com/2017/03/16/ARTI1PaDFjoEdY5G7BB0LYUI170316.shtml.

Chapter 5
'Belt and Road' Initiative: Building a China–South Asian Security Community

Xiaoping Yang

Historically, the transition to a new era is closely connected with big events, such as the end of the Cold War, China's joining into WTO, the 9/11 attacks, and world financial crisis of 2008. In today's era of significant changes, chaos and uncertainties, new challenges also embodied the opportunites to give birth to new concepts and initiatives. In Asia, Australia once initiated today's Asia-Pacific Economic Cooperation (APEC), Malaysian Prime Minister Mahathir proposed the East Asia Economic Caucus (EAEC) which became the predecessors of 10+1 and 10+3. And, former Japanese Prime Minister Hatoyama once initiated the East Asian Community which some believe, if goes through, would have changed the nature of Sino-Japan bilateral relations essentially.

In this process, China, as a rising power, also proposed a few intiatives, such as the "New Security Concept" in the 1990s and the "Harmonious World" in the early twenty first century, on the basis of trying to contemplate and handle global and Asian security problems from a broader prospective. Though "Harmonious world" is considered as a logic extension of "new security concept" by Chinese, internationally, it received much less attention than new security concept. In this sense, there still existes huge room for China to improve its capability to clearly display its new ideas and target the international audience according to its expected trajectory.

X. Yang (✉)
National Institute of International Strategy, Chinese Academy of Social Sciences, Beijing, China
e-mail: linayxpnew@163.com

B.R. Deepak (ed.), *China's Global Rebalancing and the New Silk Road*,
https://doi.org/10.1007/978-981-10-5972-8_5

1 Context and De-conceptualization of "Security Community"

The promulgation of the "Community of Common Destiny" concept would be a landmark in China's foreign affairs history in the sense that it, for the first time, clarifies China's long-term vision for Asian regional order. During the meeting of Central National Security Commission in April 2014, Xi Jinping pointed out that a country should "not only attach importance to one's own security but also pay attention to common security, forge a community of common destiny, push different parties to move towards the goal of mutual benefit and common security" (Zhou 2014). This echoed with the concept of "Community of Common Destiny" which comes through after the Central Meeting on the Works of Foreign Affairs (中央外事工作会议ZhongYang Waishi Gongzuo Huiyi) in October 2013. After that meeting, Xi Jinping said, we "must integrate the Chinese dream with the desire of the people of the neighboring countries for a good life, and with the prospects for regional development, let the awareness of community of common destiny take root in the neighboring countries."

But what does the *Community of Common Destiny* mean in Chinese perspective? The concept of community, if one views this from its abstract meaning, is a kind of feeling of happiness, warmth, and interdependence felt in a community (Bauman 2013). This type of community has both philosophical (e.g., communism) as well as social, especially anthropological significance (e.g., community, community theory). As far as China and the neighboring countries' efforts to build a community of common destiny are concerned, it means "not only continuous strengthening of economic cooperation, but also building-up of mutual understandings and extending of mutual support on security issues between member countries (Zhou 2014)". In this context, in Chinese perspective, the construction of security community is an important part of realizing the community of common destiny.

During the fourth Conference on Interaction and Confidence-Building Measures in Asia (CICA) in May 2014, China made its own proposition on how to realize a situation of a similar kind of community on the security level. Chinese leadership for the first time proposed (Xi 2014a, b): we "must actively advocate a *common, comprehensive, cooperative, sustainable* concept of Asian security; create security community; build regional security and new frameworks for cooperation; make efforts to walk out on a mutually built, mutually shared and win-win path of Asian security".

According to Yan (2014), the so-called "Common Security" implies double security or bi-directional security, namely one country's self-security should not pose threat to another if not helping to ensure another's security. The core is to not seek absolute security, and not pursue absolute victory in seeking security. This concept of common security is especially important as far as US (the most developed country and world's leading power) and China (the largest developing country and world's rising power) are concerned, especially in the background U.S is adjusting its global strategy to deal with uncertainties originating from the rise of China.

The so-called "Comprehensive Security" means that "security" includes both traditional and non-traditional security areas. At the same time, comprehensive security also means security has to focus on not only current prominent security problems but also future emerging security threats.

The so called "Cooperative Security" means security should not be confrontational, namely not zero-sum in nature; instead, it should reduce conflict through preventive cooperation. Here, preventive cooperation might have two layers of meaning: first, this type of cooperation is not sufficient or simply has not yet started so far; second, this type of cooperation has already started, but possibly there is a problem in its implementation. It needs a redesign of the path to conduct preventive cooperation.

Finally, "sustainable security" means a balanced national strategy between short-term economic benefits and long-term environmental friendly development model.

In a nutshell, though Chinese perspective of "Security Community" is ambiguous and not clearly-cut on how to realize it, it provides pretty different thoughts on how to shape future Asian security. It also demonstrates China's domestic efforts to seek for a sustainable, benign, win-win development (rise) model. Therefore, the construction of security community is a self-made strategic choice by China based on its caculation of its own capabilities for growth as well as the judgement for prospects of current Asia–Pacific regional geopolitics.

2 South Asian Structural Characteristics and Relevances to "China–South Asian" Security Community

As a unique geostrategic unit, South Asia has its regional characteristics. It could be generalized as "India Centric", "fragmented" regional integration process, and mismatch between security threat concept and real security issues. India centrism is mainly reflected in the fact that India is not only dominant in strength but also being geographically located at the center of the south Asian subcontinent. This implies that all the security considerations of other South Asian countries are primarily linked to India. Secondly, in the economic realm, India's possible denial of transit facilities to other states will result in unaffordable transportation costs. As far as economic cooperation is concerned, fragmented integration has existed, where India radiates all its eastern countries while Pakistan is trying to keep its influence in Afghanistan to its West; this disjunction potentially will widen, in parallel with deeper cooperation between India and Southeast Asia in the future (Yang 2012).

With respect to its traditional strategic thinking between its geographical features and national security, the South Asian subcontinent had been long trapped with the land security threat curse and not given enough recognition to the strategic role of the Indian Ocean. Rulers believed that threats to its security mainly came from the northwest land or nothern land and treated the ocean as a protective security screen.

Along with the deepening of economic globalization and the arrival of the Indo-Asia-Pacific era, the Indian Ocean became an important passage to enable economic and trade exchanges between the Middle East and East Asia, and the ocean itself became a subject of economic, security, development, and strategic importance. This requires the adjustments for strategic thinkings on both the land and the sea; And focus is bound to gradually shift from the land to the seas. In terms of current dominate thinking on security threats, South Asian nations have been for long time emphasizing too much on the nuclear issue, military confrontation, and internal domestic conflicts, which in essence has diverted attention from developmental issues related to "human security" in the long-run (Yang 2012).

In practice, the 'Indian-centric' fragmented regional integration has provided China an opportunity to explore the potentials to construct a security community through construction of the 'Belt and Road', By arguing this, it challenges the conventional over-simplified explanations that China's Belt and Road Initiative is just a temporary arrangement of China to counter the US's version 2.0 'rebalancing towards Asia'; Or it is just the propaganda slogan of China to divert its domestic conflicts; Instead, it is a set of strategic arrangements which possesses a series of supporting vehicles and which will impact the developmental path of China in the coming five–ten years.

And the mismatch between the security concept and the reality on the ground in South Asia has also provided possibilities for China to build a shared security community with South Asian countries. With the increasing strategic significance of the Indian Ocean, China has already been involved in some way or other in the North Indian Ocean. However, China still has not been integrated into any regional maritime security mechanism in this region, which is obviously an unfavorable situation to efficiently integrate international resources to cooperatively realize maritime security, considering the rise of non-traditional security issues in South Asian and the Indian Ocean.

Besides, some new dynamics on the groud in Southern Asia, such as stabilizing Afghanistan, implementing of China Pakistan Economic Cooridor (CPEC), re-energizing BCIM and India's *Act East* policy, also contribute to the possiblity to co-establish a security community. It's undeniable that the intra-regional overlapping has been increasing, yet there is no very effective approach to deal with the increasing complexity.

3 Main Approach to Build a Security Community Under the Framework of 'Belt and Road'

Given the structual characteristics and current new dynamics implied the possiblities of a co-building China-South Asia security community, what would be the ways to materialize it in the context of Belt and Road Initiative, especially considering the purpose of building a China–South Asia security community is to find a way that can fully realize sustainable, comprehensive, and inclusive security both for China and South Asian countries.

First and foremost, take full advantages of China's current edges/competiveness, optimize Chinese existing economic strength to facilitate regional economic integration and make it beneficial to neighboring South Asian countries, especially, via the policy of industrial integration.

Currently in South Asia, China is advocating the joint establishment of two economic corridors, namely the Bangladesh, China, India, Myanmar Economic Corridor (BCIM) and the China–Pakistan Economic Corridor (CPEC). This is designed on China's perception that India and Pakistan are the two key economies in South Asia and there exists fragmented, integration between the two in the region. And it is assumed that there are tremendous potentials for the improvements of Sino-Indian and Sino-Pakistan economic relationships respectively, as well as the India-Pakistan economic integration. At least provides the possibility that in the future China could have the option to faciliate the normalization of India-Pakistan economic integration by using its good economic relations with both India and Pakistan as a leverage.

CPEC is an inevitable choice made by China and Pakistan in the wake of Pakistan's worsening economic situation amidst its decade-long support to the US' war on terror. It is also designed to help to stablize the security situation in Afghanistan. In this sense, CPEC is also in the line with India's interests in promoting regional stability. In the 2015 joint statement between the Islamic Republic of Pakistan and the People's Republic of China on Establishing the All-Weather Strategic Cooperative Partnership, it is said that "the two sides agreed to promote a '1+4' pattern of economic cooperation featuring a leading role of the CPEC and four key areas including the Gwadar Port, Energy, Transportation Infrastructure and Industrial Cooperation… The two sides believed that the security interests of Pakistan and China are closely interconnected. They will actively advocate the Asian security concept featuring common, comprehensive, cooperative and sustainable security. The two sides will continue to enhance cooperation in fighting terrorism and national defence, and strengthen coordination on international and regional security affairs. The two sides will continue working together to resolutely combat the terrorism. (Ministry of Foreign Affairs, P.R.C, 2015)."

The Bangladesh, China, India, Myanmar Economic Corridor (BCIM-EC) is a sub-regional cooperation mechanism initiated first by Chinese local authority Yunan province. It is primarily motivated to promote industrial cooperation and cultural exchanges by taking full advantages of the geographical closeness between Yunan and neighboring countries. After more than ten years of joint hard work, India has officially started making a positive response to the BCIM. In December 2013, the first Joint Study Group meeting was held in Kunming, China, which was a milestone at BCIM process and marked the offical launch of the inter-governmental process of BCIM-EC (economic cooridor). In order to enhance the effective cooperation between BCIM members, 4 areas including physical connectivity, trade and investment, environmentally sustainable development and people-to-people contacts were marked as the primary area for cooperation.

Moreover, four countries have also reached a broad consensus on various aspects of cultural exchanges, regional economic integration, and mutual political trust.

However, there are still two structural problems as far as BCIM is concerned. First, due to security concerns, New Delhi is still hesitant to promote physical connectivity spanning through the north-eastern region of India. Second, as Myanmar is a shared neighboring country between India and China, under some certain conditions, there is a certain degree of strategic competition between India and China. Therefore, some studies hold that, by comparison with the multilateral cooperation advocated by BCIM, New Delhi is probably more inclined towards bilateral cooperation between China and India rather than multilateral cooperation, especially aiming at using Chinese capital and expertise to upgrade its infrastructure sector.

Besides the above economic integration approach, another way that China is adopting to build a China-South Asia security community is to try to enhance its mechanism building capability by connecting current South Asia security issues within other related regional mechanism such as SCO and IONS. Especially, on how to accommodate non-traditional security issues of South Asia into Shanghai Cooperation Organisation (SCO) and Indian Ocean Naval Symposium (IONS).

With the uncertainty of Afghanistan future both on security as well as on economy, the Shanghai Cooperation Organization which was established to combat "terrorism, separatism, and extremism", has the responsibility to take a role in safeguarding regional security and responding to regional security threats, in the context that the International Security Assistance Force for Afghanistan would be cut down significantly. In September 2014, during his visit to India, Chinese President Xi Jinping stated that "China welcomes and supports India to become an official member of Shanghai Cooperation Organisation" (Xi 2014a, b) for India's membership into the SCO faciliates not only the need for cooperation in anti-terrorism but also the future energy cooperation between South Asia and Central Asia, through the related institutional mechanism integration.

Similarly, in the maritime-security domain, China is so far not integrated with any regional mechanisms in the North Indian Ocean Region. But along with the rise of China, there is a huge space for all countries to cooperate for the protection of the sea lines of communication (SLOCs). The option to incorporate China into the IONS mechanism should be re-examined and in this way it helps to cooperate China's efforts in dealing with soft security issues, such as combating sea piracy and other prominent maritime-security challenges. These include but not confine to maritime terrorism, political turmoil in the coastal states, natural disasters, flight hazards, even the collision of commercial vessels. When facing these threats and uncertainties, there is a huge opportunity for cooperation.

In the field of concrete cooperation, it may start from a few neutral practices such as joint search and rescue in times of natural disasters, or patrolling for anti-piracy operations, mutual visits of ports, etc. In this way it helps to promote confidence-building measures (CBM) between China and India through these interactions. At the same time, a tri-lateral joint exercises of the Chinese, US, and Indian military forces in the Indian Ocean and Malacca Strait area is also worthy to explore. Finally even other specific cases such as information sharing is also embodied with opportunities to try to enhance regional security.

4 Challenges and Some Suggestions

The challenges for the construction of a China–South Asia security community mainly include:

First, how to deal with "China–India–South Asia" relationship? As far as India is concerned, it enjoys the leading position in South Asia and the region is often regarded as its traditional backyard. But at the same time, since the establishment of Pakistan, India's security concerns along its western borders have never been mitigated. This indirectly influenced India's judgements on China's interntions of its increasing presences in South Asia, and India's concerns mainly dwell on: (1) the China–Pakistan "all weather" strategic partnership; (2) development of a good economic and political relationship between China and other South Asian countries and it leads to India's concern for China's "strategic encircling"; (3) the increased level of the Chinese presence in the Indian Ocean Region in the context of Chinese robust economic development and then the increasing appetite for energy resources. Obviously, these hindered the possibility of cooperation between India and China to ensure the safety of Indian Ocean waterways.

Moreover, the increasing of China's presence in South Asia, to a certain extent, will objectively play a mixed 'balanced' role in transforming the regional order in South Asia. India's emerging readjustment of its neighborhood diplomacy could be interpreted as a response to Chinese assertiveness in the region.

Second, in the process of building the China–South Asia security community, it's very important to find a way to converge economic integration and dependency with mutual trust in security. On the one hand, in terms of China–India relations, how could the China–India economic relationship be promoted continuously with the backdrop of unresolved border issues? and, on the other hand, how could a healthy China–India relaitonship be possible in the midst of enhancing India-U.S security/defense relationship and increasing India-U.S strategic cooperations in the larger Asia-Pacific region? In terms of maritime security, India expressed concerns over China's presence in the Indian Ocean by believing that China is constructing a 'String of Pearls' to 'encircle India', the encirclement being not across the Himalayas, but more from the seas. At the same time, India has also strengthened its presence in the South China Sea; And it is continuously strengthening its military and economic relationships with Vietnam. These dynamics seem to be exerting forces in conflicting directions. And this is bound to affect the construction of China–South Asia security community.

As regards to how to cope with these challenges, first of all, the building of China–South Asia security community will depend on the joint efforts of various parties, especially the political will of the core countries. In other words, how various stakeholders perceive it as strategic opportunity instead of strategic risks;

how different stakeholders under current "trust deficit" atmosphere could try to be more open-minded and more constructive on how to promote essential cooperation.

Secondly, considering economic integration is a two-edged sword, China and South Asian countries should continue to promote open regional mechanisms through mutual arrangements and design; and jointly make efforts for a good environment of long-term economic growth of China's neighbors; as well as foster an environment conducive to common development. Thereby, help to satisfy the expectations of the neighboring countries about China and enhance the possibility of building of security community.

Furthermore, China needs to enhance the integration between economic mechanism and security mechanism. In the process of constructing a security community, mechanism building are important supporting layers. In the short term, it might follow the principle of easiest thing first, and little by little enhance the coordination efforts between China and South Asian countries on specific policy levels.

Lastly, people-to-people and cultural exchanges could help to promote the concept of a "community", which is crucial for building a shared community.

References

Kartikay, Mehrotra, and Unni Krishnan. 2014. Modi Wins 20 Billion$ Pledge from Xi amid Border Flare-up. *Bloomberg*, September 18, 2014. http://www.bloomberg.com/news/2014-09-17/modi-to-host-xi-for-talks-to-bolster-india-s-china-ties.html.

Ministry of Foreign Affairs. 2015. *Joint Statement between the People's Republic of China and the Islamic Republic of Pakistan on Establishing the All-Weather Strategic Cooperative Partnership (full text-Chinese)*. Ministry of Foreign Affairs, the People's Republic of China, April 21, 2015. http://www.fmprc.gov.cn/mfa_chn/zyxw_602251/t1256274.shtml.

Xi, Jinping. 2014. *Actively Establish Asian Security Concept, Jointly establish New Aspects of Cooperation in Security* (People's website). http://politics.people.com.cn/n/2014/0522/c1024-25048258.html, 2014年5月22日.

Xi, Jinping. 2014. 支持印度加入上海合组织 (China supports India to Join SCO). *Beijing Morning Post*, September 19, 2014.

Yan, Xuetong. 2014. *Pursue Common Security, Realise Long Lasting Peace*. People's Website, June 3, 2014. http://world.people.com.cn/n/2014/0603/c1002-25093694.html.

Yang, Xiaoping. 2012. South Asian Security Framework: Structural Imbalance and Fragmented Integration. *World Economy and Politics*, No. 2, 2012 (Chinese Academy of Social Sciences, Beijing). Also available at https://indiachinainstitute.org/wp-content/uploads/2010/03/Yang-Xiaoping-Security-Architecture-of-SA.pdf.

Zhou, Fangying. 2014. Community of Common Destiny—Important Element of National Security. People's Website, June 4, 2014. http://theory.people.com.cn/n/2014/0604/c112851-25101849.html.

Zou, Chunxia. 2014. 习近平首提总体国家安全观 (Xi Jinping First Time Raising Overall National Security View). Beijing *QingnianBao* (Beijing Youth Daily), April 16, 2014.

Zygmuntm, Bauman. 2003. *Community: Seeking Safety in an Insecure World*. Translated by Ou Yang Jing gen. suzhou: Jiangsu People's Publication.

Chapter 6
Bangladesh, China, India, Myanmar Economic Corridor (BCIM-EC): Security Dilemma Rider to Regional Economic Integration

B.R. Deepak

In May 2013, during the visit of Chinese Premier, Li Keqiang, point 18 of the India–China joint statement referred to the development of a Bangladesh, China, India, and Myanmar Economic Corridor (BCIM-EC). It made provisions for setting up a Joint Study Group (JSG) on strengthening connectivity in the BCIM region for closer economic, trade, and people-to-people linkages. The statement also referred to the BCIM Regional Forum and said that the two sides appreciated the progress made in promoting cooperation under this forum (MEA 2013). Is the idea of BCIM an old wine in a new bottle? How did India and China arrive at the idea of BCIM-EC? How did it evolve and will the security dilemma in the region hinder regional economic integration?

1 Locating BCIM in History

It could be established from Chinese, as well as Indian, records that the Sino-Indian interface has always been a two-way traffic and the two elements of this traffic were the material and spiritual–cultural exchanges. This two-faceted exchange was carried out through the Central Asian Route or the so-called Silk Route: the Assam–Burma (now Myanmar) and Yunnan Route or the famous Southern Silk Route; the Tibet, Nepal, and Bhutan Route; and the Sea Route or the so-called Maritime Silk Route. The Assam–Burma–Yunnan route was in fact the earliest route between India and China, and there are historical, as well as archaeological, records to prove that. The route originated in the northeastern part of India, passed through the northern part of Myanmar, and entered Tengchong, Baoshan, and Dali of Yunnan

B.R. Deepak (✉)
Centre for Chinese and Southeast Asian Studies, Jawaharlal Nehru University, New Delhi, India
e-mail: bdeepak@mail.jnu.ac.in

B.R. Deepak (ed.), *China's Global Rebalancing and the New Silk Road*,
https://doi.org/10.1007/978-981-10-5972-8_6

province, finally reaching Chengdu in Sichuan province. It further ran on through Bengal, and then finally merged with the central Asian route.

Professor Duan (2010), of the Sichuan Academy of Social Sciences, posits that while the Indus valley civilization vanished around 1,500 BC, Sanxingdui civilization in ancient Sichuan was at its prime, and, from the remains of this civilization, various products such as *cowries* from Indian Ocean regions (IOR), huge quantities of elephant tusks, willow leaf-shaped bronze daggers have definite connections with Assam in Eastern India and Myanmar. According to Professor Duan, especially the *Monetriaannulus* types of cowries that are normally only found in the IOR have also been found in various burial graves in Yunnan and can be seen in the Yunnan Museum.

The first reliable information about this route was provided by Si Maqian (BC 145–90?), the great Chinese historian in his masterpiece *Records of the Historian: Foreigners in the Southwest*. The record narrates that Zhang Qian, who was a Han envoy in the Western Region, returned to the court in 122 BC. He reported to the Han Emperor Wu Di (BC 140–87) that, while in Bactria, he saw clothes and bamboo walking sticks that had been made in *Shu* (Sichuan). He learned from the local merchants that they had procured these from a *Shu* market in *Shendu* [India], a place several thousand *li* [1/2 km] to the southeast from Bactria (ISAS 1994). Based on these records, it could be established that the Assam–Myanmar–Yunnan route was already there in the second century BC and that it was perhaps the earliest route between India and China.

It is believed that the Chinese silk was imported to India through the Assam–Myanmar–Yunnan route. Kautilya (BC 370–283), an official during Chandragupta Maurya's reign (BC 340–298) reported in his classic *Arthashstra* that the silk was produced in China. If Kautilya's statement is to be believed, Chinese silk was in vogue in India during the fourth century BC. Sichuan was one of the earliest places to raise silkworms in China. Being close to Yunnan, and Yunnan being the earliest gateway to India, silk, as a matter of fact, became one of the earliest industries of northeast India. By the seventh century CE, Assam's silk industry had reached its pinnacle and perfection. Banabhatta (in the seventh century), the author of *Harshacharita* (Biography of Harshavardhana) records that Bhaskara Varma (600–650), king of Kamarupa, presented Harshavardhana "silken towels pure as the autumn moon light… soft loin clothes smooth as birch barks (Ray 2003)."

During the Song, Yuan, and Ming dynasties (960–1644), when trade replaced religion as the main career of cross-cultural currents, the route did not lose its relevance. Six-hundred years ago, Zheng He (1371–1433) of Yunnan led a large fleet to the ports of Burma, Bangladesh, Indonesia, India, and even Africa. Even in the twentieth century, the Assam–Myanmar–Yunnan route came to the rescue of Allied powers against the Japanese during the Second World War.

2 Initiatives for the Revival of Routes

With the globalization of the world economy and an increased level of economic interdependence, various regional economic blocks, such as ASEAN in southeast Asia, the EU in Europe, NAFTA in North America, MERCOSUR in Latin America, SAARC in South Asia, and many more at sub regional levels, have emerged all over the globe, many more are on their way, for example, the EEU (Eurasian Economic Union) came into force in 2015. As regards Asia, the initiation of reforms and an open-door policy in China, especially since Deng Xiaoping's south China tour in 1992, Indian economic reforms in 1991, and the initiation of the 'Look East Policy' (LEP), or the Act East Policy since 2014, plus a similar opening from Bangladesh in the 1990s and Myanmar in the late 1980s, have created favorable conditions for further regional economic grouping and integration, notwithstanding the fact that all these four are members of one or more other economic groupings in the region. The BCIM-EC is just another block in the making in the region that has been declared a part of China's Belt and Road initiative propounded by Xi Jinping in 2013.

China's aggressive economic engagement with the ASEAN benefitted immensely the adjoining regions of Yunnan and Guangxi. Yunnan has a border line of 4,061 km, bordering on Vietnam, Laos, Burma, Southeast Asia, South Asia, and Southeast Asia. A Free Trade Area (FTA) between China and the ASEAN has further called for building state-of-the-art infrastructure in these areas. The FTA has prompted China to invest heavily in Yunnan and Guangxi and connect these provinces with the ASEAN so as to turn these bordering areas into logistical and trade centers. A 179.2-km expressway between Nanning, the capital city of Guangxi, and *Youyiguan* (Friendship Pass) connected China with Hanoi in 2006. There are over a hundred flight routes originating from Yunnan to ASEAN cities. A network of railways, highways, and waterways to Vietnam is already in place, and construction of the Kunming-Bangkok highway and Kunming-Singapore railway are under way.

Since Myanmar is a member of the Association of Southeast Asian Nations (ASEAN) and could be linked by rail and road to India, China has been keen about initiating joint development of these links. It is with this backdrop that scholars from the Chinese Academy of Social Sciences, with the support from the provincial government, floated the idea of BCIM regional economic cooperation in the 1990s. Although Oberoi (2013) gave the credit for the BCIM idea to Professor Che Zhimin (then Deputy Director of the Economic and Technological Research Centre of the Yunnan Provincial People's Government), who during his November 1998 visit floated the idea through his paper entitled 'Proposition on Formation of "Sub-regional Cooperation Zone of China, India, Myanmar and Bangladesh"', Prof. Chen (2005) of Sichuan University ascribed it to both the Chinese and Indian scholars; the articles contributed by the scholars can be accessed in Vol. 3 issue 64 of the *Southwest China Studies* journal published in June 1994. However, it is true that, as time progressed and also as Chinese government declared Yunnan as the gateway for its linkages with south Asia, the scholars from Yunnan with support from Yunnan provincial government made extra efforts in this direction. During their deliberations, they talked about rebuilding the old Stillwell Road that starts at Ledo in Assam and goes up to Mong-Yu in Myanmar. In Myanmar, it connects the Myanmar Road to Kunming, the capital city of Yunnan. Of the total 1,726 km of the Stillwell-Myanmar road, only 61 km lies in India, 688 km in Myanmar, and 976 km in China. The regions those are likely to benefit include Southwest China, Northeastern India (Arunachal Pradesh, Assam, Manipur, Meghalaya, Mizoram, Nagaland, and Tripura) and Myanmar (Yangon, Mandalay, and Myitkina).

Also, with the ASEAN, Bangladesh-India-Myanmar Sri Lanka-Thailand Economic Cooperation (BIMST-EC), the South Asian Free Trade Area (SAFTA), the Asia Pacific Trade Agreement (APTA), the Ganga-Mekong Initiative between India, Myanmar, Thailand, Cambodia, Laos, and Vietnam, etc. regional and sub regional initiatives, the scope of economic and cultural relations in the BCIM regions has widened further, and it was felt that the region must be integrated within these economic groupings. Having the backing of the provincial government, the academics from Yunnan frequented India, Myanmar, and Bangladesh and hosted scholars from these countries in Yunnan. In the course of their exchanges, they established cordial relations with the top think tanks of these countries and floated the idea of BCIM Regional Forum.

3 From 'Kunming Initiative' to BCIM-EC

Three rounds of eleven rotational meetings were concluded since the idea of BCIM was floated. Primarily, the discussions have been around the so-called 3Ts (Transport, Trade and Tourism); however, as the meetings progressed, they were diversified to other areas, including traditional and nontraditional security and many other soft issues of concern in the region.

3.1 The First Round 1999–2003

On 15–17 August 1999, scholars from Yunnan convened the First International Conference on Regional Cooperation and Development among China, India, Myanmar, and Bangladesh, under the auspices of Yunnan Academy of Social Sciences in Kunming. The conference was attended by 134 delegates from BCIM countries and signed the 'Kunming initiative (KI 1999).' Six major themes were discussed at the conference: practical and strategic significance for the regional cooperation; the feasibility of economic, trade, and technological cooperation; study of the construction of communication channels and networks; the prospects and basis for the economic cooperation; open-door policies and trade and investment environment; and a framework for regional cooperation. It proposed the establishment of a Forum for Regional Economic Cooperation, created a two-member, country-specific Working Group that was supposed to bring the outcome of the conference to the notice of the respective governments, business and chambers of trade.

The second meeting was held in December 2000 in New Delhi, attended by around 50 delegates from BCIM countries. Issues such as transportation, overland trade, tourism, exchange of information, etc. were discussed. Besides, nontraditional security, narcotics smuggling, illegal immigration, etc. were also put on table, thus broadening the scope of regional cooperation. The chief outcome of the meeting was that business charter flights between Kunming and New Delhi were initiated, thus connecting the ancient civilizations once again and ending a long hiatus of self-imposed separation. The Third Forum was held in Bangladesh's capital Dhaka in February 2002 under the auspices of the Centre for Policy Dialogue (CPD), a founding partner institution of the BCIM initiative. The meeting was grandiose in its scale with around 200 people from all walks of life participating in the opening ceremony. The meeting issued the 'Dhaka Declaration' that proposed that the 'the track II' nature of the BCIM regional forum should move towards 'track I'. It was in this meeting that 'Forum' was added to BCIM Regional Cooperation. The Fourth Forum was held in the Myanmar capital Yangon in March 2003. The meeting issued its 'Yangon Statement.' The meeting also proposed to jointly establish a 'Forum' coordination office and smaller research groups pertaining to traffic, trade, and tourism.

3.2 *The Second Round 2004–2010*

The Fifth Forum was held from 21 to 22 December 2004 in Kunming. The forum was sponsored by the Development Research Center of Yunnan, Yunnan Academy of Social Sciences, and Yunnan Foreign Affairs Office, thus transforming the forum from being a civil society initiative to one on the government level. Areas such as transportation and communication, tourism, trade, and people-to-people exchanges were further discussed. The Indian side proposed that ports such as Chittagong and Yangon could be optimally used for furthering waterway transportation. The forum expressed that, while the BCIM region was rich in tourism resources, it was however hindered by the fact that cooperation was the least in this sector and, added to that, were difficulties such as rigid visa regimes and high travel and lodging costs, as well as the lack of tourism advertising in the respective countries (Lu et al. 2004).

The Sixth Forum was held in Delhi in 2006. Besides, reiterating facilitation of the 3Ts, the forum also introduced other dimensions of cooperation, such as discourse on social and human development, including issues like HIV/AIDS and drug trafficking. A BCIM Car Rally was also proposed. The Seventh Forum was held in Dhaka 31 March–1 April 2007. The forum issued the 'Dhaka Statement 2007'; it expressed satisfaction while reviewing the progress made since 'Kunming

Initiative' in 1999 and recognized that the BCIM initiative can fructify at the official level and can evolve into sub-regional programs at both government and non-governmental levels. It was agreed that at the Eighth BCIM Forum in Myanmar, an invitation would be extended to governments to send representatives. The Eighth Forum was held in Nay Pyi Taw, the new capital city of Myanmar, 23–24 July 2009. The take away from this forum was the setting up of the BCIM Business Council. The forum also issued a statement called the 'Nay Pyi Taw Statement 2009.'

3.3 Third Round 2011–2013

The Ninth Forum was held on 18 January 2011 in Kunming, China. Some of the highlights of this meeting were the signing of 'MoUs' on establishment of the BCIM Business Council, a joint newsletter, and the route survey of the BCIM Car Rally. The forum felt that the mechanism has become a 'multi-track' platform for cooperation albeit under the leadership of 'Track-I'. It was also decided that the 'Forum on Regional Economic Cooperation among BCIM' will be officially renamed the 'Forum on BCIM Cooperation' in the next conference in India, given the widening reach of BCIM cooperation in the areas, such as trade, agriculture, tourism, culture, education, health, science and technology, poverty alleviation, climate change, rational water use, security, etc. The Tenth Forum was held in Kolkata from 18 to 19 February 2012. A Joint Statement was also signed at the meeting that called for enhancing connectivity by road, rail, water, and air. The Route Survey Team, after completing the survey, recommended that the BCIM Car Rally run from Kolkata to Kunming in 2013. This meeting also diversified BCIM cooperation in the areas of science and technology, public health, education, agriculture, climate, water resources, and energy security. The Eleventh Forum was held 23–24 February 2013 in Dhaka. The Dhaka forum deliberated on cooperation in the areas of trade, investment and finance, multimodal connectivity, energy, and institutional arrangements. A statement known as the 'Dhaka Declaration' was also issued. Meanwhile, the BCIM Car Rally named 'Building Bonds, Fostering Friendship' also started off from Kolkata, India, on 22 February and reached Kunming, China, on 5 March 2013.

As the forum had wished to convert the mechanism from 'Track II' to 'Track I', even though the Chinese scholars had started to pronounce it as 'track I.5' owing to the increased interest from Yunnan government in its proceedings, soon after the eleventh meeting, India and China formally documented it in the joint statement during Premier Li Keqiang's India visit that BCIM would be established as an economic corridor.

3.4 Joint Study Group (JSG) Meetings

After the BCIM-EC was put in the joint statement during Li Keqiang's India visit in May 2013, it was reiterated in the statement signed during Manmohan Singh's China visit in October 2013. A JSG was specially created to look into the conceptualization of areas of cooperation for the BCIM-EC, as well as the time frame and costs involved. It could be said that henceforth the track II was officially converted into track I, albeit the members primarily were mostly from the previous BCIM forums.

The first meeting of the JSG was held in Kunming on 18–19 December 2013. According to the minutes of the meeting (CGI 2013; Krishnan 2013) it was agreed that the corridor "could run from Kunming (China) in the east to Kolkata (India) in the west, broadly spanning the region, including Mandalay (Myanmar), Dhaka and Chittagong (Bangladesh) and other major cities and ports as key nodes. With the linkages of transport, energy and telecommunication networks, the Corridor will form a thriving economic belt that will promote common development of areas along the Corridor." The areas then identified for cooperation remained mostly similar to those discussed in the earlier BCIM Regional Forums conducted between 1999 and 2013, albeit it was proposed that a joint study needed to be conducted as regards these areas. The final report was supposed to be submitted by December 2014 during the third JSG meeting in Delhi. Subsequently, owing to the change in government in Delhi and India's reluctance to join the Belt and Road Initiative, the meeting could only be held in April 2017.

4 Evaluating the BCIM Regional Cooperation Progress?

Many in India believe, owing to India's reluctance in many other such regional and sub regional initiatives, that the progress achieved by another mechanism in this line would be limited. However, if we look back at where BCIM started in 1999 and take stock of the things achieved over the last 17 years, we can say that the BCIM has been successful in many areas, albeit much more needs to be done.

4.1 Air Connectivity

As discussed above, the highlight of the second BCIM meeting in Delhi in 2000 was the starting of business charter flights between Kunming and New Delhi. India and China were joined again by flights after a gap of half a century. Two years later on 28 March 2002, China Eastern Airlines conducted its maiden flight MU563 from Beijing to India, New Delhi, thus initiating the era of direct flights between China and India. The flight later originated from Shanghai to New Delhi, as Air India also operated between New Delhi and Shanghai. On 1 April 2002, Yunnan Airlines started flights between Kunming and Yangon and Kunming to Mandalay, the first international route for a regional flight from Yunnan. Also, through the good offices of the Yunnan government, since 27 October 2002, China Eastern Airlines had agreed to make a stopover at Kunming (Ren 2004). There is connectivity between Kunming–Kolkata; Kunming–Kathmandu; Dhaka–Kunming; Dhaka–Kolkata; and Dhaka–Yangon. There are other possibilities that Kunming–Guwahati, and Chittagong–Yangon are connected with direct flights (Rahmatullah 2010).

4.2 Overland and Water Routes

Here again we see that China has been able to link its regional developmental plans with those of BCIM regional cooperation or vice versa. Ever since China initiated the western development strategy in 1999, Yunnan aggressively developed its linkages with regions adjoining Southeast Asia and South Asia, which is one of the integral goals of the western development strategy, the other two being 'Green Economy' and 'National Culture' Province. According to Ren (2004), since 2004, annual outlays towards the construction of expressways amounted to 10 billion Yuan and above; by 2005, most of the places in every prefecture were connected to Kunming with expressways. Since 2004, Yunnan started the construction of ten high-grade roads with an annual investment of 16 billion Yuan. These include, especially, the Kunming–Ruili highway that connects Longchuan (Zhang Feng), Yingjiang, Pianma ports, and could further be linked to roads entering Myanmar, Bangladesh, and India. Myanmar also intensified the investment in infrastructure; in 2001, with assistance from India, it built a 160-km highway connecting India. In April 2002, Thailand, Myanmar, and India agreed to build a road connecting Morey (India)–Mae Sot (Myanmar) and Messo (Thailand). The three also agreed to open sea channels connecting Thailand to Daweideepwater port in Myanmar and the Indian ports. In April 2004, Bangladesh and Myanmar signed an agreement to build 133-km-long Dhaka–Yangon expressway.

4.3 Trade and Commerce

On this front, Yunnan is aggressively promoting business cooperation with East Asian and South Asian countries, on the one hand, and investment in the environment on the other. It has established various platforms, such as the Kunming trade fair, commodity exhibition for South Asian countries, and the South Asia Business Forum, in addition to the BCIM initiative. Yunnan's trade with India reached US$842 million in 2011, from a meager $82.24 million in 2004, registering an annual increase of 23.8%. The trade volume accounted for nearly 80% of its total trade with South Asia. However, in 2013, Yunnan–India trade volume was only

$546 million, the decrease owing to an overall decline in the India–China trade. In South Asia, Bangladesh is Yunnan's second-largest trading partner. Yunnan's trade with Myanmar reached $4.17 billion, making it the largest trading partner (Wang et al. 2014).

Along with these economic and trade exchanges, people-to-people exchanges have increased many times over. In 2013, Yunnan hosted around 30,000 foreign students; of these, more than 80% came from either Southeast or and South Asia.

5 Infrastructure Connectivity and Challenges

Transportation connectivity has been the main theme of all eleven meetings of the BCIM cooperation. Even if there have been some steps to develop the infrastructure, the task is an uphill battle, requiring huge investment and may take years before we could see the channels of communion opening up and connecting the region fully. Let's examine the present infrastructure scenario as regards roads, railways, waterways, and air transport.

5.1 *Roadways*

As far as building of roads inside India is concerned, Prof. Indiresan (2000) offers two alternatives: one, reconstruct, admittedly difficult but the shortest route to China, a 403-km-long Stillwell Road from Ledo in Assam to Mytkina in Myanmar; and two, a better link to Southeast Asia by extending the road India is already building from Moreh in Manipur to Tamu to Kalewa along the Chindwin River. This would establish a link with Mandalay, already on the railway system of Myanmar. Indiresan advises that both are important and India must take on both projects. In addition, Mizoram could be linked to Akyab (now called Shi twe) in Myanmar, and, if Bangladesh agrees, Agartala in Tripura could be connected to Chittagong. That will open up the entire northeastern region of India, making it the commercial outlet for its eastern trade. According to Rehmanullah (2010), Imphal–Dauki–Tamabi (bordering Bangladesh) is hilly and not fit for cargo trucks; however, Karimgonj (India)–Austragram (Bangladesh), which runs through Imphal and Sylhet, is a shorter route and will cut almost 400 km from the trip between Tamu (Myanmar) and Sylhet (Bangladesh). Rehmanullah prefers this road and states that, compared to the Imphal–Shilong route, this one is more stable.

In Bangladesh, Rehmanullah proposes to convert Dauki (India)–Tamabil (Bangladesh)–Sylhet (Bangladesh) and later segments into grade-II or -III two-lane roads. After crossing Bangabandhu Bridge on Jamuna, the A1 route will pass through Benepole and enter Kolkata, while the A2 route will connect Kathmandu.

China is perhaps the only country that has upgraded its road network so efficiently and aggressively. The Yunnan–Myanmar Road that connects Chuxiong,

Dali, Baoshan and Ruili has long been operational. The road enters Myanmar at Muse. Muse-Mandalay is an all-season, 451-km-long road, which connects Tamu (India) after traversing around 600 km. The project that still needs to be done is Chittagong–Yangon highway and the Kunming–Shi twe Highway.

5.2 *Railways*

Most of the countries have good railways network, but connectivity between the countries remains an issue. China is building the Kunming–Mandalay line that will approximately run along the expressway. The work on Kunming–Dali has been completed, the surveys for the next phase Dali–Baoshan–Ruili has been conducted, and work is in progress. The Chinese line will connect Muse and Lashio in northeast Myanmar. Lashio connects Mandalay; in order to connect to India, Myanmar only needs to extend the line from Kalay to Tamu on India's borders.

The Indian scene is not too bad; the line that needs to be connected is between Tamu and Jiribum that connects Mahisasan in Bangladesh with a meter-gauge line. The work on Kumarghat–Agartala line is in progress, and once completed, will connect Assam to Agartala. Inside Bangladesh, the work to make the Parvatipur–Jamtoil line broad gauge is in progress, and there are plans to extend it to Chittagong. Further, there is an urgent need to unify the gauge systems in the BICM-EC.

5.3 *Waterways*

According to Rehmanullah (2010), waterways have to be created between Yunnan–Myanmar and India–Bangladesh. As far as the Yunnan–Myanmar waterways are concerned, both can contemplate building a harbor at Bhamo on the Irrawaddy River. The carrying capacity of ships would be between 400 and 800 tonnes. As far as building waterways between India and Bangladesh are concerned, the problems are many. The Indian side has been proposing that ports, such as Chittagong and Yangon, could be optimally used for furthering waterway transportation.

6 Importance of BCIM-EC

BCIM-EC has 40% of the world's population and a combined GDP of almost $14 trillion. The corridor has huge reserves of natural wealth, be they fauna and flora, oil and gas, minerals, or hydro potential. Moreover, the world's two most populous countries, termed as the twin engines of the world economic growth, are part of this corridor. The BCIM–EC would mean deeper integration among these countries and opening vistas of opportunities in many diverse areas. The advantages and potentials areas of collaboration are discussed in the following sections.

6.1 Integrated Transportation Network

An integrated transport network would be a boon to all the participating countries, especially the landlocked areas such as the northeastern states in India, southwest provinces in China, large areas in Bangladesh, and Myanmar. Zhao (2000) citing Professor Wen Fude of Sichuan University posits that the overland route from China via Kunming, Myanmar, to Kolkata would reduce a journey of 4,000 km compared to the sea route from Guangzhou to Kolkata that had to make a detour via the Malacca Straits. Bangladesh is poised to play a greater and critical role, as far as integrated waterways are concerned, and to benefit immensely in terms of trade and investment, as will other nations since transaction costs would be greatly reduced. It would directly connect South Asia with East Asia; Chittagong in Bangladesh will rise to prominence and act as a trans-oceanic bridge.

As rightly pointed out by Prof. Chen (2005) of Sichuan University, certain areas of the BCIM region, especially southwest Yunnan, northeast India, and northern Myanmar, have been at 'extreme ends' as far as connectivity is concerned; they have come to a standstill and do not develop any further. As a result, the areas have remained 'closed or semi closed' for a long time. The area is economically the most backward and extremely underdeveloped; the backwardness of northeast India is graphically detailed in *North East Vision 2020*, prepared by the North-Eastern Council of the Ministry of Development of the North-East Region and released in 2008.[1] Transport connectivity in the region will alleviate such areas of poverty and integrate them into the mainstream economic development of the respective countries.

6.2 Linking of the Markets and Better Access

While there have been intimate trade links in the BCIM-EC for centuries, once the transport in the area is integrated by better rail and road networks, it will give better market access to many of the interested companies, especially from India and China in their respective markets. Leaving the so-called security issue behind, if we look at the positive side of the 2007 Beijing–Lhasa train connectivity, goods from Nepal, northern India and Bhutan could easily be transported not only to Lhasa, but also

[1]The report could be downloaded from http://www.mdoner.gov.in/sites/default/files/silo2_content/ner_vision/Vision_2020.pdf.

further east to Beijing. If similar connectivity is established between northeast India, Bangladesh, Myanmar and China, the goods instead of being transported by sea will move overland. Some of the sectors that will benefit would be pharmaceutical, information technology, agro products, food processing, textiles, fertilizers, and minerals. Also, the smaller partners like Bangladesh and Myanmar will benefit immensely by reaching bigger markets for their products, in addition to expanding their present capacities and diversifying products. The FDI inflows would also translate into technology transfer, thus pushing the economic growth rates further. Furthermore, the Chinese products flooding the markets through illegal routes will also come be eliminated. Interestingly, Yunnan is investing heavily in logistics. During my recent visit, facilitated by the International Department of the Central Committee of the Communist Party of China (IDCPC) for a track II dialogue that included delegates from India, Pakistan, Bangladesh, and Myanmar, I happened to have extensive deliberations with academics at the Yunnan Academy of Social Sciences, party cadres at grass root levels, and entrepreneurs at the Pan Asia Logistics Centre in the Wangchong Yunnan Industrial Park. What interested me most was the Pan Asia Logistics Centre built by Yunnan Pan Asia Logistics Group with an investment of $1 billion, completed and operational in less than a three-year period. The logistics center, which has integrated transportation, storage, loading, handling, packaging, circulation, etc., processes data with information technology and e-commerce, thus cutting logistics cost and improving labor productivity. The Logistics Centre certainly has a long-term futuristic strategy geared towards becoming a bridgehead connecting north-south China, Southeast Asia, and South Asia.

Aligning Yunnan's developmental strategies with the BRI, it is coordinating policy, planning, the allocation of resources, and integration of its markets with the countries along the Belt-and-Road routes. We were told by the chairman of the group that, by 2020, eight logistics bases would be built inside Yunnan, bordering Southeast Asian and South Asian countries, plus smaller bases with an investment of two billion RMB and even larger with six billion RMB. It has been estimated that, by 2020, present annual output of 20 billion RMB would be enhanced to 100 billion, accounting for about 10% of China's entire logistics output. The BCIM economic corridor is certainly a part of this calculus, albeit, it is not the top priority at the moment owing to its multilateral strings, as was evident with our discussions with the scholars at the Yunnan Academy of Social Sciences (Deepak 2016).

6.3 Energy Cooperation

The BCIM-EC has reserves of natural and mineral resources. For example, the south-western region of China and eastern India has unexploited wealth of oil and natural gas, coal, minerals, and water resources. The cooperation will lead to joint investment in construction of relevant industries in the areas. There is huge potential for generating hydroelectricity in the region, which will complement the industrial activity in the area. Furthermore, since these issues will essentially touch upon the trans-border and river issues, better mechanisms could be evolved to manage and solve such issues, especially between India–Bangladesh and China.

6.4 Cooperation in Tourism

Two of the BCIM-EC countries are ancient civilizations and have many places of historical and cultural significance. All the countries in the corridor have beautiful landscapes and rich biodiversity. Integrated transportation will not only foster deeper trade relations but also strengthen the tourism sector regionally, as well as internationally. The region could venture into ecology, heritage, and spiritual, as well as cultural etc., tourism areas. This will also attract investment in the adjacent areas and open employment opportunities for the local people.

6.5 BCIM-EC Will Build 'Mutual Political Trust'

At the outset, we have to recognize that it has been owing to the existing security issues between BCIM countries that the region's borders have been 'sealed' and blocked for normal human activities, including travel, trade, and transportation. Therefore, the underdevelopment and backwardness of the region is self-imposed. Looking back, did we resolve these issues, including the border between India and China, and India and Bangladesh, by inflicting isolation? We did not; on the contrary, it has made the region highly unstable and insurgency infested. Furthermore, we have also not been able to stop the arms and smuggling of other trade items across the region. Therefore, it would be on the basis of cooperation and common security and by building CBMs that we would be able to find a solution to the issues and ultimately build political trust between the respective countries. The intimate trade ties would certainly push the respective countries in this direction over the long run.

6.6 Strategic Significance for Neighborhood Policy

In recent years, India has been widely criticized for its policy paralysis, which has been reflected in dwindling economic performance and a record depreciation of the Rupee on the one hand, and dysfunctional foreign policy on the other, especially when it comes to India's smaller neighbors. In July 2013, it halted the subsidized fuel supply to Bhutan just prior to the general election. It became an election issue there, and the then prime minister and chief of the DrukPhuensumTshogpa named Jigme Thinley suffered a defeat. Secondly, the Indian Parliament scuttled the Land

Boundary agreement between India and Bangladesh at India's own peril in early September 2013, for the passage of the legislation would have enabled the swapping of enclaves, thus solving our boundary issue with Bangladesh, and also bringing relief to the hapless people living in these enclaves without any basic amenities for the past 65 years! Good sense prevailed and the deal was finally signed in 2016. India's Nepal policy has also met stumbling blocks, and there are hues and cries for revisiting the treaties we have signed with Nepal.

New Indian leadership has sent strong signals to the neighbors that it attaches priority to its neighborhood, as demonstrated by SAARC members being present at Prime Minister Modi's swearing in ceremony on 26 May 2014 and his Bhutan visit on 15–16 June, his first visit abroad. He rightly talked about stronger economic ties between India and its neighbors. The BCIM-EC offers such an opportunity to strengthen business and people-to-people relations between India and countries in our vicinity. As China has gone whole hog to open up southwest China to business and infrastructural connectivity, India too needs to make northeast India an integral and important part of its 'Act East Policy', rather than making Kolkata the center of BCIM-EC initiative. An economically stronger India and economically stronger neighbors are beneficial in every aspect, be it concerning regional integration, geopolitics, or neighborhood security.

7 Challenges

Ever since the floating of the idea of the BCIM Regional Cooperation Forum, the holding of eleven subsequent meetings of the forum in respective countries, and India and China taking the lead in creating a political platform by converting it into a BCIM-EC, there has been significant progress in the areas of flight connectivity and trade. However, in 2015, when China pronounced the BCIM as one of the corridors of the six Belt-and-Road corridors without consulting India, the already incremental progress came to a standstill. There are inherent challenges in the areas of overland and sea-transport connectivity, trade barriers, and security issues. Let's examine them in the next sections.

7.1 Regional Representation Missing

If we examine the representations from the leading players in the BCIM Regional Cooperation Forum all these years, it comes to the fore that in China it has been Yunnan-centric, primarily dominated by the scholars of Yunnan Academy of Social Sciences and the officials of Yunnan provincial government. While there has been no participation from the Sichuan, Tibet, Guizhou, and Guangxizhuang regions, after it was pushed to the political level by declaring the BCIM-EC, this representation may change. As far as India is concerned, the Institute of Chinese

Studies (ICS) in New Delhi has steered the Track II in all eleven meetings and one JSG meeting that was held in Kunming after the Forum officially became the EC. There is not a single participant from northeast India, even Kolkata is not represented. This has been noticed by the Chinese side, and it wondered whether such 'academic' forums would have any impact as far as influencing government decision making is concerned (Chen 2005).

Even though the BCIM-EC is an intergovernmental initiative, the region involved makes it clear that state governments in the respective regions would be the main drivers of such an initiative. Therefore, the concerned state organs need to be taken into confidence if such a mechanism has to succeed. Secondly, there are issues related to the scope of the area involved, e.g., the Indian side has certain doubts about opening northeast region to China. Conversely, they are also of the view that the entire southwest China should be a part of the BCIM. Bangladesh and Myanmar are better positioned as they consider all the regions of their countries as parts of the BCIM, albeit the Rohingya crisis has caused fissures in this relationship as well.

7.2 *Is the Security Environment One of the Major Negative Factors?*

India, though has agreed in principle to cooperate with China and Myanmar to open new and old routes in Northeast India, is however apprehensive about the security concerns, due to its hypersensitivity about northeastern India. It is almost a case of the 'once bitten twice shy' syndrome; especially after the Himalayan blunder, one of the fallouts of that conflict was China forging an entente with Pakistan and encouraging the Naga and Mizo insurgencies in India's Northeast between 1962 and 1979 (Wang 1998). Brigadier (Retd.) Vinod Anand (2013), a Senior Fellow at Vivekananda International Foundation, posits that the 'prevailing security situation thwarts the successful outcome of BCIM forum and work against building trust and mutual confidence.' He cites conflicts between the armed ethnic groups in the region, Sino-Indian border tensions, Rohingyas crossing over to Bangladesh from Myanmar, etc. as reasons for causing a negative impact that is not conducive to investment and development.

7.3 *Poor and Backward Transportation Connectivity*

Even though there have been attempts by the respective countries to enhance the infrastructural connectivity, so far there is a huge gap between the conceived idea of the BCIM-EC and the kind of transportation integration that is required by such a grand idea. The so-called 'Southern Silk Route', the 'Ancient Tea Horse Road', and the 'Stilwell Road' of modern times have been discussed only on paper, and there are no concrete strategies and timeframes for rebuilding these arteries of communion. Even if there are traces of these routes and people move to and fro, there are restrictions as regards people, vehicles, customs issues, etc. There are no standard norms for the development of roads, railways, and shipping facilities. Secondly, the BCIM countries need to conduct joint research on how to realize the potential and advantages of inland-water routes; finally, there should be uniformity and coordination when contemplating rail and road projects in the region.

7.4 Disequilibrium in Regional Economic Cooperation

Regional economic cooperation demands that there are preferential trade agreements, free-trade areas (FTA), uniform customs regulations, common markets and economic union, and comprehensive economic integration, etc. And if we apply these norms to the BCIM-EC, it is clear that it will take the region years before it acquires such norms and practices. For example, even though the BCIM-EC countries have good trade relations and there is an upward trend in the bilateral trade, none of the countries have liberalized their tariff practices. Besides, non-tariff barriers (NTBs) also remain a major bone of contention for trade between these countries. The NTBs that are commonly mentioned include certification and standardization, lack of harmonization of customs procedures, restrictions on transit, visas difficulties, customs regulations, limited line of credit (L/C) facilities, etc. The intra-BCIM flow of FDI, especially FDI from major players like India and China, remains extremely low.

8 Conclusion

Notwithstanding other regional and sub regional initiatives like BIMSTEC, SAFTA, APTA, Ganga-Mekong Initiative between India, Myanmar, Thailand, Cambodia, Laos, and Vietnam, the BCIM-EC is yet another initiative and a very promising one if it is taken forward with political will. The BCIM-EC has great potential in the fields of trade, transport, tourism, and many other areas of traditional and nontraditional security cooperation.

As India's Act East Policy has been widening in scope, the BCIM-EC is another area where the policy could be coordinated, especially when we are thinking of developing the landlocked and underdeveloped northeast region of India. We certainly need to take a leaf from China's experience as to how it has developed and connected its southwestern and southern states to ASEAN. Is New Delhi ready to forgo its sensitivities in the Northeast in return for the economic development of the region? Can the massive trade between China–ASEAN and India–ASEAN percolate to northeast India and northwest China? The answer to all these questions is yes, provided we start looking at boundaries as gateways and not barriers.

In the wake of India and China both signing FTA with ASEAN, the vigorous development of infrastructure in this region is even more important. The World War II-vintage Stilwell Road proved a "blood transfusion line" during the World War II; if reopened, it could prove to be an artery for economic development of the region in the twenty first century. In the wake of China's economic success story, China has shown extreme interest in the development of this road; it is up to India to cast away its apprehensions, exhibit confidence, and initiate a positive and comprehensive partnership with China and Myanmar so that the living standard of the marginalized Northeast India is enhanced and the region converted to a logistic hub for its trade with the ASEAN and China.

There are various challenges in terms of integrating transportation, trade, and tourism and enhancing traditional as well as non-traditional security in the region. But with the concerted efforts of the respective countries, the challenges could be overcome and opportunities seized. In this context, the revival of the "the southern silk route" connecting India's northeast region with Myanmar and China's Yunnan is the need of the hour. In the same vein, the spreading standard railway links and a network of waterways through river and deep water ports could be game changers as far as economic development and regional security are concerned.

References

Anand, Vinod. 2013. *BCIM Economic Corridor: Prospects and Issues*. Vivekananda International Foundation. http://www.vifindia.org/article/2014/june/02/bcim-economic-corridor-prospects-and-issues. Accessed 17 June 2014.

CGI [Consulate General of India] Guangzhou. 2013. *Minutes of the First Meeting of the Joint Study Group of BCIM Economic Corridor*. http://www.cgiguangzhou.gov.in/news/news_detail/60.

Chen, Jidong 陈继东. 2005. "中印缅孟区域经济合作的构想与地区范围问题" (The Idea of BCIM Regional Economic Cooperation and Problem Areas) 南亚研究季刊 (*South Asian Studies Quarterly*) 1.

Deepak, B.R. 2016. *Yunnan in the Belt and Road Calculus: Building Capacities for Sub-Regional Cooperation*. http://www.thedialogue.co/yunnan-in-the-belt-and-road-calculus-building-capacities-for-sub-regional-economic-cooperation/.

Duan Yu 段 渝. 2010. 中国西南早期对外交通:先秦两汉的南方丝绸之路, 四川社会科学在线 (*Sichuan Social Science Online*). http://www.sss.net.cn/ReadNews.asp?NewsID=26826&BigClassid=9&SmallClassID=24&SpecialID=0&belong=sky. Accessed on 10 June 2014.

Indiresan, P.V. 2000. Kunming Initiative. *Frontline*, 17 (4) April 1–14, 2000. http://www.hindu.com/fline/fl1707/17070980.htm.

ISAS [Institute of South Asian Studies Beijing University]. 1994. 《中国载集中南亚史料汇编》上 (*Collection of South Asian Historical Materials from Chinese Sources*), vol. I. Shanghai: Shanghai Guji Publishing House.

KI [Kunming Initiative]. 1999. http://www.ibiblio.org/obl/reg.burma/archives/199908/msg00946.html.

Krishnan, Ananth. 2013. BCIM Corridor Gets Push After First Official-Level Talks in China. *The Hindu*, December 21, 2013.

Lu, Xiaokun and Guo Huiyan 卢晓昆 郭穗彦. 2004. 孟中印缅地区经济合作论坛第五次会议在昆明召开 (Fifth Meeting of the Forum on BCIM Regional Cooperation Convened in Kunming) *YASS [Yunnan Academy of Social Sciences*]. http://www.sky.yn.gov.cn/dtxx/ynskj/6823128929834129273. Accessed on 12 June 2014.

MEA (Ministry of External Affairs, India) Joint Statement on the State Visit of Chinese Premier Li Keqiang to India, May 20, 2013. http://www.mea.gov.in/bilateral-documents.htm?dtl/21723/Joint+Statement+on+the+State+Visit+of+Chinese++Li+Keqiang+to+India.

Oberoi, Patricia (2013). *The BCIM Forum: Retrospect and Prospects*. ICS Working Paper 2013/11/1. http://www.icsin.org/ICS/WorkingpaperPdf/1.pdf. Accessed on 12 June 2014.

Rahmatullah, M. 2010. 推进孟中印缅交通连接及对策建议:孟加拉国的思考 (Facilitating BCIM transportation connectivity and policy measures: perspective from Bangladesh). 《东南亚南亚研究》 *Southeast Asia and South Asian Studies* 3.

Ray, H.P. 2003. *Trade and Trade Routes Between India and China*. Kolkata: Progressive Publishers.

Ren, Jia et al. 任佳、王崇理、陈利君. 2004. 孟中印缅地区经济合作的回顾与展望. Yunnan Ribao, December 22, 2004. http://news.sina.com.cn/c/2004-12-22/12354597561s.shtml.

Wang, Hongwei. 1998. 《喜马拉雅山情节》 (*The Himalayas Sentiment: A Study of Sino Indian Relations*). Beijing: China Tibetology Publication.

Wang, Lin, Shi Guanglin, and Zhao Yuning 王林、史广林、赵宇宁. 2014. 云南阔步"孟中印缅经济走廊 (*Yunnan's Stride in BCIM Economic Corridor*) Zhongxinshe June 1, 2014. http://www.yn.chinanews.com/pub/2014/yunnan_0602/82157.html. Accessed on 13 June 2014.

Zhao, Weiwen. 2000. 《印中关系风云录*1949-1999*》 (*Records of Turbulences in Sino-Indian Relations: 1949–1999*). Beijing: Current Affairs Publishers.

Chapter 7
The China–Pakistan Economic Corridor (CPEC): A Game Changer for Pakistan's Economy

Ahmad Rashid Malik

Today, the China–Pakistan Economic Corridor (CPEC) has become a buzzword and the focus of academicians, strategists, policy formulators, and media alike. Reports, analyses, and opinion pieces are being written across the globe. There are positive, as well as negative, analyses, more so on the geopolitics and less on the geo-economics of it. The subject has become popular among scholars of international relations, political science, security studies, etc. In spite of entertaining a large number of political analyses, contradictory views, and concerns, the Governments of Pakistan and China are, however, strongly determined to go ahead with the CPEC and are continuously striving hard to make it a successful bilateral economic model for China and Pakistan, as well as the other countries.

This study is not on the geopolitics of the CPEC; rather it analyzes and focuses on the economic fundamentals of the CPEC to see how viable it is for the economy of Pakistan in concrete terms rather than discussing regional and global political concerns of the CPEC besides the domestic politics surrounding it.

The CPEC is a pilot and the flagship project of the Belt and Road Initiative or the 'One Belt One Road' (OBOR) that aims to build a number of economic corridors. President Xi Jinping considers Pakistan as an important partner in the OBOR; the agreement was signed when he paid a visit to Islamabad 20–21 April 2015. He expounded the idea of OBOR when he visited Kazakhstan in September 2013 and Indonesia in October of the same year. The OBOR is actually the new name of the ancient Silk Road, connecting China with Central Asia, the Middle East, and onward to Europe. China was the home and the starting point of the Silk Road. The basic idea behind the OBOR is to revive the ancient Silk Road spirit that had facilitated trade, discoveries, cultural cohesion, and cross-civilizational bonds among nations in the past. At least six economic corridors have been designed under the OBOR at the moment, namely; the China-Mongolia-Russia Economic

A.R. Malik (✉)
Institute of Strategic Studies, Islamabad, Pakistan
e-mail: dr.arm@hotmail.com

B.R. Deepak (ed.), *China's Global Rebalancing and the New Silk Road*,
https://doi.org/10.1007/978-981-10-5972-8_7

Table 1 Pakistan-China bilateral decade-wise trade 1960–2010

Decade	Trade
1960	18.3
1970	73.4
1980	401.6
1990	424.6
2000	722.1
2010	10,854.7

Source: IMF: *Direction of Trade Statistics.* Washington: International Monetary Fund, 2015

Corridor (CMREC), the New-Eurasia Land Bridge (NELB), the Bangladesh-China-India-Myanmar Economic Corridor (BCIMEC), the China-Pakistan Economic Corridor (CPEC), the China-Central Asia Economic Corridor (CCAEC), and the China-Indochina Peninsula Economic Corridor (IPEC). Besides, there is a Maritime Economic Corridor (MEC) being built under the name of the 21st Century Maritime Silk Road.

The major focus of the OBOR is on the following areas: policy co-ordination, connectivity, unimpeded trade, financial integration, and people-to-people bonds (NDRC et al. 2015). Of these six important economic corridors, the CPEC was an early starter, and it was considered to be the pilot and flagship project of the OBOR and whose success would determine the feasibility of all the other economic corridors.

The reason that the CPEC was started much earlier than all other corridors reflects the deep-rooted and trusted friendship between Pakistan and China over the past 65 years. Both countries developed robust defense ties by the late 1960s, following the Sino-Indian border clash of 1962 and the Pakistan-India war of 1965 (Malik 2016). However, economic ties between the two countries remained relatively inactive as reflected in Table 1. There was no dynamic balance in trade commensurate with their diplomatic and defense ties. This situation continued for over six decades. However, there was a need to reboot the economic relationship and forge ahead in the direction of building robust economic and commercial ties between the two countries.

1 The Rationale for the CPEC

The CPEC was not developed overnight. Incremental approaches have been noted in the evolutionary process of the CPEC. Besides deep-rooted mutual ties, the CPEC is based on reasons rooted in history.

The CPEC was offered by China to Pakistan five months earlier than the OBOR when Premier Li Keqiang visited Pakistan in May 2013, urging the all-weather friends to boost cooperation in business, trade, energy, and infrastructure and build a long-vaunted economic corridor (SCMP 2013). While addressing the Senate of Pakistan, he said that "we are ready to work with Pakistan to speed up the project of upgrading the Karakoram Highway, actively explore, and develop the long-term plans of building a China-Pakistan economic corridor, expanding our shared interests."

Even the proposal for oil and gas pipelines between the two countries was discussed much earlier than 2013. The decision to construct the Gwadar Deep Sea Port during the visit of Premier Zhu Rongji in 2001 led to building a land route and oil-and-gas pipeline between Gwadar and Kashgar (Lu 2015).

The idea of the CPEC was further expounded under China's "Western Development Program" conceived in 2002. The policy covers six provinces, namely: Gansu, Guizhou, Qinghai, Shaanxi, Sichuan, and Yunnan; five autonomous regions, namely; Guangxi, Inner Mongolia, Ningxia, Tibet, and Xinjiang; and one municipality, i.e., Chongqing (Lai 2002). The total economic output of these regions as part of Chinese Gross Domestic Product (GDP) was quite low. Among these regions, the Xinjiang Autonomous Region borders Pakistan and could be developed if it could get sea access via Pakistan and could be well-connected with the latter via a communications net.

Some would even suggest that the Karakoram Highway (KKH) that was built during 1956–78 was the main motivating factor for building Pakistan–China land-route cooperation. Therefore, there are historical reasons behind the CPEC rooted in the lasting cooperation between China and Pakistan.

The progress on the CPEC projects is going well since the signing of 51 agreements in April 2015 (Haider 2015). Five energy projects were inaugurated on the occasion, namely: the Karot 720-mW hydropower project, the Dawood 50-mW wind-power project, the Sachal 50- mW wind-power project, the Zonergy 900-mW solar project, and the Jhimpir 100-mW wind-power project.[1]

A Joint Cooperation Committee (JCC) was formed during Prime Minister Nawaz Sharif's visit to China in July 2015, and five Working Groups were formed, namely; (1) the Long-Term Planning, (2) energy, (3), transportation infrastructure, and (4) the Gwadar Port.

Subsequently, the Chinese Government made CPEC a part of its 13th Five-Year Plan (2016–2020).[2] The proposal was approved by the Communist Party of China (CPC) at the Fifth Plenary Session of the 18th Communist Party of China (CPC) Central Committee held in Beijing in November 2015. It stipulated that the building of the CPEC needed to be based on scientific research and designed by short-, mid-, and long-term planning. This initiated the process of integrating the economy of Pakistan with the Chinese global economy—the world's fastest growing economy.

Many projects under the Early Harvest Program (EHP) will be completed by 2018–2020, which will give a new boost to CPEC projects to be undertaken in the

[1]"Pakistan, China ink 51 MoUs in diverse sectors", *The News International* (Rawalpindi), 20 April 2015.

[2]"CPEC made part of China's 13th 5-year development plan"; *Pakistan Today* (Islamabad), 23 November 2016.

second phase up to 2030 (see Appendix 1). All energy projects are investment-based on the IPP (Independent Power Projects) mode producing electricity in Pakistan. Most of the investment comes from the Import-Export Bank of China (EXIM Bank) and commercial banks in China. The IFC World Bank and the Silk Road Fund (SLF) also provide funding to energy projects in Pakistan. Some of the energy projects have been receiving grants from the Chinese Government. Some of them are undertaken as joint ventures with local companies rather than using soft loans.[3] Each project is determined on the basis of the type of final needs and financial arrangements, such as investment, aid, equity, etc.

2 Unimpeded Trade

Traditionally, economic and trade relations between Pakistan and China have remained extremely lackluster and inconsistent for several decades (Malik 2013). Since the cultivation of strong diplomatic and defense ties, economic relations have not seen any noticeable improvement. If bilateral trade is viewed from the Asia-Pacific perspective, the trade has very little value (Malik 2013: 206). In South Asia, India is the largest trading partner of China, followed by Pakistan, Bangladesh, and Sri Lanka, respectively. The decade-wise trade between the two countries was reported to be under.

Bilateral trade stood at around US$18 million and had only increased to US $73 million by 1970. Bilateral trade was hardly US$401 million by 1980 and US $424 million in 1990; the total only increased to US$722 million in 2000. After 2004, both countries have taken a number of steps to expand trading ties. In October 2004, both countries signed the Preferential Trade Agreement (PTA) to upgrade existing trade ties. The EAP was launched in November 2006. In 2007, both countries signed the Free Trade Agreement (FTA), which took effect from July the same year to boost bilateral trade, which stood at US$7.5 billion at that point. While China managed to export 57% along its line of preference under the FTA, Pakistan's utilization was a mere 5% along the lines which Pakistan had managed to 'negotiate' as concessions (Abduhu 2015). Pakistan could then export a number of commodities to China at zero duties, but Pakistan lacks that capacity to enhance its exports to China. This capacity needs to be enhanced, and Pakistan should take advantage of this facility. The FTA is now in the second phase, which will remove duties by 90%. Therefore, a free-trade regime would emerge between the two countries under the CPEC perspective.

After the signing of the FTA and inauguration of the CPEC, bilateral trade has been speedily turning around, and it reached US$17 billion in 2014. At present,

[3]Roundtable Talk given by Zhao Lijian, Deputy Head of Mission, Embassy of the People's Republic of China, Islamabad, at the Institute of Strategic Studies Islamabad (ISSI), on 14 July 2016.

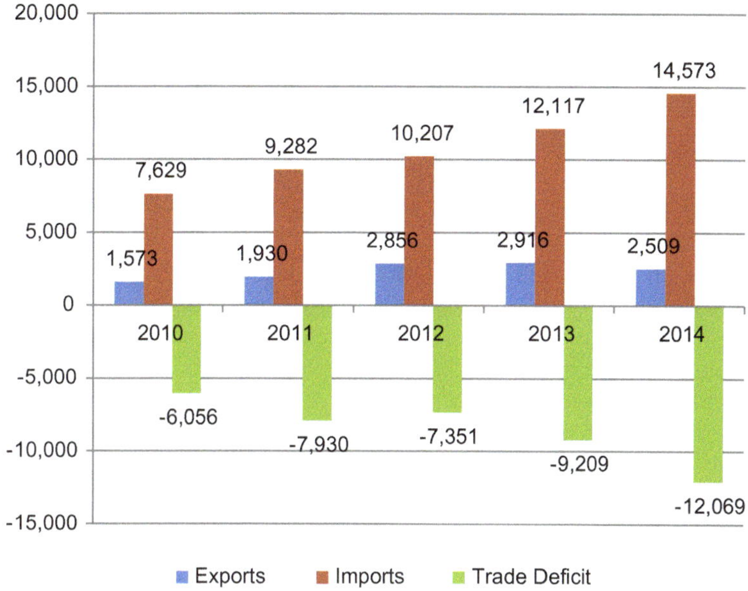

Fig. 1 Pakistan's exports, imports, and trade deficit with China 2010–2014 Source: IMF: *Direction of Trade Statistics*. Washington: International Monetary Fund, 2015

bilateral trade has surpassed total trade with the US, reported as US$19 billion[4] (Table 2).

At the moment, Pakistan imports much more from China than it exports, i.e., exports are only one-third as imports from China. Its trade deficit is also with China (its largest with any nation) reached over US$12 billion in 2014. The Government is devising strategies to increase Pakistan's exports to China (Fig. 1).

Meanwhile, at the same moment when bilateral trade had just turned around, the CPEC was inaugurated on 20th April 2015 following President Xi Jinping's visit to Pakistan. While addressing the Joint Session of the Parliament in Islamabad, on 20 April 2015, he said:

> The planning and layout of the Economic Corridor should cover other parts of Pakistan as well so that the fruits of its development will reach both all the people in Pakistan and the people of other countries in our region.[5]

At that time, as many as 51 agreements worth US$46 billion were signed. Most of the agreements were related to energy projects worth US$35 billion, planned to generate 10,400 mW of electricity.

---

[4]"Sino-Pak bilateral trade reaches dollar 18.9 billion: Chinese ambassador", Pakistan Today (Islamabad), 28 September 2016.

[5]Speech by H.E. Xi Jinping, President of the People's Republic of China, At the Parliament of Pakistan, Islamabad, 21 April 2015, Ministry of Foreign affairs, Beijing. http://www.fmprc.gov.cn/mfa_eng/wjdt_665385/zyjh_665391/t1257158.shtml. Accessed 18 October 2016.

Table 2 Pakistan–China bilateral trade 2011–14

Year	Trade
2011	11,211.6
2012	13,061.14
2013	15,033.02
2014	17,082

Source: IMF: *Direction of Trade Statistics*. Washington: International Monetary Fund, 2015

However, the CPEC has the capacity to lower the trade deficit and boost its exports to China for a variety of reasons. This is so especially once the shortage of electricity in Pakistan has been decreased following the inauguration of energy projects in 2017 and some others the following year. Therefore, the greater impact of the CPEC would be on Pakistan's trade with China and also with other countries.

Furthermore, the CPEC is converting Pakistan into a 'Transit State' in South Asia catering to the needs of China, especially of Xinjiang, Afghanistan, Central Asia, and perhaps even including Russia, which had a long-fervent desire to reach the warm-water ports of the Arabian Sea because the Cold War but had been hampered by a number of difficulties. Mongolia could also take advantage of Gwadar Port. Iran, Afghanistan, and Russia have shown interest in the CPEC and under the Shanghai Cooperation Organization (SCO), such a possibility for regional trade connectivity has increased. Iran does not consider Gwadar Port as rival to its Chabahar Port, rather these ports supplement the needs of each country.[6] After the lifting of international trading sanctions on Iran in January 2016, it is interested in exporting more oil and enhancing its trade with China. Afghanistan also fully supports the CPEC because it is desperate to achieve economic development.[7] Russia is also desirous of enhancing its trade with Central Asia and Afghanistan besides Pakistan, and the CPEC provides that opportunity.[8]

A pipeline will also be built from Gwadar to Kashgar to transport oil from the Persian Gulf and Iran. One million barrel are expected to be exported to China because it is getting ready to shift 17 oil exports from the Gulf via Gwadar. Construction of the Gwadar–Kashgar pipeline would be started by 2017 and completed by 2021 (Yousafzai 2016). When more oil is exported to China via the Gulf and Iran, a major source of Chinese oil imports, this could also very likely boost Pakistan's trade. The Pakistan that emerges under the CPEC would be a 'gateway' to China and Central Asia. Additionally, CPEC would also boost regional trade. The results are in the pipeline.

[6]See the statement of the Iranian Ambassador to Pakistan, Mehdi Honardoust, "Iran desires a role in CPEC", *Dawn* (Islamabad), 10 September 2016.

[7]See the statement of Ambassador of Afghanistan to Pakistan, Dr Omer Zakhilwal, "Afghanistan desires role in CPEC: Zakhilwal", *Pakistan Observer* (Islamabad), 15 October 2016.

[8]See the statement of Dr Natalia Zamaraeva, Senior Researcher, Institute of Oriental Studies at Russian Science Academy, Moscow, "Russian Researcher Describes CPEC Game-Changer for Region", *Radio Pakistan*, 28 September 2016. http://www.radio.gov.pk/28-Sep-2016/russian-researcher-describes-cpec-game-changer-for-region. Accessed 27 October 2016.

Table 3 Pakistan's regional trade with neighbors 2014

S. No.	Country	Exports	Imports	Total
1	China	2,509	14573	17,082
2	India	481	2400	2,881
3	Iran	501	1,801	2,302
4	Afghanistan	2,222	195	2,417
	Total	5,713	18,969	24,682

Source: IMF: *Direction of Trade Statistics*. Washington: International Monetary Fund, 2015

Pakistan exported goods worth US$5.7 billion and imported goods worth US $18.9 billion in 2014, thus reaching a total trade of US$24.6 billion. A new trading infrastructure and industrial zones would drastically increase Pakistan's trade with these countries (Table 3).

In the future, the trade would be quadrupled, with China having a lion's share of Pakistan's total trade. Therefore, one point is clear: the CPEC would boost bilateral trade between the two countries, as well as regional trade. Solid bilateral trade ties are in the making.

The setting up of industrial and mineral zones is the backbone of the CPEC projects under the policy coordination between the two governments to develop the relatively under-developed areas (Liang 2014: 174–84). The CPEC will give an unprecedented boost to build at least 29 industrial zones and 21 processing zones in various parts of Pakistan along the CPEC routes during the first phase of the projects.[9] (See Appendix 2 for details.)

3 Economic Turnaround

The CPEC is a long-term comprehensive economic project. It is having multiple effects on the economy of Pakistan, ranging from infrastructure building to social, educational, and health development. The package has already boosted Pakistan's economy to a great extent within less than two years. The results are encouraging. With the change in the economic outlook and positive trends, many milestones have been achieved that contribute to a vibrant and sustainable economy. The Government has forecast a 5.7% growth rate for the next fiscal year.[10] International rating agencies have upgraded the trends of Pakistan's economy. This included the Japan External Trade Organization (JETRO), Standards and Poor's, Moody's, and many other rating agencies. According to Morgan Stanley Capital International,

[9]"Govt proposes 29 industrial parks, 21 mineral zones under CPEC", *The News International* (Rawalpindi), 26 July 2015.

[10]"Message from Minister for Finance, Revenue, Economic Affairs, Statistics and Privatization", *Business Recorder* (Islamabad), 27 September 2016.

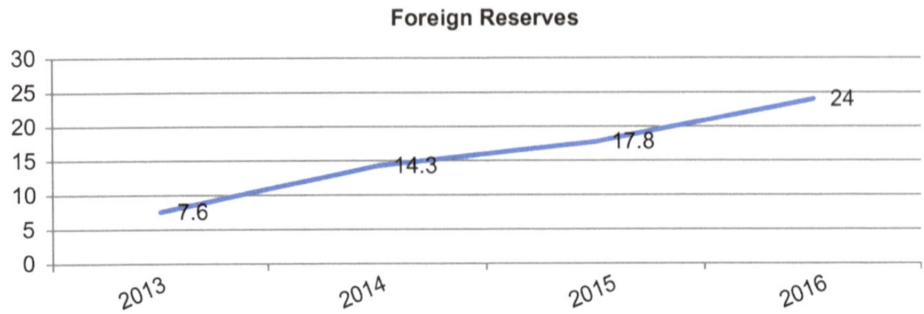

Fig. 2 Pakistan's foreign reserves 2013–2016. Source: *Business Recorder Times* (Karachi), 5 October 2016

Pakistan is becoming an emerging market because of improvements in transparency, liquidity, and the stock exchange.[11]

At present, the total GDP of Pakistan is only US$269.7 billion,[12] which is small compared to other Asian countries. The CPEC package of US$46 billion has injected new impetus into Pakistan's GDP, which is around 17% of Pakistan's total GDP. The CPEC projects have been showing encouraging progress. Chinese companies have invested US$14 billion in the 30 Early Harvest Programs, which are under construction.[13] Some of these projects are already completed, and some are nearing completion in a year or so. The momentum of development of energy, roads, and infrastructure projects is growing, and it is likely to continue to do so after the EHP at an even faster pace.

Investment is an integral part of trade. Ever since the CPEC has been offered to Pakistan, its foreign reserves have been showing an upward trend over the past three years. Pakistan's foreign reserves climbed to US$24.4 billion by October 2016, and this has been confirmed by the World Bank (Saeedi 2016) (Fig. 2).

In addition, there would be an active mobilization of the workforce. The CPEC projects would create at least two-million new job opportunities.[14] The Multan–Sukker Motorway, for instance, has created just over 10,000 jobs.[15] Every project is going to generate unprecedented job opportunities, which would also reduce unemployment and poverty in the country. The CPEC could become an environmental corridor to spearhead the development of regional renewable-energy trade,

[11]"Pakistan upgraded to emerging markets status", *The Express Tribune* (Islamabad), 15 July 2016.

[12]World Bank, *World Development Indicators Database,* 22 July 2016. http://databank.worldbank.org/data/download/GDP.pdf.

[13]"China has so far invested $14 billion in 30 CPEC projects", see the statement of Zhao Lijian, Deputy Chief of Mission, Embassy of the People's Republic of China at Islamabad, *Pakistan Today* (Islamabad), 28 September 2016.

[14]*The News International* (Rawalpindi), 5 July 2016.

[15]*Pakistan Today* (Islamabad), 22 September 2016.

and add Pakistan to China's nationwide carbon market, which is already the world's largest, thus creating a regional market (Sheikh 2016).

The CPEC package has a financial significance for Pakistan as well. As far as Pakistan's Foreign Direct Investment (FDI) is concerned, the CPEC package is the largest of all the FDI that Pakistan has received from various sources over the past 60 years. The CPEC package is the biggest package ever offered to Pakistan by a foreign donor or an aid agency. It is almost half of all the loans contracted by Pakistan since 1947. Now, under the CPEC, China has been massively investing in FDI in Pakistan during the last three years. Chinese FDI has reached US $593.9 million in 2015–16, and China has been Pakistan's largest FDI partner for the last three years.[16]

4 Regional Connectivity

The CPEC focuses on regional integration. In fact, the CPEC is more about regional trade connectivity and transportation by providing a modern and efficient corridor for regional trade. The CPEC, in other words, is a symbol of trade connectivity. Because of the difficult terrain and the region's long-term geographical disconnectivity, all of which was intensified by exploitative colonialism in China, South Asia, East Asia, and Central Asia, these economies have been disjointed and remained neglected for centuries.

It was not in the interest of the British during the colonial period, for instance, to promote trade between the Indian sub-continent and China, and also with Japan and other countries. By exporting opium from India into China, in the 19th century, the British virtually destroyed trade between the Indian subcontinent and China. So did the French. Japan, on the other hand, fully exploited China and the Korean Peninsula for quite some time until 1945. The Spaniards, Portuguese, Russians, and Americans also exploited their "sphere of influence" rather than genuinely integrating parts of East Asia, China, South Asia, and Central Asia, as this was not in their interests.

Rather, the British in India and the Japanese developed an understanding and signed an agreement not to interfere in each other's respective and exploitive spheres of influence in South and East Asia until the early 1920s. Trade was also discouraged between British India and Japan during the colonial era.

After the end of colonialism, by the 1940s, Asian nation-states mainly remained busy with nation-building processes. Little effort was paid to regional trade integration and connectivity. The Association of South East Asian Nations (ASEAN) emerged as the main locomotive for intra-ASEAN trade integration by the late 1960s.

[16]Board of Investment, "Country-wise FDI Flow". http://boi.gov.pk/ForeignInvestmentinPakistan.aspx. Accessed 29 September 2016.

The incorporation of China into the ASEAN process in 1995 was a significant milestone in the promotion of regional-trade connectivity. China emerged as the major trading partner of a number of ASEAN members. The country also emerged as the source of in-bound and out-bound investment. Chinese infrastructure-related companies are rapidly becoming more prominent in the infrastructure-development landscape in ASEAN. They have participated in building infrastructure across all sectors in the region. These players are not only operating as contractors but are also investing in and owning infrastructure.[17] As a result, trade and investment flourished between the ASEAN nations and China. In the nourishment of ASEAN-China trade, it was the ASEAN members who played the leading role in bringing China into ASEAN's fold.

The two decades of promising relations between ASEAN nations and China have resulted in China's Belt and Road initiative as espoused by President Xi Jinping during his visit to Jakarta in October 2013. The underlying rationale was to maintain and grow the continuity of trade relations as developed by ASEAN and China by significantly broadening the canvas through the incorporation of, inter alia, East Asia, South Asia, West Asia, as well as the African and European continents.

This was the Chinese thinking, in contrast to the imperialist and colonialist thinking. China does not promote either exploitation or imperialism, but rather a cooperative relationship. It would like to share its development experience across the whole world. China has been offering the world's ever largest trade connectivity by integrating the whole Asian continent, as well as providing benefits to nearby Africa and Europe.

China is among the five largest international traders, namely, the US, Germany, Japan, and the Great Britain. China conducts around US$5 trillion trade in merchandise via the Indian and the Pacific Oceans.[18] The trade routes can be very long, stretching up to 16,000 km, and there are some choke points at the Straits of Malacca and the South China Sea. If some trade was diverted to land routes through Pakistan, this would be safer, as well as economical. The route from Gawader to Kashgar is approximately 2,500 km, and an oil pipeline would be safer and quicker.

Given this regional context of the OBOR's regional connectivity in the Indian Ocean and South China Sea, the CPEC, in fact, promotes Pakistan's regional trade by introducing new trading routes and by modernizing the old trading routes. The CPEC is not just the name of a road or a route, but rather a system of communication networks to connect all parts of Pakistan, as well as the region. A new network of roads and railway lines is under construction in Balochistan, Sindh, Punjab, Khyber Pakhtunkhwa, Azad Kashmir, and Gilgit–Baltistan. This would transform Pakistan into one of the "most physical infrastructural developed country" in Asia on modern telecommunication lines.

---

[17]The ASEAN Secretariat and United Nations Conference on Trade and Development, *ASEAN Investment Report 2015: Infrastructure Investment and Connectivity*. Jakarta: ASEAN Secretariat, November 2015, pp. 85–89.

[18]The World Trade Organization (WTO), *World Trade Statistical Review*, 2016.

Provinces and major cities will be connected by high-speed, limited-access highways, motorways, bridges, tunnels, and railway tracks. China plans to ply high-speed railways in Pakistan. Chinese high-speed railways run at speeds between 200- and 350-km per hour. China is a global leader in high-speed railways and far ahead of Japan, the US, Germany, etc. At the moment, China's railway industry is engaged in infrastructure negotiations with at least 30 countries. China's high-speed rail bids are much lower than those of developed countries. Over the past twelve years, China has built 16,000 km of high-speed track within its borders —longer than the rest of the world's network combined. China has been building high-speed railways in Indonesia and Russia, and it has been investing in high-speed rail in California. China trounced Japan in the Indonesian high-speed railway's bid this year.

If moderately fast bullet trains (e.g., 200-km per hour) run between Karachi-Peshawar, it would just take nine hours from Karachi to Peshawar and one hour 15 min from Islamabad to Lahore. Days-long trips between all cities will be reduced. There will be a miraculous improvement in rail transportation in Pakistan with the completion of the Chinese rail projects planned under the CPEC. Construction of an intra-city Orange Line Metro train is already underway in Lahore. This will change the outdated railway system of Pakistan because it will be built on modern patterns.

China will invest U$18 billion to build a 200-km-long tunnel at Babusar, which will ensure year-round rail service, something that will revolutionize inter-regional travel and freight transport (Sering 2016). An optic-fiber cable has been planned from Kashgar to Rawalpindi to provide faster and safer internet services between Pakistan and China.

All type of industries will be built. The CPEC would turn Pakistan into a knowledge-based corridor and develop it into a "truly Asian tiger" exporting hub economy, thus meeting the growing demands of China and Central Asia.

5 Conclusion

The OBOR and CPEC have touched the hearts and minds of people in Pakistan. This is their hope. China is the only country among all of Pakistan's friends that qualifies as the most trusted and true friend under all circumstances. Both are developing countries, and China teaches Pakistan how to build a sustainable economy for a large population, while possessing fewer resources. The CPEC is a shining example of South-South cooperation. Pakistan is lucky to have China on its border. It is a matter of pride and jubilation. For Pakistanis, China has a soft image and a sustainable economy, and they are striving hard to learn from China. The CPEC is bringing about an economic miracle on the Indus River similar to the miracles that happened in Japan after 1945, in ASEAN in the 1980s, the Han River miracle in South Korea, and the Yellow River miracle in China (Malik 2016).

Analysts are of the opinion that this is the time for the Indus River miracle. The CPEC is greatly transforming the economy of Pakistan. The CPEC is also a knowledge corridor to educate people and to invest in science and technology. China is now a popular destination for young Pakistani students studying science and technology in various fields. The CPEC would bring about a civilizational transformation in the wider Asian continent, with Pakistan as the focal point. The CPEC is Pakistan's shared destiny, not only with China but with the other Asian countries. The CPEC symbolizes iron friendship between Pakistan and China. The CPEC is the most powerful tool to illuminate the Pakistan-China friendship at this point in time by leaders, diplomats, and scholars. The bright future of Pakistan's economy would be greatly linked with the CPEC and China's global economy. This would greatly help convert Pakistan's economy along modern, completive patterns. In a nutshell, the CPEC is actually an "economic game changer" for Pakistan's trade, regional road connectivity, and its economy.

Appendix 1 The On-Going CPEC Projects

1	KKH II (Thakot–Havilian)
2	Multan–Sukkar
3	Railway Projects
4	Quaid-e-Azam Solar Plant
5	Haier Ruba Industrial Park Phase I:
6	Port Qasim Coal-Fired Power Project
7	Gwadar East Bay expressway,
8	Gwadar Port Capacity Recovery of Phase
9	Maintenance Dredging
10	Expansion of Stock Yard and New Bulk Cargo Handling Equipment
11	Restoration of Structures, Facilities and Site
12	Purchase of a 5000-HP Tugboat and Certain Transportation Vehicles
13	Production and Living Facilities Improvement and Security
14	Multipurpose wharf Zone
15	Breakwater
16	Gwadar International Airport
17	Gwadar East Bay expressway
18	Gwadar Smart Port City Master Plan
19	Gwadar Power Plan
20	Desalination Plant
21	Sewage Plant
22	Gwadar Faqueer Primary School
23	Gwadar Hospital Up Gradation
24	Gwadar Vocational Technical Institute

(continued)

(continued)

25	Scholarship Programs for Gwadar
26	Expansion of Existing Multipurpose Terminal of Gwadar Port
27	Phase-II of East Bay Expressway from Makran Coastal Highway to New Gwadar International Airport
28	Fresh Water Supply, distribution
29	Wastewater Treatment Project for Gwadar City
30	Khuzdar–Besima Highway
31	KKH Up Gradation Phase III (Raikotto Thakot)
32	D.I Khan–Quetta, Up Grading to Four Lanes
33	Haveliandry Port
34	Lahore–Multan Motorway
35	Multan–Hyderabad Motorway
36	Kemari–Hyderabad Motorway
37	Dawood 50-mW Wind Farm, Sindh
38	Uep 100-mW Wind Farm, Sindh
39	Sachal 50-mW Wind Farm, Sindh
40	Zonergy 300-mW Quaid-E-Azamsolar Park, Punjab
41	Port Qasim 2 × 660-mW Coal-Fired Power Plant
42	Sahiwal 2 × 660-mW Coal-Fired Power Plant, Sindh
43	Karot Hydropower 720-mW Plant, Punjab
44	Thar Mine Mouth Coal-Fired Power Plant, Sindh
45	Suki Kinari Hydropower Station, 873 mW, KP
46	Mine Mouth Coal Fired Power Plant at Thar Block II, 2 × 330 mW
47	Matiari (Port Qasim)–Lahore Transmission Line
48	HUBCO Coal Power Plant 660 mW
49	Matiari (Port Qasim)–Lahore Transmission Line
50	Matiari (Port Qasim)–Faisalabad Transmission Line
51	China-Sunec Wind Farm, 50 mW
52	Mine Mouth Coal Fired Power Plant at Thar Block I, Sindh, 2 × 660 mW
53	Rahimyar Khan 2 × 660-mW Coal-Fired Power Project
54	Gwadar Coal-Fired Power Plant
55	Wind Farm Phase II at China Three Gorges
56	Kohala Hydro Power Station
57	Gadani Electricity Park
58	Hubco Coal Power Plant II
59	Salt Ranges Mine Mouth Coal Power Plant
60	Thar Mine Mouth Coal Power Plant
61	Muzaffargarh Coal Power Plant
62	Gas Power Project
63	Gwadar Free Zone Development
64	Haier Industrial Park Phase II

(continued)

(continued)

65	Gwadar–NawabShah Gas Pipeline and Gwadar LNG Terminal
66	Orange Line Train, Lahore
67	Gwadar--NawabShah Gas Pipeline and Gwadar LNG Terminal
68	China-Pak Cross Border Optical Fiber

Source: Embassy of the People's Republic of China, Islamabad

Appendix 2 CPEC Proposed Mineral and Industrial Zones

Mineral Zones
Thar (coal), Larkana (coal), Salt Range (antimony), Chiniot (iron ore), Dargai (chromite), North Waziristan (chromite), Kurram (antimony), Waziristan, (copper), Chitral (antimony), Besham (iron ore, lead), Nizampur (iron ore) Mohmand (marble), Khuzdar (chromite, antimony), Chaghi (chromite), Qila Saifullah (antimony, chromite), Saindak (gold, silver), RekoDiq (gold), Kalat (iron ore), Lasbela (manganese), Gwadar (oil refinery), Muslim Bagh (chromite)

Source: *The News International* (Rawalpindi), 26 July 2015.

Industrial Zones
Sukkur, Larkana, Karachi, Bin Qasim, Korangi Creek, Khairpur, Hattar, Gadoon Ghazi, D I Khan, Jalozai, Nowshera, Bannu, Chitral, Risalpur, Quetta, Dostan, Gwadar, Khuzdar, Uthal, Hub, Dera Murad Jamali

Source: *The News International* (Rawalpindi), 26 July 2015.

References

Abduhu, Salman. 2015. Pakistan Suffers Trade Gap of $4.39b with China. *The Nation* (Islamabad), April 4, 2015.

Haider, Irfan. 2015. Details of Agreements Signed During Xi's Visit to Pakistan. *Dawn* (Islamabad), April 20, 2015.

Lai, Hongyi Harry. 2002. China's Western Development Program: Its Rationale, Implementation, and Prospects. *Modern China* 28(4) (October 2002) Beijing.

Liang, Tong. 2015. CPEC Industrial Zones and China-Pakistan Capacity Cooperation. *Strategic Studies* 34 & 35(4 & 1) (Winter 2014–Spring 2015).

Lu, Shulin. 2015. China-Pakistan Economic Corridor: A Flagship and Exemplary Project of One Belt One Road. *Strategic Studies* 34 & 35 (4 & 1) (Winter 2014–Spring 2015) (Islamabad).

Malik, Ahmad Rashid. 2013. The Sino-Pakistani Trade and Investment Relations. *Margalla Papers* XVII (1): 201–221.

Malik, Ahmad Rashid. 2016. The Growing Defence Ties Between Pakistan and China. *Issue Brief* (Islamabad: Institute of strategic studies Islamabad, October 7, 2016). http://issi.org.pk/wp-content/uploads/2016/10/Final-Issue-brief-Ahmad_R_Malik_dated_07-10-2016.pdf. Accessed 17 Oct 2016.

NDRC, MoFA and MoC [National Development and Reform Commission, Ministry of Foreign Affairs & Ministry of Commerce]. 2015. *Vision and Actions on Jointly Building Silk Road Economic and 21st Century Maritime Silk Road*. Beijing: Foreign Languages Press.

Saeedi, Tariq Ahmed. 2016. World Bank Forecasts Growth at 5 pc for FY17, 5.4 pc for FY18. *The News International* (Rawalpindi), October 5, 2016.

SCMP [South China Morning Post]. 2013. Li Keqiang Urges Development of China-Pakistan Economic Corridor. *South China Morning Post* (Hong Kong), May 23, 2013. http://www.scmp.com/news/china/article/1244267/li-keqiang-urges-development-china-pakistan-economic-corridor.

Sering, Senge H. 2016. China's Rise is a Source of Optimism for Many in Pakistan. *The American Bazaar* (Germantown), November 3, 2013. https://www.americanbazaaronline.com/2013/11/03/pakistan-chinas-soft-power-gilgit-baltistan/. Accessed 28 Sept 2016.

Sheikh, Ali Tauqeer. 2016. How CPEC Can Help the SDGs. *Dawn* (Islamabad), October 22, 2016.

Yousafzai, Fawad. 2016. China to Build Mega Oil Pipeline from Gwadar to Kashgar. *The Nation* (Islamabad), June 13, 2016.

Chapter 8
China–Pakistan Economic Corridor (CPEC): Regional Cooperation in the Wider South Asian Region

Siegfried O. Wolf

1 Introduction

The focus on Economic Corridors (EC) has become a trend of strategic development in various countries and regions worldwide (Safitri 2012). Basically, an EC is a development project aiming at the increase of economic growth over a certain period of time and in a specific area.[1] Therefore, ECs link economic agents along a defined geographical entity and provide important connections among major economic nodes or hubs centered in urban landscapes (Brunner 2013). Consecutively, ECs link production, trade, and infrastructure within a specific geographic framework of the center of economic activities and extend benefits to rural areas through transport development and expansion of production activities (Ishida et al. 2012). As such, an EC is designed to create global, regional, and domestic value chains through the creation and/or connection of economic centers and ideally produces positive multisectoral spillover effects.

Having such a conceptual framework in mind, the China-Pakistan Economic Corridor (CPEC), a multi-billion-dollar infrastructure investment project, is heralded as a game changer for Pakistan's economy and regional cooperation. Being a crucial part of a major development initiative led by China, known as 'One Belt, One Road' (OBOR), to connect Asia with Europe and the Middle East with Africa

[1]See, AGIL (2000: 2).

S.O. Wolf (✉)
South Asia Democratic Forum, Brussels, Belgium
e-mail: siegfried.wolf@sadf.eu

B.R. Deepak (ed.), *China's Global Rebalancing and the New Silk Road*,
https://doi.org/10.1007/978-981-10-5972-8_8

via a 'land (belt)'[2] and 'sea (road)',[3] for the CPEC project and for those involved it evokes hopes and a myriad of interests and spurs a significant geopolitical shift (Shi 2015). Praised as a new economic lifeline, the CPEC is an essential link between the belt and road. In order to provide this connection, the CPEC should connect Kashgar in China's western, landlocked province of Xinjiang with Gwadar port on the Balochistan coast in Pakistan's southwestern region (Aamir 2015). According to the plan, the CPEC will be implemented through a '1+4 cooperation structure' as follows (Khan 2015a, b): the Economic Corridor as an overall, multisectoral development project at the center and Gwadar Port, energy, infrastructure, and industrialization as its four key areas of collaboration. To operationalize this plan, the corridor combines several cross-sectional components, such as infrastructure, trade, connectivity, transport, energy, and services. More concretely, it consists of various components: roads, railways, airport (Gwadar), local transportations (e.g., metro), and pipelines for oil and gas. In this context, in addition to building a completely new supporting infrastructure to create connectivity, several major upgrades of existing outdated infrastructure systems are required (e.g., the Karakorum Highway). Besides infrastructure, the major focus [around two-thirds of the investments, roughly $35 billion (Markey et al. 2016)] will be placed on the increase of energy capacities—both renewable and non-renewable—such as solar, wind, and hydro-power energy and coal. The planned pipeline projects are also expected to improve the imports of gas and oil. Additionally, all these projects are flanked by substantial security measures to guarantee a safe environment for the CPEC development (BBC 2015a). Essentially, the CPEC encompasses three routes through Pakistan, plus a northern extension: first, the so-called route of Eastern Alignment, which passes mainly through central Punjab and Sindh (Rana 2015). Second, the Central Route passes partly through Khyber–Pakhtunkhwa (KPK) and hitherto unconnected parts of Punjab and Sindh. The third route, known as the Western Alignment, passes through the relatively underdeveloped areas of KPK and Balochistan (Zingel 2015: 14–24). Finally, there is also a so-called Northern route (drawing on the existing Karakorum highway), which will connect all the three Pakistani alignments with the Pakistani–China border at Kunjarab and will continue to the Chinese territory. The whole project, which is mainly financed by China, is expected to be totally completed in 2030 (i.e., the long-term projects) and some parts within the next one to three years (i.e., the early harvest projects). However, it is important to note that China has four major conditions for Pakistan to implement the CPEC: First and foremost, Pakistan needs to establish a stable

---

[2]The sum of all land-based routes of OBORS are also known as the Silk Road Economic Belt (SREB).

[3]Sea-road part of OBOR is also known as 21st Century Maritime Silk Route Economic Belt, a sea-based path through the South China Sea, South Pacific Ocean, and Indian Ocean in order to complement the land routes (SREB). It is the modern-day equivalent of ancient sea lanes and aims to link China with the Mediterranean Sea via the Persian Gulf.

security environment; it must ensure national harmony and consensus; and it must achieve timely implementation of the CPEC projects. In other words, 'the faster, the better', and thus the 'mantra' will be, 'the Easiest First'.

2 Expected Benefits from the CPEC for China and Pakistan

A multifaceted development project like the CPEC influences many aspects of state and society: it relates to the economic, political, and social spheres, as well as foreign policy objectives and geopolitics.

2.1 Pakistani Interests

From an economic point of view, Pakistan's main interest is to attract foreign capital. In other words, the CPEC comes at a time when a surge of major investments in the country is imperative (Chang 2014). Through the successful implementation of the respective projects, Islamabad hopes to improve the infrastructure and energy situation and to generate a positive spill-over effect in all other economic sectors. In this context, through the build-up of special economic zones, the CPEC not only aims to be a transit route for commodities and raw materials but also to become a catalyst for industrialization and spur the development of manufacturing hubs. These hubs must boost Pakistan's underperforming economy and create opportunities for entrepreneurs. By identifying economic nodes in established industrialized-urban centers, as well as disadvantaged rural areas, the government hopes to generate a nationwide economic boost that reaches Pakistan's poorer provinces (Rafi 2015). To achieve these goals, Pakistan will link the country's major cities in order to serve as junctions in a new nationwide infrastructure. With the expected economic growth and Chinese technical support, Islamabad hopes that it will be able to address the problems of unemployment, lack of know-how, and insufficient management capabilities, and to bridge the gap in trade and transport capabilities. Keeping these goals in mind, the CPEC might also initiate an impetus to reverse negative processes of brain drain and capital flight that are at high levels (Wolf 2016a, b, c). If the projects prove successful, the CPEC could have a positive impact on the population's overall mindset: on one hand, attracting educated youths from abroad, as well as getting those who were planning to leave the country and (re-)engaging them in Pakistan's future. On the other hand, it could convince non-state investors to provide venture capital. In the context of Pakistan's overall financial indicators, one is hopeful that foreign exchange reserves will significantly increase as the CPEC progresses. Needless to say, Islamabad wishes to further deepen Pakistani and Chinese cooperation as the Chinese are finally willing to broaden bilateral ties beyond geopolitics and towards mutually entrenched economic and socio-political relations. In the words of Iqbal (2015), Pakistan's minister for planning and development, who believes that the CPEC will change the scope of Sino-Pakistan ties "from geopolitics to geo-economics" which will have "significant transformative effect on Pakistan's economy". As the CPEC is implemented, "the entire geostrategic importance of Pakistan will change."

Furthermore, it is important to note that Pakistan aims at the diversification of its foreign aid and investment portfolio. Traditionally, US financial support was a major source for inflows of financial assets, however, the provision of capital by the US (and Europeans) is usually linked to political conditions or prerequisites. After the cool-down in US–Pakistan relations, Washington reduced its engagement in the region and left Islamabad looking to replace the 'unreliable' US support. However, the CPEC investments by China do more than simply fill this void, and Pakistan's decision makers are convinced that China is not just an 'all-weather friend', but also a valuable ally who will become a political and economic superpower within the next decade. Therefore, Islamabad will further strengthen its relationship with Beijing at the expense of its ties with the US. Taking into account the various perspectives of Washington and Beijing on issues such as the South China Sea, North Korea, trade, counter-terrorism, and especially Taiwan ('One-China Policy'), one can also see a broader alignment of Pakistani and Chinese views than those possible between Pakistan and the US. The current uncertainties within the international community regarding the foreign policy of US President Donald Trump will further enhance the convergence of Sino-Pakistani interests. This trend will only continue to grow, since it seems that Washington is willing to increase pressure on Pakistan to end its support for cross-border terrorism (Dorsey 2017).

There is no doubt that the above mentioned economic opportunities will have significant political and social impacts. One may expect: firstly, improving relations between the various provinces, as well as better center-state relations. Secondly, expectation is the notion that a successful or complete implementation of the CPEC will improve the credibility and capacities of the civilian government and, as such, strengthen processes of good governance. Thirdly, all these could potentially lead to a new international status and improved regional standing (Rafi 2015) for Pakistan based on the emergence of a "new economic self-confidence". With this in mind, Islamabad's decision makers aim to overcome the country's regional 'diplomatic isolation' (Fazil 2015) and to subsequently improve the economic and political cooperation with Afghanistan, Iran, central Asian states, and Russia (Barber 2014). Finally, extraordinary growth predictions will generate positive results for the common people. In this context, there is great hope that the subsequent improvement of the living conditions will also help contain political radicalization, Islamization, militancy, and Jihadism. In brief, the CPEC might help to eradicate terrorism in Pakistan (Haider 2015).

However, besides these expected positive impacts, one must be also aware that there are critical voices pointing out that, due to Pakistan's handling of the CPEC project, there is a lack of national consensus and harmony among the provinces and other disadvantaged areas, especially between Balochistan, Khyber Pakhtunkhwa

(KPK), and the Federal Administered Tribal Areas (FATA), on one side, and Punjab and Sindh on the other side, plus between the regions and the federal government. Hence, the following complaints by some regions have been put into the forefront in the context of the implementation: no adequate inclusion of regions in decision-making processes; exploitation of regional resources without adequate remuneration; land acquisition; forced displacement of local people and guided internal migration to change the social demography in restive regions especially in Balochistan and Gilgit-Baltistan; and severe distortion of fair and free economic competition. In consequence, there is the rationale that the CPEC enforces already existing center–regional conflicts, and intensifies socio-political unrest and protest movements (Wolf 2016a, b, c).

2.2 Chinese Interests

According to analysts, China has plenty of incentives to unleash these vast investments for the CPEC, despite facing a multitude of threats that challenge the establishment and smooth functioning of the initiative.[4] Beijing is convinced that, in the light of its many security problems, Pakistan is in need of major development projects to bring stability to the country (Small 2015a, b; Tiezzi 2015). From Beijing's point of view, this will protect Chinese economic interests and reduce the terrorist threat coming from Pakistan. It believes that sustainable economic prosperity in Pakistan will help to contain the terrorism that challenges Chinese economic interests, territory, and security. In other words, it aims to secure a win-win situation by eradicating the threat within Pakistan and protect its economic interests in the country (Fullerton 2015). As reported by Small (2015a, b), "Chinese investments have been constrained by Pakistan's instability and security threats to Chinese workers. By some measures, 'Pakistan has been the most dangerous place to be for an overseas Chinese.' Therefore, China demands a clear commitment from Pakistan accompanied by clear and concrete actions to protect the sovereignty and territorial integrity of the People's Republic and Chinese citizens on Pakistani soil. Namely, to undermine all efforts from Pakistan based terrorists and separatists to destabilize 'mainland China', especially Xinjiang province.[5] Furthermore, Beijing expects that Pakistan continues its diplomatic support for the 'One-China' policy".[6]

Additionally, the land-based CPEC provides China with another access route to the Indian Ocean and allows it to by-pass the Malacca Straits to reach Africa and the Middle East (BBC 2015a). Strategists have long perceived the corridor as a

[4]Andrew Small quoted in Gabriel Domínguez, Author Interview with Andrew Small: Bilateral relations: The Sino-Pakistani axis: Asia's 'little understood' relationship, *Deutsche Welle*, January 15, 2015. http://www.dw.de/the-sino-pakistani-axis-asias-little-understood-relationship/a-18194448.

[5]Daily Times (2015), The New York Times (2015).

[6]Xinhua (2016).

strategic liability; they see it as a means look to immunize China from a potential blockade by the US and its allies in the Asia-Pacific region (Joshi 2013). The current diplomatic turmoil with the new US administration and increasing tensions in the South China Sea are indicators for the likelihood of such a scenario. This so called 'Malacca-Dilemma' further gains significance if one takes into account that around 80% of Chinese energy imports flow through the Malacca route (Sahgal 2015). While the CPEC is expected to be shorter, cheaper, and avoid the risk of piracy (Detsch 2015), it is doubtful that any land corridor could fully substitute the economic usage of the Malacca Strait. Nevertheless, it would significantly reduce Beijing's reliance on the Malacca passage.

Another reason why an improved connection with the Middle East and Africa is gaining significance is the presence of the large number of Chinese companies and employees and development activities in the respective regions (BBC 2015a). As such, the CPEC also touches on China's overseas interests and would provide additional logistic support and coordination for Chinese 'global business activities (Ze 2015)'.

China hopes that the CPEC can also provide a boost to China's slackening economy, especially in the western, landlocked province of Xinjiang (Tharoor 2015). The project should help bridge the development imbalance between the prosperous eastern and underdeveloped western parts of the country (Xu 2015). The corridor should create incentives for both state and private enterprises to expand economic activity, create jobs, and raise consumption levels in this underdeveloped region (BBC 2015a). By doing this, China similarly expects to stabilize the region by improving the economic conditions in the western periphery; the region currently constitutes one of Beijing's top domestic security concerns (Dominguez 2015). However, Uighur militants, who are leading a separatist movement in Xinjiang, might perceive its development as a way to exploit the region's resources. Overall, China expects that improving economic conditions in Xinjiang will bring sociopolitical stability and subsequently help undermine the 'three evils': separatism, terrorism, and religious fundamentalism (Davis 2008).

3 India's 'Uneasiness' with the CPEC

As already elaborated, the OBOR in general and CPEC in particular seem to offer many possibilities for regional cooperation, especially for New Delhi (Ranjan 2015). But, until today, India has hardly responded to any invitation to join the CPEC nor spent much concrete efforts to push its own envisaged economic corridor with China via Bangladesh and Myanmar, in short, the BCIM-EC, which is the second South Asian part of OBOR (Sajjanhar 2016). Now, the questions arise as to why India has remained reluctant to define its position towards and perhaps adopt a potential role within the OBOR? What are the causes for New Delhi's obvious uneasiness with the CPEC? Basically, besides all the opportunities associated with the OBOR, there are certain issues that make New Delhi uncomfortable in joining the Chinese initiative.

Firstly, there are concerns among India's decision makers about the increase in Pakistan–China security cooperation alongside the CPEC. Furthermore, there is the severe fear in India that the Gwadar Port may one day become a Chinese naval base for maritime expansionism. As such, Gwadar—as part of a series of strategically well-located port projects in the Indian Ocean to realize the so-called 21st Century Maritime Silk Route Economic Belt—is fostering fears in New Delhi of a Chinese encirclement of India by a so-called 'string of pearls' or 'pincer strategy' (Rahman 2012).

In other words, the CPEC heightens the notion that the Sino–Pakistani partnership poses a challenge to India's regional standing and attempts to contain New Delhi's influence in South Asia and beyond (Ashraf 2015).

Secondly, the fact that the corridor crosses Gilgit–Baltistan, a part of the disputed area in Kashmir, is a major roadblock to India's participation in the project. Any potential cooperation that includes India in the CPEC development might be interpreted as a legitimization of the status quo regarding the territory controlled by Pakistan but claimed by India (Fazil 2016; Sering 2014).

Thirdly, there is much suspicion revolving around the overall OBOR project, especially regarding China's real intentions. Basically, it is understandable to observers that Beijing is aiming to push its own stagnating economy and to develop its remote western province, Xinjiang, by increasing connectivity with Central and South Asia. Additionally, taking the tremendous demands and nature of China's manufacturing industry into account, it is also not surprising that the country is launching vast activities to ensure energy security and the supply of resources, as well as access to new markets. As such, major Chinese development projects outside its own soil are not rare and can be traced back to earlier economic development schemes like the 'Going global' strategy with which Beijing tried to encourage Chinese companies to invest abroad and/or to establish the so-called Chinese Overseas Special Economic Zones (Bhattacharjee 2015). What is entirely new, however, is that China is attempting to transform—in a coherent and conceptual way—its economic success abroad into political power on a larger international stage for the first time. Therefore, the OBOR is the most visible expression of Beijing's desire to create a new multipolar world order that sufficiently addresses Chinese national interests (Sárvári et al. 2016). Against this backdrop, many Indian observers are not convinced about the Chinese intention to create 'mutual benefit' on a collective basis, and they identify the OBOR as a unilateral measure to ensure Chinese national interests (Madan 2016).

By looking at the tremendous geographical (around 60 participating states) and financial dimensions (regarding which The Economist[7] published figures estimate there are around 900 deals under way, worth US$890 billion), it becomes apparent that the OBOR is far more than just a 'development initiative'. Even if the Chinese

---

[7]The Economist (2016).

officials refuse to use another term than 'initiative,' it is clear that OBOR is China's 'New Grand Strategy' that constitutes the main focal point of its foreign policy and diplomacy.

However, New Delhi is not only puzzled about the magnitudes and security-related aspects of the New Silk Road. Even though Beijing is emphasizing that all its foreign investments are based on mutual benefit and not designed to create a hegemonic position, the way OBOR is carrying out its projects does not help to dilute India's concerns, especially due to the lack of transparency of decision making, combined with an insufficient level of communication by Chinese authorities and the questionable profitability of several projects (Wells et al. 2017). All these aspects are now deepening Indian skepticism about the OBOR even more. The fact that China refuses to negotiate OBOR in multilateral arrangements seems to confirm the criticism about the amorphous character of the project, which is complicating a constructive debate about India's view on that matter. This is an unfortunate development because India would not only miss a much-needed improvement of regional connectivity and economic opportunities but will also complicate India's access to markets and resources in Central Asia and Africa. In sum, New Delhi should take a decision as soon as possible on whether to join the OBOR, especially the CPEC, or not. In case of non-cooperation, India will have to come up with an alternative concept if it doesn't want to be part of the Chinese-initiated economic integration in the new 'Eurasia'.

4 Impacts of CPEC on Regional Cooperation

Insofar as CPEC may have positive impacts on regional cooperation, this depends on its ability to increase regional connectivity as much as possible. Therefore, it is imperative that the CPEC will be integrated in transport, energy, and trade infrastructure networks beyond the Pakistan–China nexus. As the CPEC is linked with Kashgar and its growing special economic zone (Wells et al. 2017), a successful entrenchment within the northern networks is ensured, connecting the CPEC with Central Asian States, Russia, and Europe (Barber 2014). However, it is of the utmost importance that Pakistan includes its neighbors as they would greatly benefit from this project if it succeeds. Subsequently, Pakistan should open up the CPEC to the west (Iran and Afghanistan) and to the east (India); only then can it make a significant impact on regional connectivity and become a game changer for regional cooperation in South Asia. For any real change to occur, a normalization of Pakistan–India relations and a constructive Pakistan–Iran relationship are essential preconditions. Furthermore, a fundamental reassessment of Pakistan's predominantly-security based approach towards Afghanistan and India is needed (Malik and Naseer 2015a, b). However, this requires a decisive change in the mindset of regional decision makers, especially in Islamabad and New Delhi; the tensions in the India–Pakistan relationship continue to obstruct any noteworthy regional collaboration. Regarding Afghanistan, Pakistan must finally drop the vision of 'strategic depth' and/or similar notions and adopt a nonpartisan policy approach towards Afghanistan's internal affairs (Rizvi 2013).

Therefore, Pakistan should redefine its regional profile and normalize economic and diplomatic relations with its neighbors (Rizvi 2013; Khan 2015a, b). With the formulation of its 'Vision 2025' (ISSRA 2014), Islamabad took the first step, at least in theory; however, Pakistan must also develop a foreign policy free from ideological parameters that will allow more rational behavior in its bilateral relations. More concretely, Pakistan needs to put greater emphasis on trade and economic cooperation rather than focusing primarily on security (Barber 2014). Until now, the country's military and intelligence services did not play any constructive role in Pakistan's relations with its neighbors. The latest invitation by representatives of the Pakistani army to India to join the CPEC is rather half-hearted (IANS 2016). Furthermore, the cross-border activities of Pakistan-based terrorists undermine any sustainable rapprochement between Islamabad and New Delhi, as well as Kabul. On this matter, China sides with Pakistan on several issues,[8] nevertheless it does not want to deepen involvement in India–Pakistan disputes. As such, Beijing could play an essential role as interlocutor and make it clear "that the proposal to open access to the economic corridor for India has credible commitment at the highest levels in China". Beijing is most likely the only stakeholder that could encourage a change in Pakistan's mindset. Only then can regional connectivity be improved and can Pakistan, China, and the whole extended region enjoy maximum benefits from the Economic Corridor. In order to work towards sustainable regional cooperation, the integration of a stabilized Afghanistan into the CPEC, as well as other economic corridors, must be ensured. Therefore, Beijing has vested interests in a stable Afghanistan that is no longer under the control of Jihadist elements who will give shelter to Muslim Uighur separatists challenging law and order in Xinjiang (Wolf 2012a, b, c; Shams 2015). Furthermore, it is of the utmost importance that Afghanistan will not turn into a base for forces aiming to destabilize 'Central Asian Republics',[9] which is one of the most crucial areas for the overall success of the OBOR. This raises the questions of how much influence China has on Pakistan's security-sector agents in order to convince them to eradicate Pakistani-based, cross-border terrorist groups. As long as Islamabad follows an appeasement strategy by providing shelter to Jihadists operating in neighboring countries, the prospects for a peaceful environment for OBOR projects in the wider region looks rather grim.

While it may be tempting to assume Chinese influence in this matter, assessing the genesis of foreign leverage in Afghanistan shows that Pakistan and China have differing priorities: Beijing's primary interest is to produce sufficient peace and stability in Afghanistan to contain the negative spill-over effects towards Central

---

[8]For example, in the territorial dispute with India over Gilgit-Baltistan or the case of Indian and US attempts to designate Pakistan based-militants on the United Nations Security Council Sanctions Committee list of terrorists. Dawn (2017).

[9]Namely Kazakhstan, Kyrgyzstan, Uzbekistan, Turkmenistan and Tajikistan.

Asia. However, as long as Afghanistan's internal socioeconomic and political trajectories do not threaten Chinese interests, they are not perceived as major concerns in China. On the other side, Islamabad looks to exercise influence over domestic power dynamics and to keep its rival India out of Afghanistan.[10] It is interesting to note that in the past "China used to outsource its Afghanistan policy to Pakistan but is now taking a far more active role in the planning in the wake of the West's drawdown" (Small 2015a, b). The latest 'trilateral talks' between China, Russia, and Pakistan are a clear indication that Beijing is aiming to evolve from a bystander into a stakeholder in Afghanistan's security affairs (Bai 2016). However, Beijing "expects Pakistan to take Chinese concerns into account" (Small 2015a, b). This could help to improve relations between Kabul and Islamabad and may improve Pakistan–Afghanistan economic cooperation. Severe litmus tests for future constructive collaboration between Kabul and Islamabad include the envisaged Turkmenistan-Afghanistan-Pakistan-India (TAPI) pipeline, an Afghanistan-Pakistan Transit-Trade Agreement, and the Central Asia South Asia Electricity Transmission and Trade Project (CASA-1000).

The second crucial aspect of the increase of CPEC's 'western connectivity' is the collaboration with Iran. A successful eastward orientation would not only help deepen regional cooperation but offers tremendous opportunities for the CPEC in general and the Western alignment of the Economic Corridor in particular. The cooperation in energy and trade would benefit considerably from a rapprochement between Islamabad and Tehran. Furthermore, the construction of an Iran–Pakistan–India pipeline would create other avenues of potential cooperation between India and Pakistan, as well as Afghanistan. Until recently, it seems to many observers that the 'Joint Comprehensive Plan of Action'—the deal reached between Iran and other world powers to limit Tehran's nuclear program and subsequent removal of sanctions—will re-established Iran's position in international relations in general and will open up new opportunities for cooperation, especially with Pakistan in particular. But in the wake of the latest US–Iran tensions after Washington enacted new sanctions against Teheran,[11] it seems that the expected outcomes of the negotiated 'nuclear deal' must be reassessed, especially its impacts on relations with the Middle Eastern country. Tehran has been put "on notice" by Washington and punitive measures by Trump administration are announced in cases of further violations of the JSPOA or continuation of state-sponsorship for terrorism. Here, the US expects from its allies and partners to follows its Iran policy. More concretely, individuals and companies that are on the US sanction list are "barred from doing business with US companies, and that companies around the world will be

[10]*Daily Times*, April 21, 2015; Dominguez, January 15, 2015.

[11]On February 3, the new US administration enacted fresh sanctions on Iran. The sanctions list includes three separate networks linked to supporting Iran's ballistic-missile development program and those providing support to the Islamic Revolutionary Guard Corps Force. The measures are partly a response to Tehran's test of a medium-range missile on 29 January 2016, as well as Tehran's support for foreign-armed groups like the Yemeni Shia Houthi rebels or the Lebanese Hezbollah, among others. Jin (2017), Borger and Smith (2017).

blacklisted by the US if they do business with them (Aleem 2017)". Despite the fact that the latest US sanctions also target Chinese individuals and companies (Jin 2017), Beijing will most likely try to follow a 'neutral approach' within US-Iran confrontation in order to avoid being drawn into a major conflict between and 'Iranian led Shia camp' and 'Saudi Arabia guided Sunni camp'[12]. This would harm the OBOR in general and Chinese interests in the Middle East in particular. Nevertheless, Beijing will not allow the US to interfere decisively in Sino-Iranian ties in such a way that China's long-held dominant investment position in, and economic cooperation with, Iran will be challenged (Jin 2017).

While much depends on how the US–China relation develops, nevertheless it will not challenge the overall success of the OBOR. Besides all the apocalyptic critical forecasts, there are also numerous voices stating that US President Trump, despite his 'noisy and unconventional rhetoric', is open to rational economic arguments and will not change fundamental parameters of Washington's foreign policy as long as they do not touch substantially US domestic affairs and national security. As such, in the long run (if there will be no critical escalation), one could speculate that Mr. Trump, who is inspired by a 'Dubaization of America', will be rather interested in major infrastructure projects like the OBOR. However, regarding the facts on the ground, at the moment it is apparent that not only Pakistan, but also Iran, is moving towards closer cooperation with China and Russia. The cancelation of the Trans-Pacific Partnership (TPP), the Russia–Pakistan rapprochement, increasing Russia–China cooperation, and the growing interests of Turkey in the OBOR are other favorable conditions for the development of OBOR and the CPEC. However, these trends do not necessarily lead to an improvement in Iran–Pakistan cooperation.

No doubt that any rapprochement has to take both 'Pakistan's special relations with Saudi Arabia' and subsequently 'Riyadh's sentiments towards Tehran' into account. Riyadh and Islamabad share a long history of cooperation on defense and security, and Saudi Arabia has often helped the Pakistani government with precarious financial situations (Vandewalle 2015). Nevertheless, the CPEC may initiate a gradual shift in Pakistan's regional outlook and its relations with Iran and Saudi Arabia. On the one hand, Pakistan considers Iran a potential partner to cooperate in the field of energy, transport, and trade, but, on the other hand, it does not want to offend Saudi Arabia further by getting too close to Tehran (Sham 2016). This will be a difficult balancing act for Islamabad due to the growing Saudi–Iranian hostility in the Middle East. For example, Saudi Arabia was displeased that Pakistan's parliament voted against joining the Saudi-led attacks (Operation

[12]The differentiation between 'Iranian led Shia camp' and 'Saudi Arabia guided Sunni camp' must be understood as ideal types. There are several cases in which a clear-cut distinction between both types are not possible because they are both intervening. Iran's military intervention in Syria and its collaboration with Sunni, as well as with Shia groups, can be seen as a proof therefore. Another example is Iranian support for the (Sunni) Taliban in Afghanistan, or the use of Shia communities by Pakistani governments 'settlement policies' to change the social-religious demography of restive areas in Pakistan.

Decisive Storm) against Iranian supported Houthi rebels in Yemen.[13] Against this backdrop, Pakistan will most likely approach the situation with great caution to not further alienate Saudi Arabia. The difficult task of balancing the relations between Islamabad with Tehran and Riyadh is only one challenge in the context of the CPEC. At this time, it is unclear whether Iran will turn out to be a competitor or a partner. As previously indicated, the Chinese government is concerned with the ongoing political conflicts that obstruct implementation of the CPEC, security problems, delays, and more. Tehran may offer an alternative economic partnership and corridor; Iran's main argument is that it has the functional port of Chabahar, only 36 km from Gwadar, which lies in a remote and restive area (Chang 2014). In contrast to Gwadar, Chabahar is well connected with the country's infrastructure, and Iran can guarantee the security of Chinese investments and its workers (Fazl-e-Haider 2014). In this context, it is interesting to mention that China offered to invest US$51 billion in Iran, which is more than it offered initially to Pakistan (today it seems that Islamabad will receive much more loans for investments to implement the CPEC). In sum, there is the imminent threat that a potential Iran–China Corridor turns into competition for the CPEC. However, considering Pakistan's 'strategic location' (Fazil 2015)—which is the country's major asset—and Chinese interests into account, one can state that an 'Iran option' will merely be an additional option for Beijing and is unlikely to substitute the CPEC.

5 Conclusion

The CPEC could be designed as an entity with an inclusive character, open to all actors willing to participate in a constructive manner. Therefore, Pakistan's government must work towards a national consensus and harmony. As such, Islamabad should stop disadvantaging certain areas and their respective populations, especially Balochistan and Gilgit–Baltistan, to avoid anti-CPEC unrest and protest, as well as provincial rivalries. Therefore, Pakistan should introduce an all-inclusive and transparent decision-making process. It is advisable to establish mechanisms that allow for the fair distribution of the profits generated by CPEC and related projects among the provinces. In other words, the federal government should look at the grievances of the local people. Its current policy of zero tolerance and crushing military response to any opposition in Balochistan will likely escalate the tense situation (Wirsing 2008) and increase the risks to Chinese workers and projects in the provinces. The persistent attacks on Chinese workforces can be seen as proof of this hypothesis. In this context, Islamabad "should keep in mind that development does not bring peace, rather it is peace that brings development" (Fazl-e-Haider 2014). The dream of a fully functional Gwadar port, which could turn the province into an important energy conduit in the region, can only come true if peace and

[13]BBC (2015b).

stability return to Balochistan. In this context, Gilgit–Baltistan serves as another important reference point. Islamabad expects that an improvement of the socioeconomic conditions would have a positive impact on peace and reconciliation in the conflict-ridden Gilgit–Baltistan region. Historically, the original construction of the Karakoram Highway has failed to resolve tensions between Shia and Sunni communities. On the contrary, the communal tensions have increased over time (Hunzai 2013; Wolf 2012a, b, c). On the international level, Pakistan needs a fundamental reassessment of its foreign policy to be able to enter into a constructive relationship with its neighbors. As long as Islamabad gives the impression of being unreliable, it will not be able to obtain their cooperation on the CPEC. India also urgently needs to debate and proclaim its stance vis-à-vis the CPEC; any discourse should be based on a rational evaluation of policy options, free from emotional arguments. This will not be easy, considering India's concerns regarding the CPEC. Furthermore, New Delhi's questioning of Beijing's intentions behind the OBOR is making the situation even more complicated. If these issues are not addressed, the CPEC will neither serve as a critical juncture in Pakistan's troubled economic, social, and political development, nor become a 'game changer' for regional connectivity, cooperation, and integration.

References

Aamir, Adnan. 2015. Pak-China Economic Corridor. *Pakistan Today*, February 7, 2015. http://www.pakistantoday.com.pk/2015/02/07/comment/pak-china-economic-corridor/.

AGIL. 2000. *Zona Paz Economic Corridor Strategy*. Abt Association Inc., Guatemala-CAP Income Generation Activities Project. Guatemala: Abt Association Inc. http://pdf.usaid.gov/pdf_docs/Pnacy158.pdf.

Aleem, Zeeshan. 2017. Trump's New Sanctions Targeted Iran. So Why is China Angry About Them. *Vox News*, February 6, 2017. http://www.vox.com/world/2017/2/6/14522040/iran-sanctions-china.

Ashraf, Sajjad. 2015. China-Pakistan Economic Corridor, ISAS Brief, No. 364, Institute of South Asian Studies National University of Singapore, Singapore, April 9, 2015. http://www.isas.nus.edu.sg/isaspapers/Pages/Briefs.aspx.

Bai, Tiantian. 2016. China, Russia, Pakistan Hold Trilateral Talks on Afghanistan Issue. *Global Times*, December 27, 2016. http://www.globaltimes.cn/content/1026031.shtml.

Barber, Christopher Ernest. 2014. The Pakistan-China Corridor: A New Project Will Give Pakistan the Tools of Globalization. Will it Use Them? *The Diplomat*, February 27, 2014. http://thediplomat.com/2014/02/the-pakistan-china-corridor/.

BBC. 2015a. Is China-Pakistan 'Silk Road' a Game-Changer? April 22, 2015. http://www.bbc.com/news/world-asia-32400091.

BBC. 2015b. Yemen Conflict: Pakistan Rebuffs Saudi Coalition Call, April 10, 2015. http://www.bbc.com/news/world-asia-32246547.

Bhattacharjee, Dhrubajyoti. 2015. *China Pakistan Economic Corridor (CPEC)*. Indian Council of World Affairs, Issue Brief, 2015. http://www.icwa.in/pdfs/IB/2014/CPECIB12052015.pdf.

Borger, Julian, and David Smith. 2017. Trump Administration Imposes New Sanctions on Iran. *The Guardian*, 2017. https://www.theguardian.com/us-news/2017/feb/03/trump-administration-iran-sanctions.

Brunner, Hans-Peter. 2013. *What is Economic Corridor Development and What Can It Achieve in Asia's Subregions?* ADB Working Paper Series on Regional Economic Integration, No. 117, Asian Development Bank, 2013. http://www.adb.org/publications/economic-corridor-development-and-what-it-canachieve-in-asia-subregions.

Chang, Gordon. G. 2014. China's Big Plans for Pakistan. *The National Interest*, December 10, 2014. http://nationalinterest.org/feature/chinas-big-plans-pakistan-11827.

Daily Times, Pakistan. 2015. China Launch Economic Corridor, April 21, 2015. http://www.dailytimes.com.pk/national/21-Apr-2015/pakistan-china-launch-economic-corridor.

Davis, Elizabeth Van Wie. 2008. *Uyghur Muslim Ethnic Separatism in Xinjiang, China*. Asia-Pacific Center for Security Studies, January 2008. http://apcss.org/college/publications/uyghur-muslim-ethnic-separatism-in-xinjiang-china/.

Dawn. 2017. China Blocks US Move to Designate Jaish Chief Masood Azhar a Terrorist at UN, February 7, 2017. http://www.dawn.com/news/1313303.

Detsch, Jack. 2015. China's Grand Plan for Pakistan's Infrastructure. President Xi Jinping Has Inked a Deal with Islamabad That Could Provide Beijing with Direct Access to the Indian Ocean. *The Diplomat*, April 21, 2015. http://thediplomat.com/2015/04/chinas-grand-plan-for-pakistans-infrastructure/.

Domínguez, Gabriel. 2015. Author Interview with Andrew Small: Bilateral Relations: The Sino-Pakistani Axis: Asia's 'Little Understood' Relationship, Deutsche Welle, January 15, 2015. http://www.dw.de/the-sino-pakistani-axis-asias-little-understood-relationship/a-18194448.

Dorsey, James M. 2017. Trump Pressured to Confront Pakistan on Support for Militants. *The Express Tribune*, February 10, 2017. http://mideastsoccer.blogspot.de/2017/02/trump-pressured-to-confront-pakistan-on.html.

Fazil, Muhammad Daim. 2015. The China-Pakistan Economic Corridor: Potentials and Vulnerabilities. *The Diplomat*, May 29, 2015. http://thediplomat.com/2015/05/the-china-pakistan-economic-corridor-potential-and-vulnerabilities.

Fazil, Muhammad Daim. 2016. Pakistan: What Stands in CPEC's Way? *The Diplomat*, February 15, 2016. http://thediplomat.com/2016/02/pakistan-what-stands-in-cpecs-way/.

Fazl-e-Haider, Syed. 2014. Insurgency stunts Gwadar progress. *Asia Times*, May 9, 2014. http://www.atimes.com/atimes/South_Asia/SOU-01-090514.html.

Fullerton, Jamie. 2015. China Unveils £30 bn Plan to Link to Pakistan with Economic Corridor. *The Independent*, April 20, 2015. http://www.independent.co.uk/news/world/asia/china-unveils-30bn-plan-to-link-to-pakistan-with-economic-corridor-10190916.html.

Haider, Mateen. 2015. Operations to Continue Till Pakistan is Terror Free, Says General Raheel. *Dawn*, July 3, 2015. http://www.dawn.com/news/1192103.

Hunzai, Izhar. 2013. *Conflict Dynamics in Gilgit-Baltistan*. Special Report 321, United States Institute of Peace, Washington, D.C. http://www.usip.org/sites/default/files/SR321.pdf.

IANS. 2015. India Needs to Be Part of China-Pakistan Economic Corridor. *The Economic Times*, October 10, 2015. http://economictimes.indiatimes.com/news/politics-and-nation/india-needs-to-be-part-of-china-pakistan-economic-corridor/articleshow/49298727.cms.

IANS. 2016. Shun 'Enmity', Join CPEC: Pakistan Army Commander Tells India. *The Hindustan Times*, December 21, 2016. http://www.hindustantimes.com/india-news/shun-enmity-join-cpec-pakistan-army-commander-tells-india/story-iuwc5GktYxaVi2TO7QIspM.html.

Ishida, Masami, and Ikumo, Isono. 2012. Old, New and Potential Economic Corridor in the Mekong Region. In *Emerging Corridors in the Mekong Region*, ed. Ishida, Masami. BRC Research Report No. 8, Bangkok Research Center (BRC), IDE-JETRO, Bangkok Thailand, 2012. http://www.ide.go.jp/English/Publish/Download/Brc/08.html.

ISSRA. 2014. *A Roadmap to Vision 2025*. Institute of Strategic Studies, Research and Analysis (ISSRA), National Defense University, Islamabad, Pakistan. http://aan.ndu.edu.pk/download/Post-Report-Ex-NSW-16.pdf.

Jin, Wang. 2017. US Sanctions on Iran: Good or Bad News for China? *The Diplomat*, February 7, 2017. http://thediplomat.com/2017/02/us-sanctions-on-iran-good-or-bad-news-for-china/.

Joshi, Shashank. 2013. Can India Blockade China? *The Diplomat*, August 12, 2013. http://thediplomat.com/2013/08/can-india-blockade-china/.

Khan, Aarish U. 2015a. *Pak-China Economic Corridor: The Hopes and Reality*. Spotlight. Institute of Regional Studies: Islamabad, Pakistan, 2015. http://irs.org.pk/spotlight/spjan15.pdf.

Khan, Masood. 2015b. CPEC: We Will Succeed. *Pakistan Observer*, May 28, 2015. http://pakobserver.net/detailnews.asp?id=264996.

Madan, Tanvi. 2016. *Order from Chaos: What India Thinks About China's One Belt, One Road initiative (But Doesn't Explicitly Say)*, March 14, 2016, Blog, The Brookings Institution, Washington, D.C., U.S. https://www.brookings.edu/blog/order-from-chaos/2016/03/14/what-india-thinks-about-chinas-one-belt-one-road-initiative-but-doesnt-explicitly-say/.

Malik, Shayan, and Enum Naseer. 2015a. CPEC Politics—Part 2. *Spearhead Analysis*, April 30, 2015. http://spearheadresearch.org/SR_CMS/index.php/researchopinions/cpec-politics-part-2.

Malik, Shayan, and Enum Naseer. 2015b. CPEC Politics—Part 1. *Spearhead Analysis*, April 30, 2015. http://spearheadresearch.org/SR_CMS/index.php/researchopinions/cpec-politics.

Markey, Daniel S., and James West. 2016. Behind China's Gambit in Pakistan, Expert Brief, Council on Foreign Relations (CfR), May 12, 2016. http://www.cfr.org/pakistan/behind-chinas-gambit-pakistan/p37855.

Rafi, Amna Ejaz. 2015. *Chinese President Visit to Pakistan*. IPRI Review, Islamabad Policy Research Institute (IPRI), Islamabad, April 29, 2015. http://www.ipripak.org/chinese-president-visit-to-pakistan/.

Rahman, Maseeh. 2012. Chinese Plans in Seychelles Revive Indian Fears of Encirclement. *The Guardian*, March 22, 2012. http://www.theguardian.com/world/2012/mar/22/china-seychelles-indian-fears-encirclement.

Rana, Shahbaz. 2015. China-Pakistan Economic Corridor: Lines of Development—Not Lines of Divide. *The Express Tribune*, May 17, 2015. http://tribune.com.pk/story/887949/china-pakistan-economic-corridor-lines-of-development-not-lines-of-divide/.

Ranjan, Alok. 2015. The China-Pakistan Economic Corridor: India's Options, Institute of Chinese Studies, ICS Occasional Paper # 10, South Asian Studies, School of International Studies, Jawaharlal Nehru University, Delhi, May, 2015. http://www.icsin.org/uploads/2015/06/05/31e217cf46cab5bd9f15930569843895.pdf.

Rizvi, Hasan Askari. 2013. China and Pakistan's Economic Recovery. *Pakistan Today*, July 9, 2013. http://www.pakistantoday.com.pk/2013/07/09/comment/columns/china-and-pakistans-economic-recovery/.

Safitri, Hilmayati. 2012. *Economic Corridor Policy, Land Concentration and 'Social Exclusion' Java's Economic Corridor Policy Implementation*. Indonesia, International Institute of Social Studies, The Hague, Netherlands. http://thesis.eur.nl/pub/13083/.

Sahgal, Arun. 2015. China—Pakistan Economic Corridor: Changing Dynamics of Southern Asia, Analysis. *Eurasia Review*, April 24, 2015. http://www.fsidelhi.org/china-pakistan-economic-corridor-changing-dynamics-of-southern-asia-analysis/.

Sajjanhar, Ashok. 2016. Understanding the BCIM Economic Corridor and India's Response, ORF ISSUE BRIEF No. 147, Observer Research Foundation. New Delhi, India, June 2016. http://www.orfonline.org/wp-content/uploads/2016/06/ORF_IssueBrief_147.pdf.

Sárvári, Balázs, and Anna Szeidovitz. 2016. The Political Economics of the New Silk Road. *Baltic Journal of European Studies* (Tallinn University of Technology) 6 (1)(20). https://www.degruyter.com/downloadpdf/j/bjes.2016.6.issue-1/bjes-2016-0001/bjes-2016-0001.pdf.

Sering, Senge H. 2014. Gilgit-Baltistan: Nexus of a New Asian Economic Corridor. *The Diplomat*, June 5, 2014. http://thediplomat.com/2014/06/gilgit-baltistan-nexus-of-a-new-asian-economic-corridor/.

Shams, Shamil. 2015. China Expands Influence in 'Economic Colony' Pakistan. *Deutsche Welle*, April 20, 2015. http://www.dw.de/china-expands-influence-in-economic-colony-pakistan/a-18393881.

Shams, Shamil. 2016. Can Iran's Rouhani Win Over Pakistan? *Deutsche Welle*, March 24, 2016. http://www.dw.com/en/can-irans-rouhani-win-over-pakistan/a-19138190.

Small, Andrew. 2015a. China-Pakistan Economic Corridor Will Change the Region. *Hardnews*, July 3, 2015. http://www.hardnewsmedia.com/2015/07/chinapakistan-economic-corridor-will-changeregion%E2%80%93-andrew-small.

Small, Andrew. 2015b. *The China-Pakistan Axis: Asia's New Geopolitics*. New York, USA: Oxford University Press.

Tharoor, Ishaan. 2015. What China's and Pakistan's Special Friendship Means. *The Washington Post*, April 21, 2015. http://www.washingtonpost.com/blogs/worldviews/wp/2015/04/21/what-china-and-pakistans-special-friendship-means/.

The Economist. 2016. Our Bulldozers, Our Rules. China's Foreign Policy Could Reshape a Good Part of the World Economy, July 2, 2016. http://www.economist.com/news/china/21701505-chinas-foreign-policy-could-reshape-good-part-world-economy-our-bulldozers-our-rules.

The New York Times. 2015. China's Big Plunge in Pakistan, April 23, 2015. http://www.nytimes.com/2015/04/23/opinion/chinas-big-plunge-in-pakistan.html?_r=0.

Tiezzi, Shannon. 2015. Can China's Investments Bring Peace to Pakistan? *The Diplomat*, April 21, 2015. http://thediplomat.com/2015/04/can-chinas-investments-bring-peace-to-pakistan/.

Vandewalle, Laurence. 2015. Pakistan and China: 'Iron Brothers' Forever? Directorate.

Wells, Peter, and Don Weinland. 2017. Fitch Warns on Expected Returns from One Belt, One Road. *Financial Times*, January 26, 2017. https://www.ft.com/content/c67b0c05-8f3f-3ba5-8219-e957a90646d1.

Wirsing, Robert G. 2008. *Baloch Nationalism and the Geopolitics of Energy Resources: The Changing Context of Separatism in Pakistan*. US Strategic Studies Institute (SSI), April 2008. file:///C:/Users/User/Downloads/Baloch_Nationalism.pdf.

Wolf, Siegfried O. 2012a. From Bad to Worse: Gilgit-Baltistan Between Sectarian Conflict, Socio-Economic Neglect, and Political Deprivation. *The Independent*, Dhaka, Bangladesh, December 14, 2012. http://crossasia-repository.ub.uni-heidelberg.de/2846/.

Wolf, Siegfried O. 2012b. The Good Neighbour: China's Alternative Strategy in Afghanistan. *The Independent*, Friday Features, Dhaka, Bangladesh, May 11, 2012. http://crossasia-repository.ub.uni-heidelberg.de/2826/.

Wolf, Siegfried O. 2012c. Trapped in Old Patterns? The Future of Pakistan-Afghanistan Relations. *The Independent*, Bangladesh, April 20, 2012. http://crossasia-repository.ub.uni-heidelberg.de/2820/.

Wolf, Siegfried O. 2016a. China-Pakistan Economic Corridor (CPEC) and Its Impact on Gilgit-Baltistan. *SADF Focus*, vol. 25, November 24, 2016. Brussels, Belgium: South Asia Democratic Forum (SADF). http://sadf.eu/new/wp-content/uploads/2016/11/FOCUS.25.SOW_.CPEC_.pdf.

Wolf, Siegfried O. 2016b. Betwixt and Between: The FATA Reform Process and the China-Pakistan Economic Corridor. *SADF Focus*, vol. 21, October 11, 2016. Brussels, Belgium: South Asia Democratic Forum (SADF). http://sadf.eu/new/blog/sadf-focus-21-betwixt-fata-reform-process-china-pakistan-economic-corridor-siegfried-o-wolf/.

Wolf, Siegfried O. 2016c. The China-Pakistan Economic Corridor (CPEC): Feasibility and the Need for an Assessment of India's Role. *SADF Comment*, vol. 19, March 16, 2016. South Asia Democratic Forum (SADF). http://sadf.eu/new/blog/comment-nr-19-china-pakistan-economic-corridor-cpec-feasibility-need-assessment-indias-role/.

Xinhua. 2016. Pakistan Reiterates Support 'One-China' Policy, January 20, 2016. http://news.xinhuanet.com/english/2016-01/20/c_135028885.htm.

Xu, Weihong. 2015. China-Pakistan Economic Corridor Key to Economic Upgrading in Southern Xinjiang. *Global Times*, July 5, 2015. http://www.globaltimes.cn/content/930491.shtml.

Ze, Shi. 2015. A Look at a New Concept and the Remarkable Practice of China's Development Through the "One Belt, One Road". In *Presentation at the International Conference of the Schiller Institute, Paris, France, 13–14 June, 2015*. http://newparadigm.schillerinstitute.com/media/pr-shi-ze-regard-sur-le-concept-nouveau-d-une-ceinture-une-route/.

Zingel, Wolfgang-Peter. 2015. China's Pakistan Option: Economic and Social Implications of an 'All-Weather Relationship', IIC Quarterly. Indian International Center (IIC): New Delhi, India. 42 (2(Autumn)), 14–24.

Chapter 9
China–Mongolia–Russia Economic Corridor: Opportunities and Challenges

Sharad K. Soni

Ever since China unveiled its plans for two massive trade and infrastructure networks connecting Asia with Europe and the Mediterranean through the Silk Road Economic Belt (SREB) and the 21st Century Maritime Silk Road (MSR), also known as 'One Belt, One Road' (OBOR), a number of countries across Eurasia and Central Asia, including Mongolia, have responded optimistically. The reason lies in the fact that these countries have rediscovered a kind of a new Silk Road with tremendous potential for growth. In particular, Mongolia which borders on Russia and China has been showing serious interest to be part of the OBOR initiative because it does not want to miss the chance for development as the connectivity between Beijing and Moscow is becoming more vibrant. Moreover, being in China's northern periphery, Mongolia has had direct impact of Beijing's "neighborhood" or "peripheral" policy. In the past few years, it has been revealed that China's "peripheral" policy has been yielding positive results in Mongolia so far as Sino–Mongolian relations are concerned. This is more so because Mongolia no longer views China in terms of a territorial threat but as a sustainable business partner for mutual benefits given that, today, China is Mongolia's largest economic and trade partner, and the two sides have pledged to almost double their annual trade from US$6 billion to US$10 billion by 2020 (CI 2014: 1). It clearly indicates that, ever since the normalization of Sino–Mongolian relations began in the late 1980s, the two sides have come a long way to expand the scope of their bilateral and multilateral relations. The recent thaw in their relationship also owes much to the OBOR initiative, especially after the Chinese President Xi Jinping proposed constructing an economic corridor linking China, Mongolia, and Russia.

It is in this context that the paper seeks to examine the shift in China's 'neighborhood' or 'peripheral' policy under Xi Jinping which resulted in the announcement of the OBOR initiative. It argues that the OBOR initiative is highly

S.K. Soni (✉)
Centre for Inner Asian Studies, Jawaharlal Nehru University, New Delhi, India
e-mail: sharadksoni@gmail.com

B.R. Deepak (ed.), *China's Global Rebalancing and the New Silk Road*,
https://doi.org/10.1007/978-981-10-5972-8_9

desirable to promote cooperation between China and Mongolia, in particular, and China-Mongolia-Russia, in general, by improving connectivity. Besides, it investigates the opportunities and challenges related to the construction of an economic corridor connecting China's Silk Road Economic Belt with Russia's Trans-Eurasia railway and Mongolia's Prairie Road, or what is termed as the passage-to-grassland initiative.

1 China's 'Neighborhood' Policy

Since the 1991 collapse of the Soviet Union, China's foreign and security policy has largely been concentrated on maintaining cordial relations with neighboring or peripheral countries in the Asia-Pacific region (Soni 2009: 255). From the Chinese point of view, the nature of this policy has continued to be both a "non-confrontational" relationship, as well as a "cooperative" relationship. Perhaps an understanding that rising powers have a critical need for a friendly periphery is what stimulated China to pursue its neighborhood policy more vigorously in recent times. It all began during the reform period with the idea of devising an exclusive policy that could explore "the common ground with Asian countries in both economic and security arenas by conveying the image of a responsible power willing to contribute to stability and cooperation in the region (Zhao 2004: 258)." This resulted in adopting an integrated regional policy, known as "*zhoubianzhengce*" (periphery policy) or "*mulinzhengce*" (good-neighbor policy) so far as China's relations with neighboring countries are concerned (You and Qingguo 1998: 128). Although based on pragmatism, China's neighborhood policy or more precisely good-neighbor policy can be considered as a "smart" strategic move given that establishing good relationships with neighbors was meant to endow China with "a more secure environment in its periphery as a leverage to increase its influence in world affairs (Zhao 2004: 259)."

The Chinese, however, felt motivated to pursue their good-neighbor policy due to the souring of Beijing's economic relations with Western countries after the 1989 Tiananmen Square incident. Sanctions turned China's attention to develop its political and economic relations with neighbors, particularly those sharing common borders. In 1990, Deng Xiaoping advocated two major post-Cold War foreign policy trajectories, i.e., pursuing anti-hegemonism and establishing a new multipolar international order of politics and economics (Chung 2011: 14). Such Chinese approaches with some modifications are still relevant in its good-neighbor policy. After a decade or so, in November 2002, Jiang Zemin's report to the 16th National Congress of the CPC reiterated continuation with building a good-neighbor relationship and partnership with neighboring countries, in addition to stepping up 'regional cooperation' to new heights. This was the first time that 'regional cooperation' was mentioned in the report of the National Congress of the CPC that became the key direction of China's neighborhood policy (Zhang 2013: 18). Furthermore, Chinese Premier Wen Jiabao's speech on "China's Development and Asia's Rejuvenation", which was delivered on 7th October 2003 at ASEAN Business and Investment Summit, made it clear that China pursues a policy of bringing harmony, security, and prosperity to neighbors by means of mutually beneficial cooperation, deepening regional and sub-regional cooperation, and vigorously facilitating economic integration in the region (Cao and Xu 2004: 4–5). In 2005, at the Afro-Asian Summit in Jakarta, Hu Jintao first spoke of realizing a "Harmonious World" which ultimately became a catchword of China's foreign policy in general and neighborhood policy in particular (Chung 2011: 19). Therefore, developing or improving relationships with neighboring countries caught his attention as he was well aware that, in order to realize a "Harmonious World", a peaceful and secure environment in China's periphery was crucial.

However, in the recent past there have been obvious changes in Beijing's neighborhood policy that pose challenges to China's dealings with its neighbors. One of the main issues has been China's 'peaceful' rise, which has raised serious concerns about Beijing's strategic intentions towards its Asian neighbors. There have also been accusations that China's foreign policy has become more rigid under the Xi Jinping administration than what it had been under the Hu Jintao administration (Shin 2014). This rigidity points to China becoming more aggressive now in pursuing its neighborhood policy, which is "characterised by rising confidence and assertiveness in projecting and protecting Chinese national interests" according to Zhang (2010: 40). This is evident from the high-level meeting held for the first time ever on 24–25 October 2013 to discuss China's diplomacy in its periphery and set guidelines for maintaining relations with neighboring countries. Although the meeting emphasized changing the way China had been approaching its neighbors, it also reaffirmed that maintaining a peaceful and stable periphery would remain a core priority of Chinese diplomacy. Meanwhile, Xi Jinping's keynote address to the meeting highlighted the principles of Chinese diplomacy according to four basic concepts: amity, sincerity, mutual benefit, and inclusiveness. Later, the Chinese Ambassador to the United States Cui Tiankai affirmed that Beijing "remains committed to peace and stability in the region, to good neighbourliness with others, to common prosperity and a stronger community, and to peaceful dialogue and negotiations on disputes (Cui 2014)."

Nevertheless, Chinese think tanks and academic circle are unanimous in pointing out that China's relations with its neighbors have now moved into a period of "upgrade, acceleration, and added power (Glaser and Pal 2013)." So, it is no wonder that under Xi Jinping China has reprioritized its relations with peripheral countries within its larger foreign-policy portfolio. This marks a break with foreign policy since the era of Deng Xiaoping, which placed a focus on great power relations to ensure China's growth and security. While the Xi administration continues to view great-power relations as critical to China's foreign-policy strategy, elevation of peripheral relations to a top priority is a paradigm shift. To support this shift, the OBOR grand strategy has been initiated, which focuses first and foremost on the establishment of linkages between China and its peripheral states. China, on the other hand, seeks to use the OBOR to establish more robust policy, facilities, trade, financial, and social ties with its peripheral partners to ensure greater connectivity with neighboring states. One such neighboring state is Mongolia where Beijing's reassurance of a good-neighbor policy has been paying dividend, especially after the launch of China's OBOR initiative.

2 'One Belt, One Road' (OBOR) Initiative

The 'One Belt, One Road' (OBOR) initiative can be considered as Beijing's most ambitious foreign-policy agenda since the establishment of the People's Republic of China in 1949. The initiative was unveiled, for the first time, on September 7, 2013, when the Chinese President Xi Jinping spoke of the Silk Road Economic Belt (SREB) in a speech at Nazarbayev University in Kazakhstan for reviving China's contacts with the Silk Road nations. In another speech delivered on October 24, 2013 at the Indonesian Parliament, he spoke of the importance of economic policy in China's periphery diplomacy and proposed a 21st Century Maritime Silk Road (MSR) initiative. Together they came to be known as New Silk Road or OBOR, an even broader and more ambitious vision for boosting regional integration in China's neighborhood. A recent study points to the fact that the OBOR initiative is unique in terms of China's financial engagement and the innovative network-based project design aimed at contributing to a "more inclusive global governance." Thus, it differs with the prevailing treaty-based integration concepts where the geographical scope, partner countries, strategy, principles, and rules are clearly defined at the beginning (Ghiasy and Zhou 2017).

It was in March 2015 that China came out with its document on the vision and actions of the "One Belt, One Road" initiative, which had been jointly prepared by a combined team from the National Development and Reform Commission (NDRC), Ministry of Commerce, and Ministry of Foreign Affairs. Describing the initiative as a flexible, open, and inclusive cooperative framework, the document envisions diversified means of mutually beneficial cooperation among the countries along the OBOR (Grieger 2016: 3–4). It stresses the following five major goals in terms of cooperation and connectivity to implement the OBOR initiative (NDRC 2015):

1. Policy coordination to be promoted on the basis of existing or new bilateral/multilateral cooperation mechanisms.
2. Facilitate connectivity for overland and maritime transport, energy, and communication infrastructure.
3. Unimpeded trade to be encouraged by simplifying customs-clearance systems and foreign-investment procedures, in addition to creating more free-trade zones.
4. Financial integration to be deepened by involving China-supported multilateral financial institutions besides promoting the use of Chinese currency in bilateral trade.
5. People-to-people contact to be strengthened by promoting extensive cultural and academic exchanges, personnel exchanges and cooperation, media cooperation, youth and women exchanges, and volunteer services, so as to win public support for intensifying bilateral and multilateral cooperation.

The vision document outlines the vast geographic expanse of the OBOR Initiative that would run through the continents of Asia, Europe, and Africa, connecting the exciting East Asian economic circle at one end with the developed European economic circle at the other, thus covering countries having enormous potential for economic development. While, on land the OBOR Initiative will focus on jointly building a new Eurasian Land Bridge and developing China-Mongolia-Russia, China-Central Asia-West Asia and China-Indochina Peninsula economic corridors, at sea it will concentrate on jointly building smooth, secure, and efficient transport routes connecting major sea ports along the OBOR. Since the China-Pakistan Economic Corridor (CPEC) and the Bangladesh-China-India-Myanmar Economic Corridor (BCIMEC) are also associated with the OBOR Initiative, the vision document calls for closer cooperation to develop these two corridors. Further, the document identifies specific gateways that will connect China with other countries.[1] For example, Xinjiang province in the west will be the connecting point for Central, South and West Asian countries, besides being one of the terminals of the CPEC. Likewise, China's province of Heilongjiang will turn out to be the gateway for Mongolia and Russia's Far East because the area would be central for the development of the Eurasian high-speed transport corridor linking Beijing with Moscow.

Intensifying interconnectivity in a geographical area that covers, potentially, 65 countries and 4.4 billion people, and generates roughly 55% of global GNP, represents about 70% of global population and has an estimated 75% of identified energy reserves, is expected to make a significant impact on the OBOR Initiative (Grieger 2016: 4). Moreover, the OBOR could be considered as a strategic framework enabling China to manage its infrastructure projects extending across Asia, Africa, and Europe in a better way as "it combines different foreign and domestic policies with existing and new political and financial cooperation mechanisms in a new geographical format" (Grieger 2016: 5). China's foreign investment through the OBOR can contribute much to Beijing enhancing its status as a global development leader. Commenting on the issue, Ghiasy and Zhou (2017: 7) provide the rationale saying that "current Western-led developmental institutions are not able to address Asia's vast infrastructure deficit, an estimated 4 trillion US dollars for the period 2017–20 alone", and "in meeting that need, China positions itself in a leadership role, contributing to regional development, connectivity and even stability."

As such, "economic cooperation could expand China's circle of friendship and, if executed well, has the potential to amplify its soft power and enhance its neighborhood diplomacy (Ghiasy and Zhou 2017: 7)" For the small states on China's borders, such a new approach to neighborhood diplomacy under the OBOR framework can potentially transform their domestic situations. In this vein, greater engagement and connectivity with China on both the bilateral, as well as multilateral, basis may create more opportunities for underdeveloped neighbors like Mongolia. The China-Mongolia-Russia Economic Corridor is such an initiative

[1]'One Belt One Road' initiative, 1 May 2015, http://www.frontline.in/world-affairs/one-belt-one-road-initiative/article7098506.ece.

aimed at linking the three neighbors to boost transportation connectivity and economic cooperation in border regions. However, it is important to examine how Mongolia could, in particular, and China, Mongolia, and Russia, in general, enjoy benefits from China-Mongolia-Russia Economic Corridor.

3 Opportunities Deriving from China-Mongolia-Russia Economic Corridor

The China-Mongolia-Russia Economic Corridor is one of the six corridors China has planned to establish within the framework of OBOR Initiative. In comparison with the other five economic corridors, it will cover more territory than the others and is also considered to be significant for Northeast Asian economic integration and transportation networks. So far as this corridor is concerned, SCO's Dushanbe and Ufa meetings held in 2014 and 2015 respectively were seen as proofs of China and Russia's deepening coordination, not only regarding Mongolia but also regarding the greater Eurasian continent within the ambit of the OBOR initiative. But 2016 turned out to be a landmark year as an agreement on the development plan to construct the China-Mongolia-Russia Economic Corridor was finally signed by the three participating countries. Describing the agreement as indicative of a "broad regional trend" toward deepening economic integration across the continent, Kent Calder, Director of the Reischauer Center for East Asian Studies at Johns Hopkins University's School of Advanced International Studies, has been quoted as saying that "the region's propensity toward increasing interdependence is spurred by several developments including Chinese economic growth, deepening Sino-Russian diplomatic ties flowing from Euro-Russian tensions since the Ukraine crisis, the greater autonomy of Central Asia since the collapse of the Soviet Union, and technological developments in high-speed rail and communications (Peter 2016)." Mongolia, thus, has been witnessing a new era of economic opportunity through cooperation with its two giant neighbors in the China-Mongolia-Russia Economic Corridor.

But what does an economic corridor stand for? Although no one economic corridor aligns exactly with the characteristics of another, it can broadly be defined as an integrated network of infrastructure within a geographical area intended to excite economic development. Thus, an economic corridor connects economic agents along a defined geography that provides "connection between economic nodes or hubs, usually centered on urban landscapes, in which large amounts of economic resources and actors are concentrated (Brunner 2013: 1)." Generally, an economic corridor is developed by taking into consideration the following (Otgonsuren 2015: 3):

1. Investment in the infrastructure of roads and railroads
2. Implementation of regional development plans

3. Facilitation of trade and support for cross-border trade, services, and tourism
4. Synchronization between government policy and regional development plans.

Significantly, implementation of regional development plans needs support for rural development and urbanization so as to improve infrastructure conditions. It also needs support for heavy industries and improvement of investment environment for small- and medium-sized enterprises, besides increasing investment in tourism. Moreover, it is very important to have synchronization between government policy and the regional development plans in order to establish a proper economic corridor. This is relevant in the case of China-Mongolia-Russia Economic Corridor also because its plan is in line with the individual policies of all three countries involved: China's "Silk Road Economic Belt", Mongolia's "Steppe Road" or "Prairie Road" Programme, and Russia's "Trans-Continental Rail and Road" Plan. In fact, such a vision came to the fore during a trilateral summit among the presidents of Mongolia, China, and Russia, on the sidelines of the 14th SCO summit at Dushanbe, Tajikistan, on September 11, 2014. This was the first such meeting at which Mongolian President Elbegdorj tried to position his country to take advantage of deepening Sino–Russian economic relations. Thinking that a "great game" to create a new version of the Eurasian Silk Road was being played out without any Mongolian input, he used the occasion "to make certain that his two powerful neighbors do not proceed with transportation and energy cooperation without taking into account the role of a mineral-rich Mongolia (Campi 2014)."

On the sidelines of the 15th SCO summit at Ufa in the Russian Federation, the second trilateral meeting was held in June 2015. While, during the first meeting, the three parties basically exchanged their views on possibilities to develop infrastructure and transit transportation, advance the existing railroads, and establish new railroads so as to build a China-Mongolia-Russia Economic Corridor, during the second meeting, they signed a memorandum of understanding to build this economic corridor in addition to adopting a mid-term roadmap to develop the trilateral cooperation. Moreover, underlining that connecting the three countries through infrastructures would be the first and foremost priority of trilateral cooperation, they agreed to facilitate their cooperation in mining, transit transportation, infrastructure construction, tourism, and environmental sectors. However, it was the third meeting held on the sidelines of the 16th SCO meeting in Tashkent, Uzbekistan on June 23, 2016 that the three years of negotiations between the presidents of China, Mongolia, and Russia finally saw its first tangible result when a development plan to construct the China-Mongolia-Russia Economic Corridor was signed by the three parties.

The development plan for the Economic Corridor has indeed been a long-awaited agreement which found its expression after Chinese President Xi Jinping noted that mainland companies had invested nearly US$15 billion in countries participating in Beijing's new Silk Road initiative in 2015, an increase of one-fifth compared to 2014 (SCMP 2016). The whole plan aims at strengthening trilateral cooperation through increasing the scale of trade, improving product competitiveness, and facilitating cross-border transportation between the three countries. Overall, the plan emphasizes developing transportation infrastructure and connectivity; intensifying port construction and supervision of customs, inspection, and quarantine; and promoting cooperation in production capacity and investment besides reinforcing economic and trade cooperation between China, Mongolia, and Russia. According to China's top economic planning body, the National Development and Reform Commission (NDRC), the trade cooperation between the three countries is planned to be increased in areas like agricultural products, energy, the service sector, and building materials, in addition to cooperation on software-program designing and data maintenance (GT 2016).

In order to make this economic corridor feasible, multiple channels will be used for financing, such as government investment, public-private partnerships, and investment from international financial institutions like the Asian Infrastructure Investment Bank and the New Development Bank (GT 2016). These three countries, thus, rely on each other for a large amount of their economic sustenance. China's policies, developed by central and local governments since 2014 for improving the northeast region, exactly go with the China-Mongolia-Russia Economic Corridor framework. This economic corridor can provide opportunities for Mongolian cargo to reach Vladivostok in the east via China's three northeastern provinces and reach Europe in the west via Chita (Otgonsuren 2015: 5). A high-speed rail line costing US$230 billion linking Beijing and Moscow through the Mongolian capital Ulanbaatar has already been agreed to by Russia and China, which would basically reduce time for the 7,000-km journey from six to just two days. It has been noticed that this railway connectivity has potential to boost the China-Mongolia-Russia Economic Corridor besides promoting cooperation in railways, roads, energy resources, logistics, transportation, and agriculture (Soni 2017).

3.1 Key Projects Under the Trilateral Economic Corridor

While signing the development plan of the economic corridor, the three participating countries identified 32 key projects to be implemented because they did not want the trilateral cooperation to be restricted only to the economic corridor, transportation, and customs matters. Rather, regional cooperation in terms of connectivity appears to be one of the top priorities. There has been clear support for Chinese ideas on developing cooperation of eastern regions of Mongolia, Russia, and China. Similarly, the Inner Mongolia Autonomous Region of China, which borders both Mongolia and Russia, holds importance in the planned economic corridor as it has been acting as a window to provide a northward gateway for the OBOR project. It has currently 16 national open ports, including 13 land ports and three aviation ports. However, among these 16 open ports, the following Inner Mongolian ports have special significance (Yang and Yang 2015):

1. The Manzhouli land port is presently the most convenient, economical, and important land-sea transport channels from the Bohai Rim Region to European countries like Russia;
2. The Erenhot railway port is the only railway port connecting China and Mongolia, and it is also an important international channel communicating with Eurasia; and
3. The ports of Manzhouli, Erenhot, Ceke, Ganqimaodu, Zhuengabuqi, Mandula, and Heishantou have become significant channels for import/export of China's energy resources, besides being the main platform for economic and trade cooperation between Russia and Mongolia.

In order to manage the financial issues related to programs and projects of the China-Mongolia-Russia Economic corridor, an Investment and Planning Center has also been planned to be established in Ulaanbaatar. The three countries intend to equally divide costs needed for building the Investment and Planning Center. China's National Development and Reform Commission, Mongolia's Ministry of Foreign Affairs, and Russia's Ministry of Economic Development will be responsible for implementation of projects and programs concerning the economic corridor. Moreover, the 32 key projects in the various sectors, under the development plan of the economic corridor, have been slated for implementation in the following ways (Bayarsaikhan 2016).

3.1.1 Transportation Infrastructure Sector

1. A feasibility study to be carried out on redeveloping the main railway links of the economic corridor (UlanUde–Naushki–Sukhbaatar–Ulaanbaatar–ZamiinUud–Erenhot–UlaanTsav–Zhangjiakou–Beijing–Tianjin), constructing a double-track railway and supplying electricity to it.
2. A feasibility study to be performed on northern railway links in the economic corridor (Kurangino–Kyzyl–TsagaanTolgoi–Arts, Suuri–Ovoot–Erdenet–Salkhit–ZamiinUud–Erenhot–UlaanTsav–Zhangjiakou–Beijing–Tianjin).
3. A feasibility study to be conducted on western railway links of the economic corridor (Kurangino–Kyzyl–TsagaanTolgoi–Arts, Suuri–Khovd–Takashiken–Haxi Prefecture–Urumqi).
4. A feasibility study to be carried out on eastern railway links of the economic corridor (Borzya–Solovevsk–EreenTsav–Choibalsan–Khuut–Bichigt–Zuun Khatavch–UlaanKhad–Chifeng–Jinzhou).
5. A feasibility study to be conducted on the Tumen River Transportation Corridor project, also referred to as the "Coast-2" corridor, (Choibalsan–Sumber–Rashaan–Ulanhot–Changchun–Yanji–Zarubino).
6. A feasibility study to be conducted on the "Coast-1" railway corridor (Choibalsan–Sumber–Rashaan–Manchuria–Qiqihar–Harbin–Mudanjiang–Suifenhe–Vladivostok–Nakhodka).

7. A feasibility study to be conducted on opportunities to connect Mongolia with the superhighway between Moscow and Beijing.
8. A joint discussion session to be organized on establishing a trilateral logistics company.
9. Asian Highway Networks AH-3 (UlaanUde–Kyakhta, Altanbulag–Darkhan–Ulaanbaatar–Sainshand–ZamiinUud, and Erenhot–Beijing–Tianjin) for transportation to be actively used, and a feasibility study to be conducted on building a highway joining Mongolia to AH-3.
10. AH-3 routes (Novosibirsk–Barnaul–Gorno–Altaysk–Tashanta, UlaanBaishint–Khovd–Yarantai, and route Takashiken–Urumqi–Kashi–Honqiraf) to be constructed.
11. A feasibility study to be conducted on the East Highway Corridor (BorzyaBorzya–Solovevsk–EreenTsav–Choibalsan–BaruunUrt–Bichigt–ZuunKhatavch–Xi, Ujimqin–Ulaanhad; routes between Zuun Khatavch and Chaoyang and between Chengde and Jinzhou) and the start of construction if the feasibility study shows positive result.
12. An Intergovernmental Agreement to be concluded on the Asian Highway Network between the governments of Mongolia, Russia and China.
13. Efforts to be intensified for building communications infrastructure, managing technological operations, and ensuring safety of transportation corridors running from UlaanUde to Kyakhta, as well as on the routes: Altanbulag–Darkhan–Ulaanbaatar–Sainshand–ZamiinUud and Erenhot–UlaanTsav–Beijing–Tianjin.

3.1.2 Industry Sector

1. The construction of the main part of the China-Mongolia-Russia Economic Corridor to be boosted and opportunities to be explored for establishing an industrial cooperation agreement between the three participating countries.
2. A feasibility study to be conducted on building an economic cooperation zone between Heilongjiang Province and the Inner Mongolia Autonomous Region of China, Mongolia, and Russia.

3.1.3 Border Checkpoint Reforms

1. Russian-border checkpoints in Zabaikalsk, Pogranichny, Kraskino and Mondi, Chinese-border checkpoints in Manchuria, Suifenhe, Hunchun, and Erenhot, as well as Mongolian-border checkpoints to be renovated.

3.1.4 Energy Sector

1. Opportunities to be explored for Research cooperation with Chinese companies on renewing Mongolian and Russian electricity-distribution network.

3.1.5 Trade, Customs, Specialized Inspection, and Quarantine

1. Framework Agreements established on July 9, 2015 on cooperation for the development of ports of entry and on cooperation in creating favorable conditions to facilitate trade development between China, Mongolia, and Russia to be accomplished.
2. Implementation of agreements among Russia's Federal Customs Service, China's General Administration of Customs, and Mongolia's General Taxation and Customs Administration for mutual recognition of the outcome of custom-control inspections of certain goods to be endorsed.
3. The joint declaration of China, Mongolia, and Russia on food-security cooperation made on October 3, 2015 to be implemented apart from strengthening cross-border trade control on food products and improving the trade environment.
4. Support to be lent on agreement concluded among customs authorities of Mongolia, Russia, and China on June 23, 2016 through cooperation on bolstering customs control inspections of products of animal and plant origin, preventing the spread of animal and plant diseases, and harmful biological outbreaks, as well as ensuring trade-security controls on products of animal and plant origin.

3.1.6 Environmental Protection and Ecology Sector

1. Practical cooperation on special protection areas that is beneficial to all sides to be enhanced besides strengthening relevant communication. China, Mongolia, and Russia will organize consultative meetings and improve mutually beneficial cooperation within the scope of Mongolia's Daguur Strictly Protected Area measures.
2. Trilateral cooperation to be strengthened on protection of wild animals, plants, and migrating birds, and on scientific exploration and inspection related to wild plants, animals, and water bodies.
3. Opportunities to be explored for undertaking a study on creating an information-exchange system between authorities and collaboration on environmental protection and ecology sectors.

3.1.7 Scientific and Technological Sector

1. Science and technological parks and innovative companies of China, Mongolia, and Russia will advance cooperation in transportation, environmental protection, rational use of natural resources, science and technology for sustainable livelihood, information and communication technology, nano-technology, energy, energy conservation and waste reduction, agricultural science, and new industrial technologies, as well as natural and technological disasters.
2. Scientific and technological development of information exchange to be expanded by all the three parties in addition to promoting the exchange and training of academics.
3. The scope of international student exchange to be expanded besides advancing educational exchanges for young people based on resources of educational organizations.

3.1.8 Humanitarian Sector

1. Cross-border tourism destinations, including Mongolia's Khuvsgul Lake, Russia's Baikal Lake, and China's Hulunbuir Grassland to be developed besides establishing a tourism circle across Mongolia, Russia, and China.
2. "Great Tea Road" brand for Mongolia-Russia-China tourism to be created.
3. Film trade and exchanges among the three nations to be enhanced besides developing a joint film industry.

3.1.9 Agriculture Sector

1. Protocol signed on September 12, 2015 among Mongolia's Department of Veterinary and Animal Breeding, Russia's Federal Service for Veterinary and Phytosanitary Supervision, and China's Veterinary Bureau of the Ministry of Agriculture to be accomplished.

3.1.10 Medical Science Sector

1. International seminars on medical science and health to be co-organized by three sides besides cooperating in the public health sector.

In August 2016, in order to test the proposed economic corridor, the three participating countries sent a joint convoy of nine trucks, three from each country, on a 2,152-km trial run from Tianjin in China to Ulan Ude, the capital of the Russian Federation Republic of Buryatia in Siberia. Stopping at eleven key cities along the so-called ancient "tea route", the trucks eventually reached the destination after seven days. Significantly, China's new membership in the United Nation's Transport Internationaux Routiers (TIR) Convention, which came into effect on January 5, 2017, has been a key part of this overland trade route. The TIR is the world's only universal, customs-transit system, which could increase the potential volume of international trade between Asia and Europe in addition to providing new trade routes with access to the sea for Mongolia and other landlocked areas in Russia and Central Asia.[2] Given that TIR has been in operation in Russia for 30 years and in Mongolia for more than ten years, the trucks can move throughout the planned corridor with only a single customs inspection, thus reducing drastically the waiting time due to lethargic border procedures. The cost of road transport is around one-tenth the cost of air, and this mode is essentially more adaptable than rail. This is another step in China's broader plan to improve overland-trade routes across Eurasia, lessening reliance on any one import/export method, as well as expanding the connectivity of its emerging inland cities and manufacturing zones (Shepard 2016).

4 Challenges for China-Mongolia-Russia Economic Corridor

Although the China-Mongolia-Russia Economic Corridor may bring lots of opportunities to significantly enhance trade and economic cooperation, there are certain challenges that need to be overcome. At present, there are two routes in the China-Mongolia-Russia Economic Corridor: one is 1,963-km long from Mongolian capital Ulaanbaatar to the Chinese Port of Tianjin passing through the Inner Mongolian city of Erenhot; the other is 2,264-km long from the Mongolian city of Choibalsan to the Chinese Port of Dalian through Inner Mongolian city of Manzhouli. But the planned route from the eastern part of Mongolia, i.e., Choibalsan to Jinzhou in China, which is 1,100-km long, is the shortest route and needs to be given attention. Yet, Zhang Guobao, Vice-Chairman of the National Development and Reform Commission of China has been quoted as saying that "there is great opportunity for goods transportation networks between China and Russia and China and Mongolia, connecting the two continents of Europe and Asia, but unfortunately there are no good transport relations (Orgonsuren 2015: 4)." It also should be pointed out that every country's interest in using railways is to transport goods to intended markets at low cost in the shortest time possible, and, therefore, Mongolia needs to use its existing railways as much as possible to minimize the related investment costs.

Differences in railway gauge of China, Mongolia, and Russia remain a serious challenge for the economic corridor. While the Russian railway gauge is 1,520 mm,

[2]"Trilateral transit transportation", Frontier's Strategy Note, 16 September 2016, p. 5, http://frontier.mn/index.php/research/daily-report/736-trilateral-transit-transportation.

the Chinese gauge is 1,435 mm, which makes transshipment obligatory at the borders between China and Mongolia and between Russia and Europe. How the upcoming high-speed rail line linking Beijing and Moscow via Ulaanbaatar would change the whole scenario is yet to be seen. Since the Sino–Russian and Sino–Mongolian trade structures still follow an "exchange of raw materials for end products" pattern (Orgonsuren 2015: 6), it will take time to make a transition for improving trade structures. Besides, differences in the pattern of economic development of the three participating countries are another challenge to trilateral cooperation. While Mongolia imports electricity, daily consumer goods, clothing, food, fruit, vegetables, construction material, and oil products from China, it exports untreated minerals, leather, wool, and cashmere to China. On the other hand, Russia exports forest products and minerals to China. Mongolia and Russia are, therefore, competitors in terms of mining-based exports to China. However, Russia has shown keen interest in diversifying its export composition with machinery, agricultural products, meat, and dairy products. Hence, there is a need to reflect on these specifics of the economic development and trade structure of the three countries and find ways of mutually beneficial cooperation in the interest of all the parties involved in the economic corridor (Orgonsuren 2015: 6).

Despite having plans for using multiple channels for investments in infrastructure development related to the economic corridor, there is a need for focused investments so as to expand infrastructure cooperation among the three countries. No doubt, under the OBOR initiative, involvement of private sector and public-private partnerships to invest in infrastructure sector are being promoted, and there are several other ways of investment that need to be explored. Some other challenges for China-Mongolia-Russia Economic Corridor can be identified as follows (Ganbat 2015):

1. Disparity among large and small economies causes numerous challenges, thus it is important to stick to a principle of being mutually beneficial.
2. Although the three countries who are also neighbors have somewhat high complementary capacity, it cannot be overlooked that they may become competitors.
3. In the future, environmental, and ecological vulnerability may increase and desertification may become the most challenging problem. In particular, Mongolia may face water shortage and air pollution when coal liquefaction and power plants are built and energy is exported to China.
4. Financial and investment challenges of a varied nature lay in constructing roads and railways need critical attention.

Lastly, the prospects for the economic cooperation of the Northeast Asian region within the framework of the China-Mongolia-Russia Economic Corridor look bleak. This is more because, for more than 20 years, economic cooperation within the Northeast Asian region has remained very low (Orgonsuren 2015: 4). Trade among the Northeast Asian countries accounts for only 20% of the total foreign trade of the regional countries since it is limited to bilateral cooperation only. In other words, regional economic integration and multilateral economic cooperation has not yet developed within the region, and hence it requires serious attention for the effective operation of the trilateral economic corridor involving the three major stakeholders in Northeast Asia—China, Mongolia, and Russia.

5 Conclusion

Under Xi Jinping, a shift in China's 'neighborhood' or 'peripheral' policy contributed substantially to the announcement of the OBOR initiative, which appears to be highly desirable to promote the cooperation between China and Mongolia, in particular, and China–Mongolia–Russia in general, so far as improving connectivity is concerned. This is largely due to the fact that the OBOR is not just about reestablishing and boosting transportation, but is ultimately about creating a network of special economic corridors, which are placed at strategic locations across Eurasia, with all roads leading to China. As for Mongolia, it is now determined not to miss the chance for development as Beijing remains firm in advancing its neighborhood diplomacy and Moscow eyes improving Russia's less-developed Far East region. In this vein, the China-Mongolia-Russia Economic Corridor has been described as the lifeline of the [OBOR] aorta because the SREB initiative fits together with Russia's transcontinental rail plan and Mongolia's Prairie Road or Grassland Road or the steppe road program.

Since numerous countries across Eurasia have seen challenges to their economic growth, the China-Mongolia-Russia Economic Corridor may provide them with opportunities to enter into cooperation, because it will mean more security along borders and a broader market within the framework of the OBOR. For, it is not only about putting in place physical infrastructure but, who knows, it may become a source of stability in the future development of Eurasia as a whole largely because it aims at connectivity, including greater movement of people and exchanges of ideas. Yet, the China-Mongolia-Russia Economic Corridor is not without its challenges, be they political, economic, or geopolitical. Hence, cooperation and coordination between partner countries seem to be the prescription for the successful implementation of development plans for constructing this strategically important corridor.

References

Bayarsaikhan, Dulguun. 2016. Over 30 Projects Lined Up for Trilateral Economic Corridor, June 29, 2016. http://theubpost.mn/2016/06/29/over-30-projects-lined-up-for-trilateral-economic-corridor/.

Brunner, Hans-Peter. 2013. What is Economic Corridor Development and What Can It Achieve in Asia's Subregions? ADB Working Paper Series on Regional Economic Integration, no. 117, August 2013, 1. https://www.adb.org/sites/default/files/publication/100110/reiwp-117-economic-corridor-development.pdf.

Campi, Alicia. 2014. Transforming Mongolia-Russia-China Relations: The Dushanbe Trilateral Summit. *The Asia-Pacific Journal* 12(45), no. 1, November 10, 2014. http://apjjf.org/2014/12/45/Alicia-Campi/4210.html.

Cao, Yunhua, and Shanbao Xu. 2004. China's Policy of Good-Neighborliness and China-ASEAN Relations. *Peace*, no. 72, September 2004.

Chung, Chien-peng. 2011. *China's Multilateral Cooperation in Asia and the Pacific: Institutionalizing Beijing's "Good Neighbor Policy"*. London and New York: Routledge.

CI [China Insight]. 2014. China, Mongolia Bolster Neighborly Ties. *China Insight*, August 27, 2014, p. 1.

Cui, Tiankai. 2014. China's Policy towards the Asia-Pacific. Embassy of the People's Republic of China in the United States of America, April 25, 2014. http://www.china-embassy.org/eng/sgxx/ctk/rota/t1150642.htm.

Ganbat, Damba. 2015. Silk Road Forum 2015 Essay. Internal Document, 2015. http://en.drc.gov.cn/DambaGanbat.pdf.

Ghiasy, Richard, and Jiayi Zhou. 2017. *The Silk Road Economic Belt: Considering Security Implications and EU–China Cooperation Prospects*, SIPRI, 2017. https://www.sipri.org/sites/default/files/The-Silk-Road-Economic-Belt.pdfBEL.

Glaser, Bonnie, and Deep Pal. 2013. China's Periphery Diplomacy Initiative: Implications for China Neighbors and the United States, November 7, 2013. http://www.chinausfocus.com/foreign-policy/chinas-periphery-diplomacy-initiative-implications-for-china-neighbors-and-the-united-states/.

Grieger, Gisela. 2016. One Belt, One Road (OBOR): China's Regional Integration Initiative. Briefing European Parliamentary Research Service, July 2016, 3–4. http://www.europarl.europa.eu/RegData/etudes/BRIE/2016/586608/EPRS_BRI(2016)586608_EN.pdf.

GT [Global Times]. 2016. New Details of China-Mongolia-Russia Economic Corridor. *Global Times*, September 13, 2016. http://www.globaltimes.cn/content/1006360.shtml.

NDRC [National Development and Reform Commission] of the People's Republic of China. 2015. Vision and Actions on Jointly Building Silk Road Economic Belt and 21st Century Maritime Silk Road, March 28, 2015. http://en.ndrc.gov.cn/newsrelease/201503/t20150330_669367.html.

Otgonsuren, B. 2015. Mongolia–China–Russia Economic Corridor Infrastructure Cooperation. ERINA Report, no. 127, December 2015, p. 3. http://www.erina.or.jp/wp-content/uploads/2015/02/se12710_tssc.pdf.

Peter, Bittner. 2016. China, Russia, Mongolia Sign Long-Awaited Economic Partnership Agreement. *The Diplomat*, June 28, 2016. http://thediplomat.com/2016/06/china-russia-mongolia-sign-long-awaited-economic-partnership-agreement/.

SCMP [South China Morning Post]. 2016. China, Russia, Mongolia sign economic corridor plan: Xinhua. *South China Morning Post*, June 24, 2016. http://www.scmp.com/news/china/diplomacy-defence/article/1980597/china-russia-mongolia-sign-economic-corridor-plan.

Shepard, Wade. 2016. How China's Belt and Road Economic Corridors Are Enhanced by the UN's TIR Convention. *Forbes*, August 22, 2016. http://www.forbes.com/sites/wadeshepard/2016/08/22/how-the-emerging-china-mongolia-russia-economic-corridor-is-enhanced-by-the-uns-tir-convention/#447989da5079.

Shin, Kawashima. 2014. Line Between Cooperative Good Neighbor and Uncompromising Foreign Policy: China's Diplomacy Under the Xi Jinping Administration. *Diplomacy*, no. 22, July 3, 2014. http://www.japanpolicyforum.jp/en/archives/diplomacy/pt20140703152152.html.

Soni, Sharad K. 2009. China's Periphery Policy: Implications for Sino-Mongolian Relations. *India Quarterly* 65 (3): 2009.

Soni, Sharad K. 2017. Gauging the Importance of China-Mongolia-Russia Economic Corridor in 'One Belt, One Road'. *The Dialogue*, January 16, 2017. http://www.thedialogue.co/gauging-the-importance-of-china-mongolia-russia-economic-corridor-in-one-belt-one-road/.

Yang, Chenhua, and Qinyu Yang. 2015. Jointly Building China-Russia-Mongolia Economic Corridor: New Development Opportunity Sharing. Internal Document for Silk Road Forum 2015. http://en.drc.gov.cn/YangChenhua.pdf.

You, Ji., and Jia Qingguo (1998). China's Re-emergence and Its Foreign Policy Strategy. In *China Review, 1998*, ed. Joseph Y. S. Cheng. Hong Kong: Chinese University Press.

Zhang, Baohui. 2010. Chinese Foreign Policy in Transition: Trends and Implications. *Journal of Current Chinese Affairs* 39 (2): 2010.

Zhang, C. 2013. *Historical Changes in Relations between China and Neighboring Countries (1949–2012)*. Sweden: Institute for Security and Development Policy.

Zhao, Suisheng. 2004. The Making of China's Periphery Policy. In *Chinese Foreign Policy: Pragmatism and Strategic Behavior*, ed. Suishen Zhao. Armonk: M.E. Sharpe.

Chapter 10
Contemporary Central Asia: Balancing Between Chinese and Trans-Asian 'Silk Road' Diplomacy

Mirzokhid Rakhimov

It is well known that contemporary world history has been characterized by substantial political transformations, including the creation of the Soviet Union and its dissolution, decolonization, the East-West conflict, and many others. The international relations at the end of the twentieth and the beginning of the twenty first centuries, has been characterized by uncertainty. Regional cooperation and integration are two of the important aspects of contemporary international relations. From the mid-twentieth century to the present, in various parts of the world, political and economic regional organizations have been gradually developing. Representatives from various disciplines have searched for explanations of regional integration and the major analytical framework including functionalism, neo-functionalism, inter-governmentalism, economic theories of integration, and others. But, there are weaknesses of the various approaches to international affairs, and it is generally accepted that there is no "one size fits all" method—different questions demand different methods (Reus-Smit and Snidal 2010: 9). Many issues of contemporary international and regional relations in Central Asia require a wider view and approach. Like all post-Soviet regions in which there are limitations of approaches, this will be more efficient towards analyzing the past 25 years of complex processes that the region has faced and is still facing. Since the collapse of the Soviet Union, Central Asian republics have tried to form new bilateral and multilateral relations, and these, within a short time, were formally recognized by many countries, as they established diplomatic ties and also exchanged missions. Central Asian republics have joined the main international organizations, received memberships, and have become co-founders of regional organizations. They have also expressed their interest in developing mutually beneficial relations with various Asian regions and leading countries like Japan, the Republic of Korea, India, Iran, and others. But, there are challenges and similarities in ultra-regional relations in

M. Rakhimov (✉)
Institute of History, Academy of Sciences, 5 Shahrisabz, Tashkent 100060, Uzbekistan
e-mail: mirzonur@yahoo.com

B.R. Deepak (ed.), *China's Global Rebalancing and the New Silk Road*,
https://doi.org/10.1007/978-981-10-5972-8_10

Central Asia. Elaboration of the challenges and contradictions in the past 25 years' multilateral relations in Central Asia will make contributions to the prospective future regional cooperation and international partnerships.

1 Post-Soviet Geopolitics in Central Asian

While independence allowed Kazakhstan, Kyrgyzstan, Tajikistan, Turkmenistan, and Uzbekistan to establish external links, there were a number of problems. Firstly, Central Asian republics had no experience in world politics because, in the Soviet era, they were deprived of the possibility of directly approaching the international community. Secondly, the collapse of the Soviet Union further deteriorated the economic, political, and ethnic situation. Thirdly, the collapse of the Soviet Union created a new geopolitical situation in Central Asia.

In the post-Soviet era, there are many factors that make Central Asia an important region in the world arena, and, of these, there are three main factors: firstly, Central Asia's geographic proximity with countries like Russia, China, Iran, India, Pakistan, and others makes it a highly-contested region in terms of geopolitics; secondly, the availability of rich energy resources in Central Asia and the Caspian region raises its geo-economic profile. The proven oil reserves in Kazakhstan are estimated at 30 billion tons and natural gas at 1.5 trillion m^3. Turkmenistan and Uzbekistan hold mainly huge natural gas reserves—17.5 and 1.1 trillion m^3, respectively.[1] Kazakhstan is the biggest producer and exporter of oil in Central Asia; Turkmenistan and Uzbekistan are major producers and exporters of natural gas. Kazakhstan and Uzbekistan are also exporters of gold, uranium, and strategic minerals. Uzbekistan is the world's fifth-largest producer of cotton and second largest exporter of cotton; thirdly, the issue of Afghanistan and challenges of illegal drug production and trafficking, terrorism, and other security threats also makes the region important (Table 1).

All these and other factors have encouraged regional and global players to compete in the Central Asian region for influence. Post-Soviet Central Asia has become an important place for interests the major powers such as Russia, the US, China, the EU, Iran, India, etc. and major international organizations like the UN, NATO, OSCE, and others. Since the beginning of the twenty first century, Central Asia is confronted with new types of geopolitical transformations. One of the main challenges to regional stability in Central Asia is the maintenance of geopolitical balance, especially between Russia, China, the US, the EU, and others, as well as the creation of a multilateral system of partnerships with various countries and international organizations.

[1]British Petroleum, BP Statistical Review of World Energy. June 2015.

Table 1 Central Asian republics

Country	Population (mln)	GDP, current US $ billion	GDP grows (%)	School enrollment, primary (% gross)
Kazakhstan	17.7	189.6	1.2	104.9
Kyrgyz Republic	6	6.6	3	105.9
Tajikistan	8.4	7.9	4.2	99.6
Turkmenistan	6.8	43.6	6.5	
Uzbekistan	31	66.9	8	

Source Statistic committee of Kazakhstan, Kirgizstan, Tajikistan, Turkmenistan, Uzbekistan. Statistic committee of CIS. World Banks ECO economic update. April 2016. http://www-wds.worldbank.org/external/default/WDSContentServer/WDSP/IB/2016/05/03/090224b0842f1054/3_0/Rendered/PDF/The0impact0of00ope0and0Central0Asia.pdf

Central Asian republics have established strong partnership with leading Asian nations and received memberships in leading Asian organizations, including the Organization of Economic Cooperation (ECO), and Organization of Islamic Cooperation (OIC), as well as being co-founders of regional organizations, including Central Asian Cooperation Organization (CACO), Eurasian Economic Community (EEC), Commonwealth of Independent States (CIS), Shanghai Cooperation Organization (SCO), Eurasian Economic Union (EAEU), and others (Cooley 2002; Marlene 2013; Rakhimov 2015: 103–120). In December 2016, as a newly elected Uzbekistan President Shavkat Mirziyoyev mentioned Central Asia as the priority of his foreign policy and first two international visits were in March 2017 to Turkmenistan and Kazakhstan. Today, Central Asians are still confronted by complex threats including international terrorism, religious extremism, illegal drug trafficking, ecological degradation, and water shortage. The still evident water-sharing problem will require the countries in the region to find common approaches and acceptance of legal framework for the main regional or transnational rivers as well as the use of international best practices in solving water-sharing problems.

2 SCO and the "Belt and Road"

China is one of the largest neighbor of Central Asia. In its policy in Central Asia, China holds the expansion of trade and economic contacts with the countries of the region on a bilateral and multilateral basis; it also maintains a close policy dialogue with the possibility of an extended economic presence and the balance between political forces and stability in Central Asia as its priority. In 1996, the presidents of Russia, China, Kazakhstan, Kyrgyzstan, and Tajikistan established the "Shanghai Five" in order to resolve border disputes and to reduce armed forces stationed along their borders. At a meeting in Shanghai on June 2001, these countries, as well as

Uzbekistan, founded the Shanghai Cooperation Organization (SCO). During the summit, the presidents signed a declaration establishing the SCO and the "Shanghai Convention to combat terrorism, separatism, and extremism". It is clear that the SCO is mainly supported by China, but for Central Asian countries the interest in the organization is to facilitate infrastructure development, maintain stability in Central Asia, and build a partnership with both China and Russia. At the SCO summit in St. Petersburg in June 2002, it was decided to create a secretariat in Beijing. During the SCO summit in Tashkent in June 2004, a counter-terrorist center was officially opened in Tashkent.

The SCO passed through a number of phases in its institutional and political evolution. At present, it represents an international instrument to coordinate areas of multilateral cooperation. My survey of Central Asian experts on regional organization shows that the SCO is one of the most successful organizations in Eurasia (Rakhimov 2013: 72).

Ever since its foundation in 2001, the SCO has been expanding in its scope and reach. At present, Mongolia, Iran, Afghanistan, and Belarus have observers' status, while Turkey, Armenia, Azerbaijan, Cambodia, and Nepal are dialogue-partners. India and Pakistan were granted full membership at the SCO summits in June 2016 in Tashkent and in Astana in June 2017, which will significantly expand the political and economic scale of the organization. However, it should be noted that differences between the SCO member states on a number of economic and institutional aspects remain to be ironed out. In addition, there are new challenges and problems for the SCO. Needless to say, we need to develop cooperation between the SCO and leading European, Asian, African, and American countries and international institutions. In the long run, the SCO may open up new opportunities for cooperation and integration among member countries, at the same time it strengthens regional and global security.

In 2013, Chinese President Xi Jinping in Astana announced the creation of the "The Silk Road Economic Belt" and later the establishment of the Silk Road Fund ($US40 billion) and the Asian Infrastructure Investment Bank (AIIB) (US$100 billion) aimed at providing investment and financial support in various sectors, such as infrastructure, industry, finance, and transport communication under the framework of the "Belt and Road" initiative.

Central Asian republics have expressed their support for the "Belt and Road", and the republics were the founding members of the China-led AIIB financial institution. On 14–15 May 2017, along with 28 state and government leaders Central Asian presidents also took part at the 'Belt and Road' international cooperation forum in Beijing. Before the Forum during the offical visit of Uzbekistan President Shavkat Mirziyoyev to China two countries signed more than 100 intergovernmental and other documents in the trade-economic, investment, finance and other areas more than $23 billion.

3 Central Asia and Japan's 'Silk Road' Diplomacy

In the beginning of the new century, Japan showed keen interest in Central Asia, which was welcomed by the region. In 1997, almost 16 years before China unfolded its OBOR, Japan formulated its own "Silk Road" Diplomacy for greater trade and investment with the CARs. Tokyo recognized the growing strategic importance of Central Asia in the context of international security, and sought to play a more active role in Eurasia. During the past two decades, CARs–Japan relations grew steadily. Japan remains one of the largest donors of the CARs. There are several areas where CARs and Japan have found convergence, for example, cooperation in education, democracy, economic development, and cooperation in infrastructure and energy resources where China is a late entrant but has made huge strides. Japan's ODA program for major investment and social programs in Central Asia totaled more than US$3.5 billion, utilized primarily for the development of telecommunication networks, for renovation of construction plants, and the modernization of airports and railways.

Japanese Prime Ministers Koizumi and Abe visited the Central Asian republics in 2006 and 2015. In particular, during their visits to Kazakhstan and Uzbekistan, several agreements in energy and other sectors were signed, and Japan reiterated its commitment to assisting the CARs in building capacities in education and culture.

Is Japan carving a niche in Central Asia in the face of aggressive Chinese engagement in the region? If it is, however, there are problems and challenges too. According to my survey of the Central Asian experts, the majority (80%) was of the opinion that there was no problem whatsoever between the CARs and Japan, but 20% of the respondents mentioned some problems such as the language barrier, low level of political cooperation, moderate level of economic cooperation, weak contacts, and the lack of expertise and experience among the Japanese entrepreneurs in Central Asia (Rakhimov 2014: 79–80). However, there are potentialities for future multilateral relations. It is well known that CARs have continuously and consistently supported Japan as a candidate for permanent membership in the UN Security Council.

4 Connectivity as the Driving Force for Inter-Asian Integration

Contemporary Central Asian nations consider development of alternative, regional-transport communications important to the national and regional strategy. No wonder CARs aggressively favor revival of the Great Silk Road, supports the OBOR, and hence the development of new transport communication in all directions of the compass. Central Asia is a land-locked region, and Uzbekistan as the region's most densely populated country is one of only two (along with Liechtenstein) double land-locked countries in the world. The geographical remoteness of Central Asia from the main seaports is a serious disadvantage to the region's fledging participation in world trade. The newly independent CARs consider the development of alternative regional transport and communication networks as an important part of the national and regional strategy. This has resulted in the development of new transport communication systems and their integration with similar systems in other regions. In particular, CARs, in tandem with China, Iran, Pakistan, and the Caucasian republics, are involved in the process of organization and harmonization of the transport arteries and communications connecting Europe and Asia. This includes the famous Transport Corridor of Europe-Caucasus-Asia (TRACECA), which has received serious support from the European Union in an effort to rebuild sea, road, and railway links. In 2007, the EU Commission launched "The Reorganization of Transport Network by Advancing Rail Freight Concepts (RETRACK)" to identify the main competing overland railway corridor between Europe and China. Tejen-Serakhs-Meshkhed-Bandar-e Abbas rail link (Turkmenistan-Iran), which connects the railway systems of Central Asia with Iranian ports on Persian Gulf and passes through Turkey on the way to Europe, was completed in May 1996 In addition, in April 2016, the Ashgabat agreement between Turkmenistan, Uzbekistan, Iran, Oman, and Qatar entered into force to establish a new international transport corridor connecting Central Asia with the ports of the Persian Gulf and the Sea of Oman.

It should be noted that, ever since the rolling out of the "Belt and Road", China has intensified its participation in the development of new transport and communication links in Eurasia. In particular, these include intercontinental railroads linking China with Europe via Russia, and through an alternate route to Europe via Kazakhstan, Uzbekistan, Turkmenistan, and Iran. Its branches go in the north-west and south-west directions, passing through countries like Russia, Ukraine, Belarus, and Poland. The second branch passes through Kazakhstan, Uzbekistan, Turkmenistan, Iran, Turkey, and southern Europe. The construction of the Tashkent–Andizhan–Osh–Sarytash–Irkeshtam motor highway and railway construction project has created a conducive environment for intensive economic exchanges between China and the CARs. Nonetheless, there are problem areas too, for example, the decade old Kyrgyzstan–Uzbekistan rail project has remained a non-starter owing to disagreements among the states as regards nodes of connectivity inside the territory of the respective countries. The logic of its continuity is the new railroad, Angren (Tashkent region)–Pap (Namangan region in Ferghana valley)[2] on the territory of Uzbekistan. Construction of railways on this line was carried out by "Uzbekistan Temir Yollari"[3] and completed in June 2016. The

[2]Over 10 million people are living in the Namangan, Ferghana, and Andijan regions of Uzbekistan, and during the Soviet era highway and the train communication between Uzbek regions in Ferghana Valley and Tashkent went through Tajikistan. Since that time, it has been very strategically important for Uzbekistan to have safe and continual transport communication links between the Ferghana Valley and rest of the republic.

[3]The Angren–Pap line is 123 km long, but, in the high mountainous area, some locations are above 2000 m, the overall costs of this project is over US$1.6 billion, including more US

company predicts half a million passengers and about 4.6 million tons of cargo per annum. However, the network is not good enough to cater to the needs of the entire Ferghana Valley, and, if the potentials of Tajikistan transit are included, it falls short. CARs remain in favor of strong transport communication with China, and there is huge opportunities for opening new trans-regional routes.

While trans-regional transport and communication system are developed, the geopolitics and geo-economics of the CARs and Caspian region's hydrocarbons cannot be undermined. This is the reason for growing interest in Central Asia by major powers, especially ascendant China. In December 2005, the construction of an oil pipeline from Atasu in West Kazakhstan to the Chinese border town of Alashankou was completed. In 2009, the first gas pipeline between Central Asia and China was constructed. In the following years, second and third lines, which pass through the territories of Turkmenistan, Uzbekistan, and Kazakhstan, were completed. These lines allow the formation of a transit corridor, through which natural gas and oil would be channeled and exported to various countries. Furthermore, an intergovernmental agreement on the construction of the Turkmenistan–Afghanistan–Pakistan–India (TAPI) pipeline has also been signed; however, progress has been slow.

Stabilization of the situation and positive changes in Afghanistan would open up new opportunities for Central and South Asian cooperation Central and South Asian cooperation. Since 2002, CARs actively participated in the reconstruction of the country. The improvement of transport connections between Central Asia and Afghanistan would be a significant contribution toward future economic recovery of Afghanistan, as well as Central Asia's connectivity with South and East Asia.[4] In June 2003, Uzbekistan, Iran, and Afghanistan signed an agreement for the creation of the "International Trans-Afghan Corridor," which entails the construction of a 2,400 km expressway and an additional railway network passing through Termez–Maza-e-Sharif–Herat and reaching the Iranian seaports of Bandar-e Abbas and Chorbakhor. The Murghab–Kulma road connects Tajikistan with the Karakorum highway in China and Pakistan and gives the CARs access to the Pakistani ports of Karachi and Gwadar. Uzbekistan–Afghanistan–Pakistan is yet another trans-Afghan transport corridor. With financial support of Asian Development Bank (ADB), in 2011 Uzbekistan completed the construction of the Khairaton–Mazari–Sharif railway line, while work on the Mazari–Sharif–Herat railway line is underway.

$1 billion from "Uzbekistan Temir Yollari" and the National reconstruction and development Fund (Uzbekistan), US$350 million, and US$195 million loans from China's Eximbank and the World Bank, respectively. In 2013, construction began, and by 2016 more than ten new bridges and several railway stations had been constructed plus two tunnels, including one 19.1 km long built by the Chinese company China Railway Tunnel Group.

[4]In particularly, Tajikistan and Uzbekistan exports electro-energy to Afghanistan; in addition Uzbekistan built a number bridges, highways, and a railway in the country. Kazakhstan is exporting wheat and other goods and carries out various educational projects in Kazakhstan for Afghan students. India contributed more US$2 billion for reconstruction and various educational and social programs in Afghanistan.

Once completed, the Trans-Afghan corridor will form the shortest possible route between Central Asia and Afghanistan, which will positively impact the economic recovery of Afghanistan, and also help it to function as a node connecting Central Asia with South and East Asia.

In summation, the CARs consider development of alternative regional transport communications important to their national and regional strategies. Today, CARs are actively participating in various projects to promote economic cooperation with Asia and Europe. Most of these projects are multilateral projects, extremely important for national and international connectivity. Well-developed regional transport system in Central Asia will increase the potential for regional integration and interconnectivity. On the other hand, it would facilitate intra-regional, as well as international networks and trade, investment, tourism, and people-to-people exchange. At the same time, there is an urgent need to invest in the overhauling, modernization, and upgrading of existing highways and railways. There is also an urgent need to cooperate in the sphere of customs legislation, standardization of rail systems, and the challenges posed by traditional and non-traditional security. Undoubtedly, the CARs are gradually being integrated into the world economy; however, intra-regional connectivity and trade need to be strengthened simultaneously, since they at present remain very low.

5 Externality: From Conflicting to Cooperating Approaches

It is well-known that the main external actors Russia, China, the US, the EU, and other countries have declared their support for peace, stability, and regional cooperation in the CARs. These have, in turn, been welcomed by all the CARs. However, some contradictions remain between them. Russia traditionally has viewed Central Asia as within its sphere of influence. China expresses its understanding for Russia's leading role in the region; however, it has created a strong economic presence in the region, trouncing Russia. The EU has made some progress in the region, but it has not crafted a unified strategy toward the region. Russia and China, on the one hand and the US and the EU on the other, have diametrically opposite institutional approaches to security in Central Asia. Cooperation with NATO has become an important dialogue mechanism for the CARs, and many NATO delegations at various levels have visited the region repeatedly. Leaders from the CARs have also participated in the various NATO summits and NATO's Partnership for Peace program. At the same time, they have also joined the Russia-led Collective Security Treaty Organization (CSTO) alliance. Since 2014, the region has witnessed increased level of tensions between the US and Russia, as well as in US–China relations, which have resulted in Russia and China working more closely on bilateral and multilateral issues. However, this equation may change under the presidency of Donald Trump in the US.

The end of the twentieth century was characterized by significant geopolitical changes and transformations in the Asian continent. The CARs voiced their interest in developing mutually beneficial relations with various Asian regions and leading countries like Japan, the Republic of Korea, India, Turkey and Iran. There is potential for Central Asia's cooperation with South Asia, the Middle East, and East Asia. As regards the Central Asia and South Asian cooperation, the CARs have looked for a more proactive role from India in the region. India's major initiative in the region, the construction of the north-south trade corridor has been welcomed by all. Improvements in India–Pakistan, Afghanistan–Pakistan relations would be crucial in linking South and Central Asia in this strategy. With both India and Pakistan on board the SCO since June 2016, there may be some changes in their strategic considerations because India has increasingly expressed interest in trade and ensuring energy security. Lifting international sanctions from Iran also provides an opportunity to enhance Central Asia–Iran trade. The unfolding of China's Belt and Road, which calls for investment in infrastructure, energy resources, industries, transport, and communication along the Silk Road Economic Belt and 21st Century Maritime Silk Road, has also been seen as an opportunity to build capacities by the CARs.

Central Asian countries believe that strong cooperation with China, India, Japan, and other countries is strategically important and will contribute to closer trade ties, economic development, and the promotion of investment between Eurasia, South Asia, the Middle East, and the Asian-Pacific region.

6 Conclusion

Though CARs have established close bilateral and multilateral partnership with leading countries of the region and the world, however, there are many problems among the various stakeholders in Central Asia, originating from differing perceptions, approaches and understandings of the situation. China's engagement with Central Asia has deepened with the establishment of the SCO; it is diversifying into various areas with the operationalization of the Silk Road Economic Belt running through the region. Future prospects for multilateral regional and international cooperation in Central Asia will depend on correlations of national, regional, and global interests. The problem of reconstruction and peace in Afghanistan is critical for CARs–South Asia and East Asia cooperation and partnership.

The CARs consider development of alternative regional transport communications important for national, regional, and international perspectives. They are keen to develop new transport communication systems and link them with the respective transport systems of neighboring countries and regions. A well-developed regional transport system in Central Asia will facilitate trade and investment, bring regional prosperity, and strongly contribute to global interdependence.

The security paradigm in CARs has adversely affected the direction of integration, patterns of regional cooperation, and building of institutions. Nevertheless, these have been successful in forging strong bilateral and multilateral relations with international and regional organizations. Political, military, and economic support from many international organizations has been crucial towards maintaining peace, stability, cooperation, development, and modernization in the region, albeit they need to develop a concrete long-term strategy in Central Asia.

From the Central Asian perspectives, it is in the best interests of the region to forge a strong cooperative partnership with China, India, Japan, and other countries and international institutions at bilateral, as well as multilateral levels, on a range of issues including security, economics, and transport communication. The region was a highly-developed region during the Silk Route period; however, after the decline of the Silk Route in the sixteenth century, the development of Central Asia started to stagnate. It is time to learn from lessons of the past and resuscitate the Silk Road spirit that connected the region through various routes of communications, nodes of which reached a vast area, encouraged unimpeded trade, and facilitated bonding between the people of the various regions and countries. Can we together build those arteries of communication yet again and bring prosperity to the region?

References

Cooley, Alexander. 2002. *Great Games, Local Rules: The New Great Power Contest in Central Asia*. New York: Oxford University Press.

Marlene Laruelle, and Sebastien Peyrouse. 2013. *Globalizing Central Asia. Geopolitics and the Challenges of Economic Development.* Routledge.

Rakhimov, Mirzokhid. 2013. Transformation of SCO in the Context of Geopolitical Changes in Central Asia. In *The Shanghai Cooperation Organization and Eurasian Geopolitics: New Directions and New Perspectives*. Nordic Institute of Asian Studies Press, University of Copenhagen.

Rakhimov, Mirzokhid. 2014. Central Asia and Japan Bilateral and Multilateral Relations. *Journal of Eurasian studies*. January 2014.

Rakhimov, Mirzokhid. 2015. Central Asia and Major Powers: Complex Geopolitics. In *Central Asia. Issues, Problems, and Perspectives*, ed. Jonboboev Sunatillo, Rakhimov Mirzokhid, and Seidelmann Reimund. Göttingen: Cuvillier Verlag.

Reus-Smit, Christian, and Duncan Snidal. 2010. In *Between utopia and reality: the practical discourses of international relation in the Oxford Handbook of International relations*, eds. Christian Reus-Smit, and Duncan Snidal, p. 9. OxfordUniversity Press.

Chapter 11
India's Silk Road Strategy: Can It Meet China's Belt and Road Initiative?

Ajay Patnaik

Beginning from China, the Silk Road, through a network of other routes, connected it to the Roman Empire in Europe. The road, an early example of political and cultural integration due to inter-regional trade, promoted cultural interaction through the travel of ideas, religions, and scholars. Buddhism from India spread to Central Asia and China through the Silk Road. While in the ancient period the Kushan Empire was instrumental in promoting trade and integration, the Mongol expansion throughout the Asian continent from around 1215 to 1360 helped bring political stability and re-energize the Silk Road. In the late thirteenth century, the Venetian explorer Marco Polo (1254–1324) became one of the first Europeans to travel the Silk Road to China. With the decline of the Mongol Empire, the Silk Road also lost its significance as a facilitator of political, cultural, and economic unity. As a result, trade through this route declined. An additional factor for its decline was the growing maritime trade between Europe and Asia.[1]

When one talks about the "Revival of the Silk Road" or the "Silk Road Strategy", there are two vectors that are generally discussed. One is the Chinese one and the other is the American one. This article seeks to explore the evolution of India's own "Silk Road Strategy" and how it is different from the Chinese and the American strategies.

[1]"Silk Road" http://www.crystalinks.com/silkroad.html.

A. Patnaik (✉)
Centre for Russian and Central Asian Studies, Jawaharlal Nehru University, New Delhi, India
e-mail: Patnaik.ajay@gmail.com

B.R. Deepak (ed.), *China's Global Rebalancing and the New Silk Road*,
https://doi.org/10.1007/978-981-10-5972-8_11

1 Existing 'Silk Road' Strategy

The Chinese have gone ahead with re-establishing the East-West axis, by linking with Central Asia and the Caucasus, which was not available to it during the Soviet period. In the meantime, China's trade and commerce with Europe has grown phenomenally in the last two decades. With independence, the Central Asian states have sought to benefit from China's rise by establishing rail and road connectivity with China. As a result, China has been able to connect with Europe by a network of better and faster transport corridors. The Karakorum highway and the Gwadar port built and being operated by China links Xinjiang with Pakistan and to the Arabian Sea. During his April 2015 visit to Pakistan, Chinese President Xi Jinping announced a $46 billion future investment by China in infrastructure building in Pakistan, which would include a 3,000 km "economic corridor" between Kashgar in Xinjiang and southwest Pakistan's Gwadar Port, giving China quicker access to Europe and the Middle East.

According to Swanstrom (2011), the Chinese strategy is to intensify its trade links with Europe, which is now carried on through the choked Malacca Strait and, to a minor extent, through a Russian corridor (Trans-Sib railways) or by air. The current revitalization of the Silk Road and development of a continental transport corridor could reduce the current transport time of 20–40 days to eleven days between China and Europe. It is also rebuilding the other arterial roads to connect the other countries that will be in proximity to this corridor. The Central Asian states, Afghanistan, Iran, Mongolia, Pakistan, and Caucasian countries, are linked to the Chinese Silk Road Strategy. For China, a transport corridor to Europe is vital. It has a huge trade turnover with the EU, which is likely to grow in the future. Europeans are interested in greater Chinese engagement with the continent, whose economic revival has a lot to do with China taking interest in Europe.

The US has advanced its own Silk Road Strategy, which is also known as the 'Greater Central Asia' (GCA) project. This began with the US Silk Road Strategy Act of 1999, which talked of transporting the region's natural resources to the international markets (Purtas 2008: 115–130). The US Silk Road Strategy envisages a regional integration plan that would benefit Central Asia and Afghanistan and other South Asian countries like Pakistan and India. The US Silk Road Strategy talks of linking Central Asia–South Asia, but skips Russia, Iran, and China. Hillary Clinton's speech in Chennai in 2011 exemplifies that the West is vigorously pushing for this option, talking of the benefits that will accrue to South Asian countries through infrastructure and pipeline projects.

Speaking in Chennai, Clinton said (2011): "Let's work together to create a new Silk Road. Not a single thoroughfare like its namesake, but an international web and network of economic and transit connections. That means building more rail lines, highways, energy infrastructure, like the proposed pipeline to run from Turkmenistan, through Afghanistan, through Pakistan into India".

She further added: "Because someday, that entrepreneur here in Chennai should be able to put her products on a track on a truck or a train that travels unimpeded, quickly, and cheaply through Pakistan, through Afghanistan, to the doorstep of her customer in Kazakhstan. A Pakistani businessman should be able to open a branch in Bangalore. An Afghan farmer should be able to sell pomegranates in Islamabad before he drives on to New Delhi".

The problem with the US Silk Road strategy is that the Af-Pak region is not stable enough to open transport and energy corridors to India from Central Asia. With the US decision to withdraw from Afghanistan, terrorist attacks and instability in that country has exacerbated. Pakistan is unwilling to provide transit access for Indian goods to Central Asian countries. Other powers are also seeking to pull the region towards their economic projects, thus posing serious challenges to the US strategy. Russia is expanding its integration with Central Asia through numerous multilateral frameworks, and China's link with the region has grown quite rapidly.

2 India's Silk Road Strategy

American and Chinese Silk Road revival strategies can reconnect India with Afghanistan, Pakistan, and Central Asia. However, at the moment, these links are hostage to political relations of India with China and Pakistan, as well as to the future political dispensation in Afghanistan. Thus, prospects for India using these old corridors are more in the long-term. No doubt, once in place, these East-West (Chinese) and South-South (American) corridors would have a lot of benefits for South Asia and Central Asia.

Given the constraints, India's Silk Road Strategy should focus more on the north-south axis, which means India linking up with Russia through Iran and Central Asia–Caucasus regions. This has assumed greater prominence due to the Eurasian integration project. This axis had always existed during the heydays of the old Silk Road. In fact, Indian goods used to travel to Iran's Mashad (through Herat in Afghanistan) and then onwards to Russia's Caspian port of Astrakhan. From Iran, routes to Central Asia and Caucasus also existed.

The Khazar Empire, which reached its zenith in ninth and tenth centuries, was one of most important trading powers of the Silk Road. The Khazars, who founded Kiev, controlled much of the trade between China, Central Asia, and Europe. They engaged in direct commerce with Khwarezm and Volga Bulgaria, and with port cities of Azerbaijan and Persia. From Mashad in Iran to Sarakhs in present day Turkmenistan, a route went up to Termez in Uzbekistan. There was a route to India from Mashad through Herat and Balkh in Afghanistan. Ibn Battuta (1304–1368) of Tangiers set out in 1325 on a 24 year journey to India, reaching Delhi through Iran and Central Asia (Tucker 2003: 204, 224–225, 243, 282).

Today, again the north-south axis of the Silk Route from India to Eurasia through Iran is being revived. The International North-South Transport Corridor (INSTC) is helping to link the Iran–Astrakhan route. The Mashad-Sarakh rail link has been created and India has been using this route to transit its goods to Central

Asia. The INSTC will connect India with Caucasus–Central Asia and Russia through the Iranian port in Bandar Abbas.

This route will involve Russia, India, Iran (founding members), and other members including Eurasian states in Central Asia and Caucasus. In 2000, Russia, Iran, and India signed an agreement to develop this route. This was the year when India and Russia signed the Strategic Partnership agreement. The North–South Transport Corridor involves ship, rail, and road transportation for goods from India to Europe, through Iran, Central Asia, the Caucasus and Russia. Goods from India would move via ship to Iran, from where the freight would move again by ship across the Caspian Sea or by truck or rail to southern Russia. From there, the goods would be transported by truck or rail along the Volga River through Moscow to northern Europe. The route from the south Iranian port of Bandar Abbas to north Iranian ports of Bandar Anzali and Bandar Amirabad and onwards to the Russian Caspian ports of Astrakhan and Lagan would shorten travel time for Indian goods to Russia and Europe.

This route had been used for Indo-Soviet trade and was in decline due to deteriorating Soviet-Iran relations in the 1980s and the subsequent decline in Indo-Russian trade following Soviet disintegration. Small shipments of tea and tobacco began to be shipped to Russia from India through Iran in 2000. According to Regina Spector, Indian cargo transported via this route has increased dramatically since 2001 (Spector 2002). Indian goods would reach Bandar Abbas near the Straits of Hormuz from where the goods would be carried to Russia by rail through a specially developed railway link between Iran, Turkmenistan, and Kazakhstan.

In February 2010, representatives of the transport management in Azerbaijan, Russia, and Iran signed three cooperation documents on accelerating the development of the corridor project. Iran and Russia will cooperate in the electrification of Tehran–Bandar Abbas line, while the agreement signed by Azerbaijan and Iran stipulates cooperation in building the railway section linking them. At that juncture, the only missing section of the corridor was the 375 km-long Qazvin–Astara–Rasht line between Iran and Azerbaijan (Ilie 2011).

Most of the section (300 km) is located in Iran, which has no rail connection to the Azerbaijan border. The new line will be equipped with systems for changing the wheels and a bridge, as well as the necessary customs and frontier infrastructure. According to the technical and economic specifications, the capacity of the new line Rasht (Iran)–Astara (Azerbaijan) could reach 9 million tons in 2015 and more than 19 million tons by 2030 (Ilie 2011).

The Kazakhstan section of the railway line is complete. Turkmenistan and Iran have begun the construction of line Uzen–Gorgan in parallel with the Caspian Sea coast to replace the current, longer route to Iran, according to Vadim Morozov, Vice-President of the INSTC project. He further highlighted that "The construction of this route will make possible for the first time in history the development of a railway connection of about 4,500 km from St. Petersburg to the port of Bandar Abbas (Iran) in the Persian Gulf and a shorter connection between northwestern and central Europe with the countries in Middle East and South Asia (Ilie 2011)".

International Union of Railways (UIC) through a feasibility study conducted in 2008 concluded that, in the long term, this is the most viable route. Also, there are alternative routes or back-up sections in case the main section fails (maritime transport through the Caspian Sea or railway transport through Azerbaijan), i.e., a route along the western coast of the Caspian Sea between Turkmenistan and Iran. According to Russia's Railways Minister Vladimir Yakunin freight—transport flow through this corridor is estimated at 40 million tons per year (Ilie 2011).

A three-day meeting of experts of 16 countries on 30 May 2012 in New Delhi discussed the bottlenecks faced by the International North-South Transport Corridor and at least six supplementary routes. As per reports, the meeting aimed at achieving progress on four fronts: the remaining section to be constructed on the main north-south corridor and the time frame for completion of the work; and an action plan for the resolution of identified problems, along with the time frame for harmonization of customs and insurance documents. The meeting also discussed complementary routes and their status and actionable points for member-countries (Dikshit 2012). According to some reports, the North-South Transport Corridor can link Mumbai to St. Petersburg, with a 40% cut in cost and time (Sharma 2012).

There is another route to Eurasia that is being promoted by India through Chabahar port in Iran to Afghanistan and then onward to Eurasia. This port is meant to give India access to Afghanistan and Central Asia through Iran and also give Kabul access to warm waters without going through Pakistan. The need for a Chabahar port acquired urgency in view of the potential Indian investment in the mining sector of Afghanistan. In November 2011, Afghanistan awarded four of the five blocks at the Hajigak iron-ore deposit to a consortium of seven Indian firms led by the state-owned Steel Authority of India with the support from India's government (the final block was awarded to Canada's Kilo Goldmines Ltd.). The export of iron ore from Hajigak would mainly have to be through the Chabahar port. The agreement between India, Iran, and Afghanistan was formally signed on 23 May 2016.

3 Why the Russian Vector Is Important?

Russia is India's strategic partner and has been one of India's longest-standing friends. However, the level of trade is far below the potential. Russian President Vladimir Putin highlighted this during his visit to India in December 2012, when he announced that the goal is to take the bilateral trade from US$10 billion to US $20 billion by 2015. Then India's External Affairs Minister S.M. Krishna after his meeting with Russian Deputy Prime Minister Dmitry Rogozin also articulated his concern over the low trade turnover and said: "We exchanged constructive views on various aspects of India–Russia trade and investment cooperation. We sought definite solutions to certain outstanding problems confronting our business communities and explored ways to enhance our trade turnover (PTI 2012)".

Energy is a sector where there is great scope for cooperation, and, in the last decade or so, both countries have showed signs of improved engagement in energy, trade, and other sectors. In 2001, ONGC-Videsh Limited acquired 20% stake in the Sakhalin-I oil and gas project in the Russian Federation. Major investments by Indian companies in Russia's energy sector are: ONGC Videsh Ltd. in Sakhalin-I Project (US$2.2 billion) and Imperial Energy (US$2.1 billion), India's investment is going to gain greater momentum given the priority both countries attach to their relationship.

Expanding Russian influence since the end of 1990s makes it a preeminent factor in Eurasia. India can expect to benefit from this context. The then Russia's Prime Minister Vladimir Putin, in 2011, published a manifesto on economically integrating the "post-Soviet space". Putin's integration project, according to Vladimir Socor, takes the form of concentric circles of Russian dominance and influence in Eurasia and beyond. As the driving force in the Single Economic Space from 2012 onward, Russia proposed to advance from that integration core to a Eurasian Economic Union (EEU), ultimately covering most of the post-Soviet space as an "integrated region." Such a bloc would operate from "joint positions on the issues facing our region," with Russia "coordinating" these joint positions, underlined Socor (2011).

3.1 Russian Initiatives for Eurasian Integration

On 4 October 2011, in an article in *Izvestia*, the then Prime Minister Putin articulated his vision of a future Eurasian Union. The formation of a Common Economic Space from 1 January 2012 involving Russia, Belarus, and Kazakhstan would constitute in Putin's words (2011), 'a historic milestone for all three countries and for the broader post-Soviet space'. For sceptics who doubt the future of the CIS, he answered by saying, "To all intents and purposes, the selected model helped preserve the myriad of ties, both of civilisation and culture, which unite our peoples and also forged links in production, the economy and in other vital areas essential for our lives".

The Customs Union of Russia, Belarus, and Kazakhstan preceded the formation of a Common Economic Space (CES) of the above three and began to function on 1 July 2011. While the Customs Union facilitated free movement of goods, the CES created a huge market encompassing over 170 million consumers (including 10 million in Belarus and about 15 million in Kazakhstan) with unified legislation and the free flow of capital, services, and labor. The best thing was the creation of a common market without tariff or non-tariff barriers (Putin 2011).

Russia announced the start of the Eurasian Economic Union (EEU) from 1 January 2015 with Russia, Kazakhstan, and Belarus as members. Armenia joined a day later, and Kyrgyzstan signed a treaty in December 2014 to join the Union. Russia has committed a grant of US$200 million over two years to facilitate

Kyrgyzstan's accession to the Eurasian Economic Union. The EEU is going to create a common space for free movement of goods, services, capital, and labor.[2]

Today, Eurasia is in the throes of a great transformation since the Soviet disintegration. The Eurasian integration process is likely to make the former Soviet space very attractive for trade and investment. The combined GDP of Kyrgyzstan, Belarus, Kazakhstan and Russia was about US$1,680 billion in 2010, with Russia making up the lion's share (US$1,480 billion).[3] A completed Eurasian Union could control up to 33% of the world's proven natural-gas reserves (Russia currently has 25%).

The problem of market-size in Central Asia can be addressed through the Eurasian Economic Union/Customs Union, which could open up huge opportunities for India in Eurasia. India and Russia have very close ties in defense, science and technology, and the nuclear and space sectors. They have been trying to plug the gaps to overcome low bilateral trade for a number of years with modest success. "We are ultimately looking at a common Eurasian market," said government sources while referring to Vladimir Putin's vision of having a customs union with several republics of the former Soviet Union, according to an Indian media report (Dikshit 2011).

India has initiated a study to work out a Comprehensive Economic Partnership Agreement (CEPA), an omnibus free-trade agreement with the Customs Union. During Prime Minister Manmohan Singh's visit to Russia in December 2011, the talks on this were taken forward. According to press reports in India, government sources have indicated that most of the issues relating to CEPA have been sorted out with Russia. For India, according to Sandeep Dikshit, tailoring the CEPA to fit in with Russia's Customs Union with Kazakhstan, by far the largest Central Asian country, and Belarus will help enlarge the market for Indian entrepreneurs (Dikshit 2011).

India and Russia have decided to jointly study the possibility of India joining the group. The Joint Statement that the two leaders—Indian Prime Minister and Russian President—adopted at the end of their summit meeting in December 2011 noted that "the two sides decided to jointly study the possibility of a CEPA between India and the Belarus–Kazakhstan–Russia Customs Union".

The joint statement after the meeting of 14th India–Russia annual summit in 2013 also reiterated, "Both sides agreed to work towards the creation of a Joint Study Group for studying the possibility of signing a Comprehensive Economic Cooperation Agreement (CECA) between India and the Customs Union of Belarus,

---

[2]Presidents of Russia, Kazakhstan, and Belarus signed The Eurasian Economic Union Treaty on 29 May 29 2014. Dinara Urazova, 'Eurasian Economic Union enters into force', *Tengri News*, 3 January 2015. http://en.tengrinews.kz/politics_sub/Eurasian-Economic-Union-enters-into-force-258209/; Also, *Sputnik*, 23 December 2014. http://sputniknews.com/business/20141223/1016151391.html (Accessed on 19 June 2015).

[3]The combined GDP of all the 14 former Soviet republics (barring Russia) in 2011 was $663 billion. "Putin's Dream of Eurasian Union Could Control World's Energy", *Forbes*, 11 November 2011. http://www.forbes.com/sites/greatspeculations/2011/11/11/putins-dream-of-eurasian-union-could-control-worlds-energy/.

Kazakhstan and Russia". It is said that if the Agreement materializes duties on most tradable goods would significantly reduce besides liberalising norms for service and investments.

Though a new government assumed power in India in May 2014, the commitment to pursue the negotiation for an Agreement with the Customs Union continued. *The Economic Times of India* quoted in October 2014 a senior Commerce Department official who underlined that the CEPA could be the first free-trade pact negotiated by the new government and said that, in this context, "We have sent a Cabinet note for setting up of a joint study group for comprehensive economic cooperation agreement (CECA) with the Customs Union (Seth 2014)".

The next step was taken before the visit of President Putin to Delhi to attend the 15th annual India–Russia summit on 10–11 December, 2014. Before the visit, a Russian-Indian working group was established in November 2014. This was to help the process move forward within the Eurasian Economic Commission, which is the permanent regulatory agency of the Customs Union and the Eurasian Economic Community (Srivastava 2014). According to Rajeev Kher, Indian Deputy Minister of Commerce and Industry, the Russian–Indian working group would put forward proposals within the next six months and then the negotiation process would start (RIR 2015).

The most important state in Eurasia of course is Russia, with which India shares a great historical relationship and currently a strategic partnership. The creation of the Customs Union was a defining moment in the reintegration process of the post-Soviet space. The Customs Union is going to be a resource multiplier for all the participating countries. Other initiatives like the Eurasian Economic Union are going to add more force to this process. India needs to work out an arrangement to overcome barriers to trade in Eurasia.

4 Conclusion

India's economic success has changed the nature of its ties with Central Asia and Eurasia. The attractiveness and capacity for India's involvement in the region has grown. Yet, India's push into the region has faced obstacles in the form of a lack of land access, competing interests of China, and the US hostility towards Iran. The shortest land routes to Central Asia via Pakistan and Afghanistan are inaccessible due to difficult relations with Pakistan and instability in Afghanistan.

There are various 'Silk Road Revival' strategies pushed by the United States and China. Of course, if the political situation in South Asia remains peaceful and stable, these strategies would benefit India and Central Asia. However, the situation at present does not look so favorable for India to be a part of either the US-backed GCA project or China's Silk Road strategy. India has to evolve its own "Silk Road" strategy that should focus on the north-south axis. With Russia and three Central Asian states as strategic partners, this "Look North" policy would serve India's interest in Eurasia better.

Eurasian integration offers an opportunity to India for expanding its trade with a much larger region. Indian goods entering a member country would easily and freely access markets of other member states. The first step to access the member states has been taken with the transportation links being created through the North-South Transport Corridor and another route through Iranian port of Chabahar that would link India with Eurasia through Afghanistan and Central Asia. The next step for accessing the Customs Union countries is being worked out through a Comprehensive Economic Partnership Agreement. If all these materialize in the near future, India is poised to play a much larger economic role in Eurasia. But for this to happen, deepening India's strategic relationship with Russia is most critical.

References

Clinton, Hillary Rodham. 2011. *Remarks on India and the United States: A Vision for the 21st Century*. Speech delivered at Anna Centenary Library, Chennai, India, July 20, 2011, US Department of State. http://www.state.gov/secretary/rm/2011/07/168840.htm.

Dikshit, Sandeep. 2011. India and Russia to Discuss Comprehensive Economic Pact. *The Hindu*, December 17, 2011.

Dikshit, Sandeep. 2012. Despite U.S. Opposition, Iran to be Transport Hub for North-South Corridor. *The Hindu*, May 31, 2012. http://indrus.in/articles/2012/11/29/northsouth_transport_corridor_offers_many_opportunities_for_indo-ru_19421.html.

Ilie, Elena. 2011. North-South Corridor: Accelerating the Construction of the Missing Section. *Railway PRO*, May 17, 2011. http://www.railwaypro.com/wp/?p=5513.

India agrees for FTA with Belarus, Kazakhstan, Russia. *The Hindu*, October 22, 2013. http://www.thehindu.com/todays-paper/tp-business/india-agrees-for-fta-with-belarus-kazakhstan-russia/article5259247.ece.

PTI. 2012. India, Russia Agree on Comprehensive Economic Cooperation Agreement with Belarus-Kazakhstan. *Press Trust of India* (PTI) July 17, 2012. http://articles.economictimes.indiatimes.com/2012-07-17/news/32714224_1_trade-target-india-russia-trade-and-investment-cooperation.

Purtas, Firat. 2008. The Greater Central Asia Partnership Initiative and Its Impact on Eurasian Security. *Journal of Central Asian and Caucasian Studies* (JCACS) 3 (5): 115–130 (Johns Hopkins University—SAIS, Washington D.C. http://www.turkishweekly.net/article/319/the-greater-central-asia-partnership-initiative-and-its-impacts-on-eurasian-security.html).

Putin, Vladimir. 2011. A New Integration Project for Eurasia: The Future in the Making. *Izvestia*, October 4, 2011. http://premier.gov.ru/eng/events/news/16622/.

RIR [Russia and India Report]. 2015. India to Negotiate Free Trade Zone with Russia-led Customs Union. *RT.com*, cited in *Russia & India Report*, February 27, 2015. http://in.rbth.com/news/2015/02/27/india_to_negotiate_free_trade_zone_with_russia-led_customs_union_41667.html.

Seth, Dilasha. 2014. India to Begin Trade Pact with Former USSR Nations Rich in Natural Resources. *The Economic Times*, October 23, 2014.

Sharma, Rajeev. 2012. Transport Corridor Offers Many Opportunities for Indo-Russian Trade. *Russia and India Report*, November 29, 2012.

Socor, Vladimir. 2011. Putin's Eurasian Manifesto Charts Russia's Return to Great Power Status. *Eurasia Daily Monitor* 8 (185) (October 7, 2011).

Spector, Regine A. 2002. The North-South Transport Corridor. *CACI Analyst*, March 7, 2002. http://www.cacianalyst.org/?q=node/165/print.

Srivastava, Shruti. 2014. FTA with Customs Union on the Table During Putin Visit. *The Indian Express*, December 9, 2014.

Swanstrom, Niklas. 2011. China and Greater Central Asia: New Frontiers? *Silk Road Paper* published by Central Asia-Caucasus Institute & Silk Road Studies Programme, 2011. http://www.silkroadstudies.org/new/docs/silkroadpapers/1112Swanstrom.pdf.

The Hindu, December 24, 2012.

The Wall Street Journal, November 30, 2011.

The Weekly Voice. http://www.weeklyvoice.com/south-asian-news/india-may-join-russian-led-customs-union/.

Tucker, Jonathan. 2003. *The Silk Road. Art and History*. Philip Wilson Publishers: London.

Chapter 12
'One Belt-One Road Initiative' and ASEAN Connectivity: Synergy Issues and Potentialities

Bruno Jetin

The "One Belt-One Road" (OBOR) strategy was launched in September 2013 by President Xi Jinping in Kazakhstan as regards the mainland area and in October 2013 in Indonesia as regards the maritime area. This is by far the largest project of interconnection between Asia, Europe, and Africa that will last for decades, entail vast amounts of resources, and involve a large multilateral collaboration. The OBOR has two main components that try to revive the memory and symbolic significance of the ancient Silk Road: a land road, also called "Silk Road Economic Belt" and a "21st Century Maritime Silk Road" (see Fig. 1).[1] Starting in Xi'an in China, the mainland road will cross Central Asia, Russia, and reach Germany and the rest of Europe. Another road will connect the south of China to Singapore across mainland ASEAN. Finally, a road will start from Central Asia to West Asia and then to the Mediterranean Sea by combining land and sea routes. The 21st Century Maritime Silk Road will link the coast of China to the Pacific on one side and another road would cross the disputed South China Sea, the Indian Ocean, and then head to Africa and Europe. Many other subsidiary land and maritime roads are envisaged in the Greater Mekong Sub-region (GMS), in the South China Sea, and Java Sea, plus specific projects such as the high-speed train that will connect the south of China to Tibet and from there will join the China-Pakistan Economic Corridor. These projects are grand and involve so many diplomatic, political, and economic issues that one may wonder whether they will ever materialize in their

[1]There are no official and final maps of OBOR but just tentative ones because the projects are not defined in detail and are pending on future negotiations. However, this map gives a good idea of the broad project.

B. Jetin (✉)
Institute of Asian Studies, University of Brunei, Gadong, Brunei Darussalam
e-mail: bruno.jetin@ubd.edu.bn

B.R. Deepak (ed.), *China's Global Rebalancing and the New Silk Road*,
https://doi.org/10.1007/978-981-10-5972-8_12

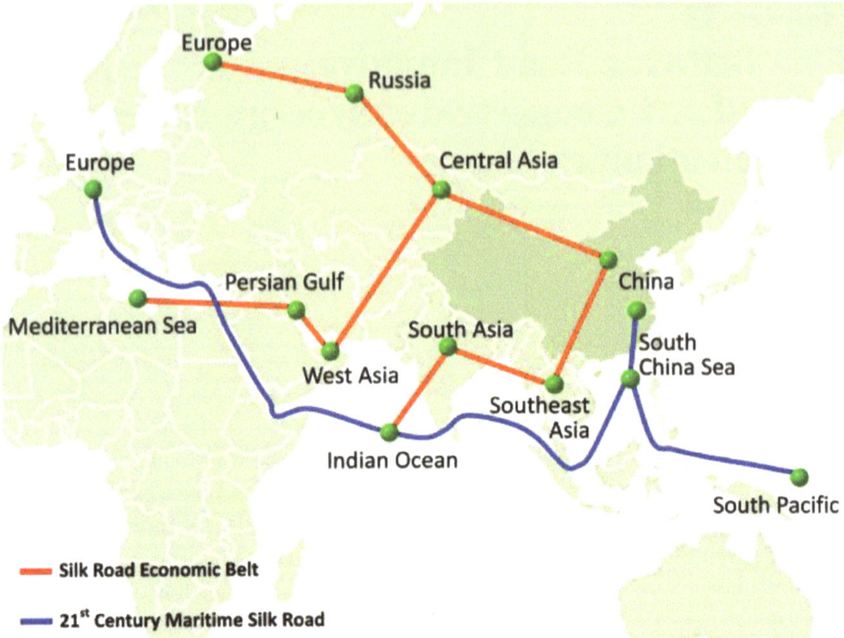

Fig. 1 Main land and maritime routes. *Source* Legislative Council of Hong Kong, China

entirety. The areas covered produce 75% of the world's gross national product and regroup 70% of world population and 75% of known energy reserves (Godement 2015). The total cost of OBOR could amount to US$1.4 trillion, an equivalent of twelve times the Marshall Plan, which amounts to about US$120 billion in today's value (Zhu 2015). Even if only part of this very ambitious plan is implemented, it will give an edge to China which can expect to open up new opportunities and markets to its heavy industry which is plagued by chronic overcapacity, while providing neighboring countries the development of much-needed infrastructure. Its realization will boost national economies, above all China's, with an additional stimulus provided by new facilities for international trade.

The OBOR strategy is the most widely-promoted initiative but is not the only one. The Republic of Korea (ROK), India, and Japan have announced their own infrastructure initiative. The implementation of all of these may potentially create a complex Asian landscape not unlike the famous "noodle soup effect" stemming from the proliferation of free-trade agreements in the Asia–Pacific region. This leaves a priori ASEAN, which has its own "ASEAN Master Plan for Connectivity" (AMPC), in a rather positive situation since it would have the choice between different solutions to remove the infrastructure bottlenecks that are hampering its growth and trade.[2] However, this depends on ASEAN's capacity to assert its centrality in Asia which implies that ASEAN stays united and speaks with one voice. Given the nature of ASEAN, maintaining unity is anything but certain: ASEAN is an intergovernmental association which takes decisions when a consensus is reached and implements them only when it is in each ASEAN member state's (AMS) interest (Jones 2016). This is especially the case because of the asymmetric trade relations between China and ASEAN. Since 2009, China is the largest country of destination for ASEAN's exports, but ASEAN is only the third largest trading customer of China. At the country level, bilateral relations between China and AMS are even more unbalanced. In these circumstances, the risk is that the OBOR strategy may deepen existing divides, for instance, between mainland ASEAN and maritime ASEAN, while the purpose of connectivity is precisely to alleviate them. This chapter will analyze these issues and explore the solutions to achieve a synergy between China's OBOR and AMPC. Section 1 summarizes ASEAN's connectivity needs and challenges. Section 2 focuses on the possible synergy between AMPC and OBOR. Section 3 examines the alternative infrastructure initiatives and concludes that rivalry between Asia's superpowers may be the surest way to achieve synergy.

1 ASEAN's Connectivity Needs and Challenges

ASEAN's connectivity needs are all the more obvious when one looks at the trade flows and the cost of trade.[3] The launch of the ASEAN Economic Community (AEC) on 31 December 2015, which officially rests on a single market and a single production base, does not mean that AMS are already fully integrated (Chia 2016). In fact, it appears that ASEAN's integration is still incipient and that some AMS are more integrated with northeast Asia(n) countries than with other AMS. According to Duval and Feyler (2016), nontariff comprehensive trade costs (NTC)[4] within ASEAN-4 (Indonesia, Malaysia, Philippines, and Thailand) remain higher (77%) than those within China, ROK, and Japan (51%), although there are no formal trade agreements between the northeast Asian countries. This runs contrary to the

[2]The "ASEAN Master Plan for Connectivity" (AMPC) was first adopted in 2010 at the 17th ASEAN Summit in Hanoi to build a physical, institutional, and people-to-people, well-connected ASEAN made necessary by the launch of the ASEAN community in 2015. An updated master plan, the ASEAN Connectivity 2025 (MPAC 2025), was adopted in Vientiane on 6 September 2016 focusing on five strategic areas: sustainable infrastructure, digital innovation, seamless logistics, regulatory excellence, and people mobility.

[3]This section draws on the main results of a book I have coedited with Mia Mikic (Jetin and Mikic 2016). However, the views presented here are my sole responsibility.

[4]Trade costs involve observable costs such as tariffs and nontariff trade costs such as compliance costs, transportation costs, behind-the-border barriers, and costs associated with the performance of trade logistics and facilitation services, as well as barriers linked to differences in language, culture, and currency.

expectation of low trade costs between AMS after several decades of integration culminating with the AEC. NTC of ASEAN-4 are also much higher with Cambodia, Lao PDR, Myanmar, and Vietnam (164.5%) than with China, ROK, and Japan (76.5%). This evidence shows the pre-eminence of Global Value Chains (GVC)[5] in shaping Asia's integration and the dominant position of China which lies at their core (Athukorala 2016). It also stresses the magnitude of inequality among AMS whose living standards have started to converge only recently (Jetin 2016). Improving connectivity between AMS is crucial for the reduction of the divide between the poorest and richest AMS and between mainland and maritime ASEAN. In this regard, one may be more optimistic for the poorest AMS's connectivity improvement because they are located in the Great Mekong Sub-region (GMS) than for closing the gap between mainland and maritime ASEAN. Up to now, mainland ASEAN integration is far more advanced than maritime ASEAN integration due to the flurry of connectivity developments in the Great Mekong Sub-region (GMS) (Wade 2010). Other ASEAN sub-regions are much less advanced. This includes the Indonesia–Malaysia–Thailand Growth Triangle (IMT-GT) and the Brunei Darussalam, Indonesia, Malaysia, and the Philippines East ASEAN Growth Area (BIMP-EAGA). These sub-regional economic zones were created in the 1990s but remained only on paper for many years. ASEAN is aware of these spatial inequalities and adopted the MPAC at the 17th ASEAN Summit in Vietnam in 2010 to develop physical, institutional, and people-to-people connectivity. It is not only about reducing business transaction costs and time and travel costs, but also to distribute all the expected benefits to all parts of ASEAN, thus reducing the development divide in ASEAN. The MPAC states: "the challenge is in ensuring that GMS and ASEAN programmes and projects mesh together very well" (ASEAN 2011).

ASEAN's problem is that it has not the financial means to carry out successfully the ambitious projects of the AMPC. According to the Asian Development Bank (ADB 2012), Asian countries will need to invest US$8 trillion in national infrastructure and another US$320 billion in inter-regional infrastructure between 2010 and 2020. ASEAN region alone requires US$60 billion in investment per year in road, rail, power, water, and other critical infrastructure (ADB 2016). As is well known, the ASEAN Infrastructure Fund (AIF) has a total equity of only US $485.3 million, far below the necessary amounts to make large loans each year. It means that the AMPC depends on external capital. The ADB has been until now one of the major investors in infrastructure in the region. But its lending capacity is

[5]Global Value Chains (also called Global Production Networks) imply the geographic dispersion of the stages of production of goods and services across national borders led by multinational firms that play a central role in leading and coordinating these processes. The objective is to reduce costs, specialize each production and distribution site, and avoid the risks involved in the concentration of activity in one sole country. In Asia, many Southeast Asian countries produce components and parts that are later exported to China where they are finally assembled and then exported all over the world. Mobile phones and computers are emblematic of this dominant form of industrial organization.

limited to US$13 billion each year. Moreover, the ADB has been much more involved in the implementation of the integration process in the GMS than in the IMT-GT (Fau 2016). It played a central role in the GMS since 1992 but became really involved in the IMT-GT only in 2007, whereas this cooperation zone was created in 1993. Contrary to AMPC's promises, the infrastructure connection between the GMS and the IMT-GT has never really been considered.

Additional obstacles have hampered the implementation of the AMPC: policy and institutional barriers have not been reduced. Rules, regulations, and standards have not been harmonised between AMS. Political instability contributes to delays. For instance, in Thailand, the mega-projects which include the high-speed train linking south and north Thailand and beyond Vientiane and Kunming became a politically controversial topic. Since 2006, changes of governments and two coups d'états delayed the start of the works for ten years until 2016 when an agreement with China was finally signed. Additional delays come from the difficulty in reaching an agreement on how the project will be funded and what the conditions will be (Peel and Hornby 2016). The first 250-km phase of the project within Thailand costs around US$5.2 billion while the China–Laos railway will cost around US$6 billion. Because Thailand and especially Laos have limited financial capacities, the bulk of the financing will come from China in the form of long-term loans. Negotiations over the interest rates and guaranties have been tough. For instance, Lao PDR will excavate five potash mines and use the income to repay a US$480 million loan within five years instead of 30 years.[6] But even if the loan is repaid without difficulty, there is no certainty that the project will be profitable, and the potential loss will be met by the state-owned China Railway Corporation. Similar problems will probably occur with other segments of the land and maritime projected roads because most of the countries involved are poor or middle-income countries, sometimes with a high level of sovereign debt. China has large but not unlimited financial capacities, and these projects are very costly. Another possible issue is the construction itself. In many countries, big infrastructure projects, when financed by China, are realized by Chinese companies with Chinese workers which reduce job opportunities for local workers. In Laos, it has been reported that more than 50,000 mostly Chinese workers will be hired to build the project, while the number of Lao workers to be recruited at the start of the works was still unknown.[7] For the 250-km Thai section between the north-eastern city of Nakhon Ratchasima and Bangkok, after long delays over the cost of the project, the Thai government decided in September 2016 that Thailand would bear the full costs of construction, while China would provide a loan for technical systems. Thailand had first envisaged a barter deal to export rice to China to pay back part of the loan made by China. But finally, because of a disagreement over the interest rate, Thailand

[6]Source: "Laos And China Come to Terms on Loan Interest Rate For Railway Project", Radio Free Asia, 01-04-2016.

[7]Source: "Clearing for Lao-China Railway Begins, but Questions About the Project Still Remain". Radio Free Asia, 01-04-2017.

decided to pay in cash. Even concerning the loan to import technical systems, disagreements persisted, as well as the currency to be employed, yuan or the US dollar. According to the Thai minister of Transport, "China is asking for development rights for land along the railway as well as an agreement to let China take concession of other development projects in Thailand if the railway project fails "that Thailand cannot accept: The project is in Thailand and we have the sole rights for it. They cannot take the benefit of the project".[8] This example shows how many political hurdles involving sovereignty issues have to be overcome to implement these big infrastructure projects beyond the technical and economic issues that should also not be underestimated and result in additional delays.

Other potential political uncertainties point to the potential fragility of the OBOR strategy. The relations between China and the Philippines have long been tainted by the contentions over the South China Sea. The conflict climaxed when an arbitration court in the Hague ruled in favor of the Philippines about the Scarborough Shoal. The announcement by the new president of the Philippines Rodrigo Duterte "to separate from Washington" and to find a compromise with China is undoubtedly a success for the Chinese diplomacy and will surely facilitate the integration of the Philippines in the maritime link. The recent agreement on naval cooperation between China and Malaysia is also a success for China. But questions arise whether these successes are only circumstantial. Future heads of states may take contradictory decisions. Our point here is that investments in infrastructure not only require appropriate financing, but also long-term commitments and institutional relationships to manage them, which in turn implies long-term political stability and not short-term diplomatic success.

The shock election of Maithripala Sirisena, Sri Lanka's new president in January 2015, who defeated Mahinda Rajapaksa, the former president who had awarded Beijing-controlled companies large infrastructure projects, shows precisely what may happen in the future in other countries where China has made massive investments. Works on the $1.4 billion Colombo Port City property development have been suspended since March 2015 following a decision to review the project and the conditions of the Chinese loans.[9] A previous Chinese-sponsored port, the Hambantota port, completed in 2010, turned out to be up unprofitable and piled up debt, forcing the new government to agree on "debt-to-equity swap granting state-controlled China Merchant Holdings 85% of the port and a 99-year concession to develop its operations, announced on January 7, 2017".[10] This triggered political protests in the streets, and the legislative opposition challenged the agreement in court.

The political conflict in Pakistan between the government and the army about which entity will take leadership over the China-Pakistan Economic Corridor

[8]Source: "China and Japan set for another high-speed railway fight". Nikkei Asian Review, 06-02-2017.

[9]Source: "Sri Lanka to review terms of Chinese loans". Financial Times, 01-03-2015.

[10]Source: "Chinese investment adds to Sri Lankan debt pile". Financial Times, 24-02-2017.

(CPEC) worth US$46 billion in infrastructure projects in part reveals other types of political hurdles that OBOR will have to resolve. This is in addition of the huge security issues. Most of the infrastructures are located in regions at war and a 15,000-strong-army-led security force is necessary to protect the Chinese workers assigned to the project. The same mix of internal political tensions and security issues exist in Myanmar, where pipelines and access to the Indian Ocean are critical to the success of OBOR.

In summary, OBOR's success of depends on many diplomatic agreements and political compromises that are not easy to secure in the long-term and make OBOR a very complex and uncertain strategy.

2 AMPC and OBOR: A Possible Synergy?

China, with US$3 trillion in foreign exchange reserves, has much more financial clout than any other superpower or institution in the region. China can use various avenues for financing infrastructure investments in Southeast Asian countries. In 2009, it created the China-ASEAN Investment Cooperation Fund (CAF) with a capital of US$10 billion and a US$15 billion credit line for infrastructure projects in ASEAN. In October 2014, China won a major diplomatic success with the launch of the Asian Infrastructure Investment Fund (AIIF) with an authorized capital of US$100 billion of which China provides US$50 billion. This multilateral bank with initially 21 member states gained momentum when, against America's advice, Western countries like the UK, Germany, and France joined the AIIB, followed by Australia, New Zealand, South Korea, Russia, and others, amounting to 57 total members at the end of 2016. Twenty-five new members from Europe, Africa, and Latin America are due to join in 2017. The US and Japan are the only significant countries to stay outside the AIIB, which is viewed as a competitor to the World Bank and the Asian Development Bank where the two countries exercise decisive influence. The OBOR and the AIIB are "twin brothers" according to Chinese officials quoted in Ye (2015). The action of the AIIB is completed by a "Silk Road Fund" with a capital of US$40 billion. While the AIIB is a multilateral development bank, in which 75% of the capital comes from Asian member states, all of them in AMS, the Silk Road Fund is a Chinese investment fund that can decide unilaterally to invest in OBOR project, for instance in the Chinese-Pakistan Economic Corridor. With such huge financing at its disposal, the question is: Will the greater integration of ASEAN with China contribute to the reduction of spatial inequality within ASEAN? Potentially, the answer is yes.

If we take again the example of the railway project in mainland ASEAN, the recent agreement between China and Thailand, should the problems be finally resolved, shows that the OBOR can give the final impetus and achieve what AMS alone has never been able to do. Initially proposed by former Malaysian Prime Minister Mahathir Mohamad at a 1995 ASEAN summit, the Singapore-Kunming Rail Link (SKRL) was later included in the AMPC in 2010 but never built. Under the OBOR umbrella, it has a greater chance of being finally achieved. But this does not mean that other elements of the AMPC will receive the same boost. Other projects are still on hold, such as the railway from Kong Ming to Vientiane in Laos and from Phnom Penh to Ho Chi Minh City (Le 2015). This means that the OBOR may stimulate the realization of large projects that are better aligned with the needs of China's economic interests, while minor projects remain idle, although they may be important for people at the local level. The risk is to create a core-to-periphery structure of connectivity, China being the hub and other countries the spokes of the system which fits well the logic of global value chains.

As regards maritime ASEAN, there may be the same tendency to give priority to large projects that fit the needs of China's foreign trade. According to Pitlo III (2015), "state-owned COSCO acquired a 49% stake in the COSCO-PSA terminal in Singapore. Beibu Gulf Holding Co. Ltd bought a 38% equity share in a consortium that received a 30-year concession to manage Kuantan Port in Malaysia poised to serve the Malaysia-China Kuantan Industrial Park". China is also investing large amounts of money in Indonesian infrastructure to improve access to Indonesian natural resources. But China does not invest a great deal in ASEAN Roll-on Roll-off network (ARN) projects which are also part of AMPC. ARN projects are key to the development of IMT-GT and BIMP-EAGA. These sub-regions of ASEAN are far from Chinese ports and are not located on the main "Maritime Silk Roads".

One area for the OBOR to address connectivity at the local level is to look for potential synergies with national connectivity-development plan. President Jokowi of Indonesia announced at an international audience, during the Ninth East Asia Summit in Naypidaw 2014, a new maritime policy called "Global Maritime Fulcrum" that aims at making Indonesia a maritime power to better manage its maritime resources, improve the connectivity of the archipelagic state, and strengthen its maritime defence force and maritime diplomacy. This new maritime policy plans to build 35 new deep-water and ordinary ports, but it is clear that Indonesia cannot finance on its own the required colossal investments. This is why Indonesia has agreed to articulate its Global Maritime Fulcrum with the 21st Maritime Silk Road. A joint statement, published when President Joko Widodo visited China in March 2015, promised a "maritime partnership" and described the two maritime policies as "complementary". From China's point of view, Indonesia is a key partner in Southeast Asia, not only because it is ASEAN's largest economy and located at the juncture between the Indian and Pacific Oceans, but also because it has sea lanes of communication that pass around the Sunda and Lombok Straits, which offer an alternative to the Strait of Malacca (Len 2015), provided that new ports and relevant infrastructure are built.

These three examples show that China's funding support for ASEAN's AMPC will be provided when there is compatibility with the OBOR projects. But if China really wants the OBOR to be a success, it will have to go beyond its direct interest and contribute to reducing the gap between mainland ASEAN fast-developing connectivity and the lagging maritime ASEAN. Otherwise, the latter may turn to other regional powers such as Japan.

3 Alternative Infrastructure Initiatives in Asia

The OBOR initiative is not the only one in Asia. In fact, there is a proliferation of infrastructure initiatives (Szczudlik 2016): India's "Blue Economy" and "Act East Policies" now rebranded as "project Mausam" by the government of Prime Minister Modi; Korea's "Eurasia Initiative"; and Japan's "Partnership for Quality Infrastructure: Investment for Asia's Future". This proliferation calls for multilateral talks. Infrastructure investments mobilize huge amount of money and are not always profitable. It does not make sense to compete in a field where large economies of scale are necessary. So, at one point, the search for synergy will have to include not only OBOR and AMPC but also avoid overlapping. But another possibility is that the various initiatives cover different geographical areas and/or needs. This is the case of India's and Korea's initiatives although the OBOR also includes South Asia and Eurasia. Japan's initiative is aimed at Southeast, Southwest and Central Asia, so it is potentially competing with the OBOR. But Japan is trying to differentiate from OBOR and to focus on quality infrastructure investment so it can potentially fill the gap left by the OBOR. In his regard, Japan can leverage its high technology capacities, its reputation for quality products, and the reliability of its industrial organization. It can make a difference when Chinese products and firms' reputation have sometimes been marred by quality issues and substandard technology, as in Indonesia concerning the construction of a ten-million-mw power plant (Fitriani 2015). Japan's initiative relies on creating jobs for local people and increasing local skills, while Chinese firms abroad tend to employ mainly Chinese workers. Japan also wants to prioritize countries' development plans so that synergy is built-in. It also emphasises ADB's role in Southeast Asia of which Japan is the biggest stakeholder and which has been one of the largest funding institutions of AMPC. Japan has also long been directly one of the major funders of AMPC with two priorities: the East-West and Southern economic corridors and the maritime ASEAN corridor. Japan can reinforce its influence by financing projects of the AMPC that are not considered as priorities by China in the Great Mekong Sub-region. The Japanese alternative can be attractive to the maritime AMS and a way to finance ARN. Two additional elements weigh in favor of Japan. Firstly, Japan is providing new patrol vessels to the Philippine and Vietnam Coast Guard and aid to Indonesia to procure three new ones in a clear move to counterbalance China's domination over the South China Sea (Lee 2015). Secondly, the Japanese Parliament approved on 11 May 2016 a milestone change to the operating charter of the Japan Bank for International Cooperation (JBIC). This change will allow the bank to make riskier infrastructure investments through a special account so that it can compete more aggressively with China.[11] Too stringent risk guarantees are one of the reason why Japan lost the bid for the first high-speed rail project in Indonesia

[11]Source: "Japan Inc. to raise investment in ASEAN infrastructure". Financial Times, 14-06-2016.

in 2015 in favor of China (Adi Syailendra 2015). With the amendment, Japan expects to bid competitively for large-investment infrastructure projects like the Kuala Lumpur–Singapore high-speed rail project.

4 Conclusion

The OBOR strategy has a huge potential for integrating Asia internally and Asia with the rest of the world. This potential is all the most important in Southeast Asia where it could help implement the AMPC for the mutual interest of China and ASEAN. To achieve this goal, a fine balance must be reached between ASEAN and China's interests to develop not only connectivity between the two entities but also the connectivity between AMS. It means that China has to include in the OBOR infrastructure smaller projects that are not directly linked to China's international trade and strategic interests but which also benefit the local economy, which has different connectivity needs. For instance, improving coastal trade in the case of maritime transport or secondary routes in the case of land transport may have a larger and more direct impact on small and medium enterprises and the local economy. This implies selecting sustainable projects that regional authorities and people may appropriate and control. It is crucial that infrastructure projects be inclusive and based on dialogue because they have a strong impact on the use of land and the environment on which depends the economic opportunities and well-being of many people at the lower end of the income distribution. Large and small infrastructure projects can be better selected and combined if based on a process of dialogue with local communities and if impact analyses on social and environmental issues are initially conducted. This would prevent these projects from resulting in excessive sovereign debt and making huge losses. In short, the OBOR should not only be an initiative for economic but also for human development. For instance, mechanisms for inclusiveness or social and environmental conditionalities could be included in the selection process of the AIIB. For the moment, nothing of the sort seems to be planned.

A necessary condition for the OBOR to synergize with AMPC and better serve human development is that ASEAN speaks with one voice in its dialogue with China. The AMPC, which represents ASEAN collective interest, should be the base of this dialogue to be sure that a coherent connectivity scheme is promoted that benefits all ASM and reduces development gaps between rich and poor ASM and between continental and maritime ASEAN. For the moment, negotiations are carried out in a piecemeal fashion between each ASM and China on a bilateral basis. ASEAN as such has not published any statement on the OBOR, expressing ASEAN's view on OBOR and how the AMPC could synergize with OBOR. The new "Master Plan on ASEAN Connectivity 2025" (ASEAN 2016), adopted in Vientiane on September 6 2016, does not mention OBOR, not even in the "ten trends that have important implications for the ASEAN connectivity agenda" (p. 35). The existence of the AIIB is mentioned on page 31 as a new funding vehicle among others but without further elaboration. This lack of recognition reveals the inability of ASEAN to play a strategic role at a time precisely when regional leadership is most needed. ASEAN could be the vehicle of negotiation between Southeast Asia and China to make sure that the AMPC benefits from the various financing vehicles linked to the OBOR. One way to do it would be to act collectively in the AIIB, which is a multilateral institution where projects to be financed will be discussed. Other financing vehicles, such as the Silk Fund, leave ample room for bilateral relation between China and individual AMS to attract additional funding for specific local infrastructure projects. An ASEAN collective action could also be useful to coordinate the Japanese and Korean infrastructure initiatives so that they do not compete directly but complement each other to avoid duplication and the waste of resources. Finally, the security issues are also key to the long-term outcome. The territorial dispute over the South China Sea is certainly an obstacle for the full development of the New Maritime Silk Road as it creates tensions and wariness. Separating sovereignty conflicts on one side and cooperative projects on the other side may work in the short-term but certainly not in the long-term if these conflicts do not find solutions that involve diplomatic initiatives and political compromises.

References

Asian Development Bank. 2012. Infrastructure for Supporting Inclusive Growth and Poverty Reduction in Asia, Mandaluyong City, Philippines.

ADB. 2016. ASEAN Infrastructure Fund. Retrieved from http://www.adb.org/site/aif/main.

Adi Syailendra, E. 2015. The End of the Line for Japanese Influence in Indonesia. *East Asia Forum, 10 December.*

ASEAN. 2011. *Master Plan on ASEAN Connectivity*. Jakarta.

ASEAN. 2016. *Master Plan on ASEAN Connectivity 2025*. Jakarta.

Athukorala, P.-C. 2016. Southeast Asian Countries in Global Production Networks. In *ASEAN Economic Community: A Model for Asia-wide Regional Integration?*, ed. B. Jetin and M. Mikic, 79–100. New York: Palgrave Macmillan.

Chia, S.Y. 2016. ASEAN Economic Integration and Physical Connectivity. *Asian Economic Papers* 15 (2): 198–215.

Duval, Y., and E. Feyler. 2016. Intra-and Extraregional Trade Costs of ASEAN Economies: Implications for Asian Regional Integration. In *ASEAN Economic Community: A Model for Asia-wide Regional Integration?*, ed. B. Jetin and M. Mikic, 153–172. New York: Palgrave Macmillan.

Fau, N. 2016. Investment in Infrastructure and Regional Integration: Will Connectivity Reduce Inequalities? *ASEAN Economic Community: A Model for Asia-wide Regional Integration?* 291–310. New York: Palgrave Macmillan.

Fitriani, E. 2015. *China's 'One Belt One Road' Initiative: An Indonesian Perspective*. The Belt and Road Initiative and Its Implications for Cambodia, Intercontinental Hotel, Phnom Penh, Cambodia.

Godement, F. 2015. One Belt, One Road: China's Great Leap Outward. *European Council on Foreign Relations China Analysis, June.*

Jetin, B. 2016. Reduction of Absolute Poverty, Increase of Relative Poverty, and Growing Inequalities: A Threat to Social Cohesion. In *ASEAN Economic Community: A Model for*

Asia-wide Regional Integration? ed. B. Jetin and M. Mikic, 267–289. New York: Palgrave Macmillan.

Jetin, B., and M. Mikic (eds.). 2016. *ASEAN Economic Community: A Model for Asia-wide Regional Integration?*. New York: Palgrave Macmillan.

Jones, D.M. 2016. ASEAN's Imitation Economic Community: The Primacy of Domestic Political Economy. In *ASEAN Economic Community: A Model for Asia-wide Regional Integration?*, ed. B. Jetin, and M. Mikic, 11–31. New York: Palgrave Macmillan.

Le, H.H. 2015. *China's Maritime Silk Road and ASEAN Connectivity: A Vietnamese Perspective*. The Belt and Road Initiative and Its Implications for Cambodia, Intercontinental Hotel, Phnom Penh, Cambodia.

Lee, J. 2015. Japan's Strategic Role in Southeast Asia: A cause for concern? *ISEAS Perspective* (28).

Len, C. 2015. China's 21st Century Maritime Silk Road Initiative, Energy Security and SLOC Access. *Maritime Affairs: Journal of the National Maritime Foundation of India* 11 (1): 1–18. doi:10.1080/09733159.2015.1025535.

Peel, M., and Hornby, L. 2016. China regional rail venture struggles with high-speed train project but wrangles remain. *Financial Times,* September 25, 2016.

Pitlo III, L.B. 2015. ASEAN Connectivity and China's One Belt, One Road. Retrieved from http://www.eurasiareview.com/author/lucio-blanco-pitlo-iii/page/2/.

Szczudlik, J. 2016. Many Belts and Many Roads: The Proliferation of Infrastructure Initiatives in Asia. *PISM Policy Paper* 148 (7).

Wade, G. 2010. ASEAN Divides. *New Mandala*. Retrieved from http://asiapacific.anu.edu.au/newmandala/.

Ye, M. 2015. China and Competing Cooperation in Asia-Pacific: TPP, RCEP, and the New Silk Road. *Asian Security* 11 (3): 206–224. doi:10.1080/14799855.2015.1109509.

Zhu, Z. 2015. China's AIIB and OBOR: Ambitions and Challenges. *The Diplomat,*October 9, 2015.

Part III
The Maritime Silk Road, the United States and the Asia Pacific

Chapter 13
21st Century 'Maritime Silk Road' and Sino-Indian Maritime Cooperation

Guoxing Ouyang

The 21st century 'Maritime Silk Road' (MSR) was proposed by Chinese President Xi Jinping during his visit to Indonesia in October 2013. According to the 'Vision and Actions on Jointly Building Belt and Road' (Xinhua 2015a), the proposed MSR will run through China's coast to Europe through the South China Sea and the Indian Ocean in one route, and from China's coast through the South China Sea to the South Pacific in the other. In 2014, this idea began to take shape with focusing on infrastructure and connectivity. MSR and Silk Road Economic Belt (SREB)[1] are regarded as the two pillars of the 'One Belt and One Road' (OBOR) project. China has provided strong support for the project, including the establishment of the Asian Infrastructure Investment Bank (AIIB) with the other 56 founding members, which has been implemented since the end of 2015 with an authorized capital of US $100 billion, and contributing US$40 billion to the Silk Road Fund (SRF).[2] Though China has released the plan for the 'Silk Road' cooperation, there are many discussions on the China's strategic intentions (or the possible strategic effects) behind this initiative.

[1]The SREB was proposed by Chinese President Xi Jinping during his visit to Central Asia in Septermber 2013, and focuses on bringing together China, Central Asia, Russia, and Europe (the Baltic), linking China with the Persian Gulf and the Mediterranean Sea through Central Asia and West Asia, also connecting China with Southeast Asia, South Asia, and the Indian Ocean.
[2]AIIB will be an international institution which includes 57 founding members. However, SRF's capital will be provided mainly by China's foreign currency reserves, Finance Ministry of China, and the China Export and Import Bank, and it will be merely managed by the Chinese government.

G. Ouyang (✉)
Hainan Institute for World Watch, Hainan, China
e-mail: angeloygx@163.com

B.R. Deepak (ed.), *China's Global Rebalancing and the New Silk Road*,
https://doi.org/10.1007/978-981-10-5972-8_13

1 Strategic Targets of China's MSR

First, MSR is believed to be one of the most important components of China's 'March West',[3] 'Neighboring Diplomacy' and 'Maritime Diplomacy'. Along with China's rapid rise, the regional security structure has been transforming to a new balance status. In 2013, the situation regarding China's surrounding oceans had been deteriorating owing to tensions in the South China Sea (SCS) and East China Sea. However, Chinese leaders claimed that it was the US rebalancing strategy to Asia which was the underlying cause of these tensions (Phoenix TV 2014). In order to stabilize the situation in South China Sea, the MSR initiative was firstly raised towards Southeast Asian countries to push forward the maritime cooperation between China and Southeast Asian countries.

Second, China believes that the historical concept of the Silk Road has some kind of 'Silk Road Spirit' (Xinhua 2014a) that is not only a symbol of open and inclusive regional economic cooperation but also represents cultural exchanges between China and the outside world. By reviving this ancient trade route, Chinese new leadership wants to manifest its willingness to continue the reforming and opening-up policy and the path of peaceful development to reassure its neighbors' anxiety about China's rapid rise.

Third, just nearly two months before President Xi put forward his pet project MSR during his visit to Indonesia in October 2013, he made an important speech at the National Propaganda and Ideology Work Conference (NPIWC) on 19 August of the same year and stressed the need to 'tell China's story well, disseminate China's voice well, enhance the national culture soft power' (Xinhua 2013). The ancient Silk Road is just one of the reassuring China's stories to demonstrate its peaceful rise which differs from the String of Pearls[4] that was created and hyped by some western strategists. China views this as a battle for the international perspective on the explanation of China's rise.

Fourth, this initiative meets China's needs for its own development (especially the 'Great West Development'). Now, China is accelerating the transformation of the pattern of economic development, also adjusting and optimizing the economic structure. Many Chinese scholars believe that the countries alongside the MSR are the best industrial transfer locations for China, and this initiative can also help Chinese companies export bullet-train technologies and the domestic oversupply of

[3]'March West' was first articulated by Wang Jisi, the director of the Center for International and Strategic Studies of Peking University, in his article 'March West: China's geostrategic reblancing' published on Global Times on 17 October 2012.

[4]This term as a geopolitical concept was first used in an internal United States Department of Defense report titled 'Energy Futures in Asia'; it refers to the network of Chinese military and commercial facilities along its Sea Lines of Communication (SLOC) in the Indian Ocean, arguing that China was planning to devleop overseas navel bases around India to support its extended naval deployement. The term has been criticized by official Chinese government but it is often used by some Indian media.

products (such as steel, cement, plastics) to the relevant countries.[5] Also, the development of infrastructure (including highways, railroads, and telecom networks) would help China strengthen its economic and trade relations with the neighboring countries. In addition, the Chinese government is trying to use the related financial institutions to promote the internationalization of its currency RMB[6] and exploit the opportunities of AIIB and SRF to speed up the opening of China's capital account and RMB's internationalized process (Gao 2014).

Fifth, China is the world's second-largest economy, and Chinese leaders believe that it has 'never in history have been closer to the goal of the great renewal of the Chinese nation' (Global Times 2014a). In the Ming Dynasty, China was the most powerful nation in the world, and the era also signified the golden age of the ancient MSR. China is on its way to becoming a strong maritime country, and, from this aspect, the MSR initiative is repeating history. From the beginning of the twenty first century, China has been paying more and more attention to the protection of China's overseas interests and Sea Line of Communication (SLOC) security. Especially, the 'arc of instability'[7] is a matter of life and death for China's international trade and oil routes. The Chinese navy has to play a proactive role in protecting its benefits along the arc.

2 What Are the Cooperation Priorities of MSR?

Now that the MSR is a pet project of the Chinese central government and the relevant local governments, central ministries have been actively participating in this initiative and achieving some great progress. About 50 countries have voiced willingness to participate in the Belt and Road Initiative (Xinhua 2014b).

Some analysts (even some domestic scholars) prefer to label this initiative as a Chinese version of the Marshall Plan, indicating that China would use this project to seek influence and even dominance in Asia.[8] Also, some strategists believe that this project is not as peaceful as it seems and they are more inclined to view this as the Chinese version of 'String of Pearls'. The Chinese government has criticized the

[5]Justin Yifu Lin, the former Chief Economist and Senior Vice President of the World Bank, had proposed using the 'New Marshall Plan' to restore the global economy in February 2009.

[6]A big portion of China's US$4 trilion forex reserve is invested in low-yield securities, such as U.S. Treasury bills and its annual rate of return is just about 2–3%. If China plans to offer RMB loans to the relevant countries, these countries can use RMB to buy some project materials from China, which has massive overcapacity.

[7]This term refers a swath of territory running from the Caribbean basin through most of Africa, the Middle East, and Central and Southest Asia. The US argued that many of the relevant countries had been left far behind the rest of the world.

[8]The Marshall Plan (officially the European Recovery Program, ERP) was the American initiative to aid Europe, in which the US offered $17 billion in economic support to help rebuild European economies after the end of World War II, remove trade barriers, modernize industry, and make Europe prosperous again.

above two ideas and declared that Marshall Plan had imposed conditions on recipient countries, whereas China will adhere to a policy 'not to interfere in the internal affairs of others, not to seek the spheres of influence, and not to seek hegemony' by the MSR (Xinhua 2015b). Also, the 'One Belt and One Road' project was the main topic of Central Leading Group on Financial and Economic Affairs (CLGFEA), which was held on 4 November 2014. That implies that China's top officials have confined the MSR to the economics and trade field, which differs the from String of Pearls that was essentially related to security and the military field. This initiative would have otherwise come under the scope of the newly established Central National Security Commission (CNSC). President Xi called for the preparation of timetables, road maps, and some significant projects for the MSR in this meeting.

According to the 'Vision and Actions on Jointly Building Belt and Road', this initiative initially focuses on five areas of 'connectivity': policy coordination, facilitating connectivity, unimpeded trade, financial integration, and people-to-people bonds. For policy coordination, countries along the MSR may fully coordinate their economic development strategies and policies and jointly provide policy support for the implementation of large-scale projects. Connectivity facilitation has been listed as the priority area for implementing the initiative, and its aim is to form an infrastructure network connecting all the sub-regions in Asia and push forward port infrastructure construction. For the unimpeded trade, investment, and trade cooperation that are believed to be the major tasks in building the MSR, China appeals to the relevant countries to improve investment and trade facilitation, customs cooperation, and to remove investment and trade barriers. Since financial integration has been considered as the important underpinning for implementing the MSR, China wants to build supporting systems for a stable currency, investment and financing, and credit information in Asia. As for people-to-people bonds, China appeals to the relevant countries to carry forward the spirit of 'Silk Road' to promote extensive cultural and academic exchanges, personnel exchanges, and media cooperation to win public support for the MSR initiative.

Overall, the connectivity and economic cooperation is the core of the MSR initiative. As the Politburo of the Communist Party of China Central Committee (PCPCCC) had chosen the 'FTA strategy' as the theme of the 19th collective leaning session[9] on 5 December 2014, President Xi declared that China should actively construct a free-trade zone with relevant countries along the 'One Belt and One Road' (China Daily USA 2014). Considering this background, China and ASEAN have agreed to launch negotiations on upgrading their previous FTA and

[9]The institution of collective leaning session started from the beginning of former Chinese President Hu Jintao era in 2002. CCP leaders often choose the significant issues as its theme and each session lasts two hours, one or two expert in relevant fields will be invited from unversities and main think-tanks to deliver a speech about 80 min, then the Politburo members will discuss the topic for about 30 min, followed by President's brief summary speech, which is invariably taken as indication of future policies and strategies. The Politburo of the 18th PCPCCC has held 19 group learning sessions, which come at every 40 days on average.

build up bilateral trade to US$1 trillion by 2020. Also, China and the Gulf Cooperation Council (GCC) mapped out an action plan for the cooperation in the period 2014–2017 and vowed to speed up free-trade talks. China is also trying to bring substantive progress in free-trade negotiations with South Asian countries. Considering that most of the MSR participants are left out of the US-led 'Trans-Pacific Partnership Agreement' (TPP) and Transatlantic Trade and Investment Partnership (TTIP), it is reasonable for China to build a FTA net with neighbors and make it into a platform of South-South economic cooperation, and establish a RMB swap pool among these countries.

3 India's Ambiguous Attitude Toward the MSR

From my personal perspective, there are four main reasons for India's dubious attitude toward China's MSR: First, only a few people in India know the historical Chinese sentiment about the 'Silk Road', some of the Indian scholars even take it as the ulterior concept of 'String of Pearls' and do not believe the Chinese willingness to build friendship with all the relevant countries. Second, India is a rising regional power which has its own cooperation strategies or initiatives (such as 'Project Mausam', 'Spice Road', and 'Cotton Road', etc.), and believes that it is not necessary to join China's Initiative like other small countries. Third, the Modi government is more pragmatic than the previous one, has not much appetite for the abstract concept, and is waiting for more details about this initiative and 'selectively' participating in some concrete projects like AIIB. Fourth, although more and more Indian scholars believe that China's MSR is essential an economic initiative, they still doubt the MSR's spillover effect which may pose a challenge to India's dominant role in South Asia (or IOR).

Especially, India is very anxious about the People's Liberation Army Navy (PLA-N)'s role in this initiative and believes that the concept of MSR is closely related to India and the Indian Ocean, and this initiative will help China to expand its presence in the Indian Ocean (especially in the Bay of Bengal and the Arabian Sea) which has been a kind of strategic turf for India. In order to differ its MSR initiative from the so-called 'String of Pearls', the Chinese government prefers to confine MSR within the scopes of soft power without political or military overtones. Also, the PLA-N is keeping silent about its role in this initiative. However, the appearance of Chinese submarines in IOR have suddenly raised India's doubts about the MSR. Many Indian strategists believe PLA-N has a strong desire to build a blue-water navy and will never willingly neglect the opportunities that comes with this initiative. Even the most famous ancient Silk Road was mainly developed by the navy of the Ming Dynasty.

Moreover, China is paying more and more attention to the protection of China's overseas interests and Sea Line of Communication (SLOC) security, and its maritime interests which will increase gradually along with the MSR with the implementation of this initiative. As anti-piracy and protection of overseas interests have made PLA-N a legal guardian in IOR, the Chinese navy urgently needs to reinforce this legitimate and reasonable impression under the peaceful concept of MSR, which focuses on economic cooperation, making its appearances in the Indian Ocean merely to regularize and not seem to be anything 'unusual'.

Moreover, the PLA-N has been practicing repeatedly to break through the 'First Island Chain'[10] in the western Pacific Ocean over recent years. With the US military's 'Pivot to Asia', the PLA-N's drills in this water have been subject to close surveillance and regular harassment by the US Navy and Japanese Maritime Self-Defense Force (JMSDF). Relatively speaking, there is a power vacuum in the Indian Ocean now that deems it more suitable for PLAN to run some substantial military drills and weapons testing and to get familiar with the combat environment in IOR.

The Indian Navy also knows that China is trying to make itself a maritime power, and the PLA-N has been rapidly developing from a green-water navy into a blue-water navy. It had been striving to hone its combat capability by rigorously sending more and more ships and submarines into various kinds of unfamiliar waters since the warship's combat capability is closely related to its familiarity with the ocean environment and oceanographic data (such as temperature, salinity, and other underwater data), especially for the submarine fleet. That is why the PLA-N has begun to send its submarines, the Indian Ocean since the end of 2013, and two of these submarines docked at Colombo in Sri Lanka in the name of routine deployment and replenishment.

In a nutshell, some Indian strategists believe that the establishment of deep-sea ports and logistical platforms will be the most important 'image projects' of the MSR initiative, and China has its advantages in technology and funds. And the PLA-N has the willingness to control some stable and friendly naval supply bases (which may be different from American military bases) in IOR in the near future if it wants to build a real blue-water navy.

3.1 India's Responses

Responding to the PLA-N's expanding appearance in the IOR, India has been expanding its maritime partnerships with the western Pacific Ocean countries (such as the US, Japan, Vietnam, Australia, and the Philippines) through bilateral, trilateral, and multilateral mechanisms, and making its maritime diplomacy the highlight of its 'Act East Policy' (AEP). The Indian Navy is playing the role of 'protector' of India's economic and strategic interests in relevant waters. Also, some Southeast Asian countries (like Vietnam, the Philippine, and Singapore)

[10]This term was first articulated by the former American Secretary of State John Foster Dulles in 1951 as a part of China-containment strategy which includes a series of island groups in the western Pacific Ocean regions.

believe that the Indian Navy could be a counterweight to China in the Indo-Pacific area, and the US has been calling for India to be a regional Net Security Provider (NSP) since 2009.

Now, the Modi government has adopted the 'Act East Policy' (AEP) to replace the old Look East Policy (LEP). Compared with its positive attitude towards the US's Indo-Pacific Economic Corridor project and Japan's Mekong-Ganga Cooperation initiative (Liu 2015), India has been ambivalent about participating in the MSR project because of its own security considerations. Also, Modi's maritime diplomacy not only engages in more proactive military cooperations with US, Japan, and Vietnam, but also seems to be changing its 'swing-state' position into a new status which I call the 'half-swing state'[11] and challenging China's 'core interests'[12] deliberately. In the past, India had not specifically mentioned the maritime disputes between China and other countries. However, the Tokyo Declaration after Modi's meeting with Japanese PM Shinzo Abe in September 2014 mentioned:

> They affirmed their shared commitment to maritime security, freedom of navigation and overflight, civil aviation safety, unimpeded lawful commerce, and peaceful settlement of disputes in accordance with international law (The Times of India 2014).

Modi also remarked at the Sacred Heart University in Tokyo on his visit:

> Everywhere around us, see an 18th century expansionist mind-set: encroaching in other countries, intruding in others' waters, invading other countries and capturing territory (PTI 2014).

These two statements were regarded as India's official position and criticism toward China's announcement of the East China Sea (ECS) Air Defense Identification Zone (ADIZ)[13] and oblique comments against China which has been in dispute with Japan over the Diaoyu Islands in the East China Sea. The same month, during Narendra Modi's visit to the US, there was a specific reference to the South China Sea (SCS) in the India-US joint statement:

---

[11]This term specifically refers to India's maritime relations with western Pacific countries, and the Modi government actually has adjusted India's traditonal 'swing-country' status and its positions on western Pacific maritime disputes and tends to be more supportive of China's opponents. However, the Modi government is unlikely to give up the 'swing' status completely and annoy China.

[12]This phrase was first adopted in China's foreign policy around 2005 and initially restricted to the Taiwan question to express China's firm stance on upholding the country's national unity and territorial integrity, but gradually extending the term explicitly to the East China Sea and the Diaoyu Islands in the last few years.

[13]The first ADIZ was established by the United States in 1950 when it created a joint North American ADIZ with Canada, citing the legal right of a nation to establish reasonable conditions of entry into its territory. The East China Sea ADIZ announced that it was introducing new air traffic restrictions in November 2013 by Chinese government and that its half of the area overlaps with a Japanese ADIZ, while also overlapping, to a small extent, with the South Korean and Taiwanese ADIZ.

> The leaders expressed concern about rising tensions over maritime territorial dispute and affirmed the importance of safeguarding maritime security and ensuring freedom of navigation and over flight throughout the region, especially in the South China Sea (The White House 2014).

During the Vietnamese Prime Minster Nguyen Tan Dung's two-day visit to India, the two countries signed the first significant military sales deal about selling new vessels to Vietnam, standing for freedom of navigation in the air and waters of the South China Sea.

4 The Emerging Maritime Hedging Between China and India

Based on the above analysis, we can see clearly that both countries have carried out some selective cooperation inside the MSR initiative (such as the AIIB and BCIM-EC), but they are also adopting a maritime hedging strategy[14] toward each other, which might raise the risk of a 'security dilemma'.[15]

For China, the MSR is more of an economic initiative, and it confines the MSR to economic and trade areas which differs from the 'String of Pearls'. Also, the mega economic cooperation prospect of this initiative is becoming clearer and clearer. Undoubtedly, those mega projects (especially port constructions) has some significant, uncertain strategic purposes or effects that will change the Indian Ocean security structure more or less. With the implementation of the MSR, China's overseas interests will increase gradually alongside this road in parallel with the expansion of the Chinese navy and its strong willingness to become a powerful blue-water navy. From this aspect, it is historically inevitable for the PLA-N to expand its presence into some unchartered waters, especially the Indian Ocean. In other words, although the Chinese government tends to see the MSR project from the regional economic cooperation scope, its overseas economic interests along the MSR are so significant that China dares not trust other security providers, and hence gives its navy implicit consent to expand in the IOR. All those elements cause India's serious concerns about China's initiative.

For India, its 'Look East Policy' is turning into the 'Act East Policy', implying that India is trying to enhance the cooperation between India and the western Pacific

---

[14]Hedge is an investment position intended to offset potential losses/gains that may be incurred by companion investments. Now, some strategists usually use this term as the anlaysis method in International Relations. Sino-Indian maritime hedging means the PLA-N's role in the MSR initiative and India's 'half-swing' are essentially peacefully intented. However, because of the lacking of mutual trust, the two countries are taking some seemingly unfriendly measures toward each other to cover their potential strategic losses.

[15]This term means each state perceives itself to be acting defensively to protect its national security, but these actions are perceived as a threat by the other. Each reacts by increasing its defensive preparations, which the other in turn interprets as offensive, escalating the cycle of insecurity.

Ocean countries from economics and trade into maritime security. As a stakeholder of Indo-Pacific area, it is reasonable for India to use its maritime diplomacy to deepen the relationships with western Pacific countries. At the same time, we must note that PM Modi seems to enjoy India's role as a 'half-swing' state that does not mind challenging China's 'core interests' and taking the responsibility as the net security provider in the Indo-Pacific region. In other words, India might believe that the MSR will focus on economic issues and has great interest in improving economic relations with China. However, India is also worried about the potential strategic effects of the MSR in the Indian Ocean, which is India's natural geographic and strategic primacy, so the Modi government has to look for more strategic partnerships to curb China's expansion in the IOR.

5 The Way Ahead

Historically speaking, the main sensitive issues in the Sino-Indian relationship have been steadily increasing from the traditional Tibet issue, the boundary issue, and the Sino-Pakistan quasi-alliance to the more recent trans-border rivers and the trade imbalance, and now the possible maritime issues. The reason for this tendency is not only rooted in 'trust deficit' between the two countries, but also related to their expanding 'security boundary' (安全边界)[16] with the rise of the two countries, as increasingly stronger countries always demand yet more security. Actually, we must realize that China and India do not have any maritime-border disputes but share broad common interests in maritime security. The two countries should take active measures to prevent the coming maritime hedging into another sensitive obstacle and turn the MSR initiative into a model of rare cooperation between the two countries.

5.1 Can Both Navies Cooperate in the MSR Initiative?

China and India are each making economic development their main priority. From the above analysis, by China's MSR initiative, it is trying to make friends with all the relevant countries and does not intend to make some new enemies or competitors. China is promoting industrial upgradation and views the countries along the MSR as the best industrial transfer locations; on the other hand, the Modi government is committed to the 'Made in India' plan. The port-construction projects along the MSR will also promote India's 'blue economy' and its business relations with relevant countries. Moreover, both the countries are excluded from

[16]'Boundary security' and 'security boundary' are being used by some Chinese scholars to define China's national interest range. The former means the territorial sovereignty and integrity. The latter means national interests spread from homeland to the surrounding strategic space of related overseas interests.

the TPP and TTIP, which are the great challenges for the two countries in the future, albeit the plans have been abandoned by the Trump administration. Just like Chinese President Xi said "the combination of the world's factory and world's back office will produce the most competitive production base" (The Hindu 2014).

Although there are some distinct divergences between the two countries, they do not want any face-to-face confrontations at this stage. As the rising maritime issue is at the adjusting stage, the MSR project labeled as 'regional economic cooperation' doesn't eventually mean that maritime conflict is inevitable. India's former National Security Advisor (NSA) Shiv Shankar Menon also asserted that the Sino-Indian maritime rivalry was not inevitable because both countries have a common interest in keeping the sea lines of communication open for their trade and energy flows (PTI 2013).

If we look into this hedging situation from the theoretical perspectives of international relations, geographical proximity, offensive power, and aggressive intentions affect the threat level. In terms of the MSR, China and India do not have any maritime border disputes and their maritime 'boundary security' is clearly divided into two distinct parts by the Malay Peninsula and the island of Sumatra. Although, it is historically inevitable for the PLA-N to expand its presence in the Indian Ocean under the MSR initiative, the PLA-N actually will never become a predominant threat to India in the next two or three decades for India's geostrategic location and its political and military supremacy in IOR. Obviously, the PLA-N also has the same advantages over the Indian Navy and China's core interests (like the Taiwan issue, South China Sea, and East China Sea) in the western Pacific. In other words, the PLA-N will remain focused on the western Pacific rather than the Indian Ocean. At the same time, although the Indian Navy is no longer confined to the Indian Ocean and is ready to participate in Modi's 'Act East Policy', its primary responsibility is to defend the country's area of interest between the Strait of Hormuz in the Persian Gulf and Strait of Malacca—that means largely the Indian Ocean, the Arabian Sea, and the Bay of Bengal—but not in competition with China's interests in the western Pacific (Singh 2014). That is to say, compared to its huge potential economic effects, the MSR's security impacts have been overemphasized. Actually, it is the easiest goal to cultivate military relationships between the two countries by seeking cooperation in the maritime domain. And maritime cooperation can be made into a great confidence-builder and catalyst for closer collaboration in many other fields. China and India have the opportunity to deepen their delicate military relations before this maritime issue completely evolves into a real 'security dilemma'.

6 Way Ahead

It is obvious that, with the advocacy of the MSR, China will need to convince other countries about the aims and goals of this initiative. It must offer more explanations, share the official outline, and other information regarding the MSR so as to enhance mutual trust and make other countries understand the real intentions of this project. For this, the MSR countries could seriously consider setting up two-way information sharing mechanisms which consist of government officials and think-tanks to communicate each other's real intentions.

Second, China should adhere to 'not to interfere in the internal affairs of others, not to seek spheres of influence, and not to strive for hegemony' by the MSR initiative, as it continue making the economy and non-traditional security areas as the priority and central issues for cooperation. Considering the reality of the maritime competition among the participants, the MSR countries also could consider to engage in 'maritime dialogue' to make the MSR into a confidence-building measure in the future.

Third, China and India have finished the feasibility study about the Regional Trade Area (RTA), but it is uncomfortable for the two governments to start the FTA negotiations because this is more of a political issue than an economic one. Now, the two countries are working together to achieve a regional trade agreement, namely the RCEP, which implies that it is easier for the two countries to cooperate in the field of multilateral economic cooperation systems. For India, the MSR is not merely an uncertain maritime challenge, but it should be taken as a possibility for the two countries' relationship and cooperation in regional economic integration and maritime dialogue.

Fourth, the two countries should seriously deal with the bilateral 'maritime dialogue' and learn how to start maritime cooperation. Considering that the overlapping maritime 'security boundary' will enlarge along with China's MSR initiative and India's 'Act East' over the next decades, there is no better option than bilateral maritime dialogue to minimize divergences and maximize common interests. India has set up similar kinds of maritime dialogues with major marine powers like US, Japan, even Pakistan, but the proposed Sino-Indian Maritime Dialogue has been progressing very slowly. Actually, China has been playing a more active role than India in pushing forward this dialogue, as all the suggestions have come from the Chinese side.

As early as March 2012, the former Chinese Foreign Minister Yang Jiechi (now a State Councilor in charge of foreign affairs) paid a visit to India and proposed launching a bilateral maritime dialogue, which was seen as a major confidence-building exercise between the two countries. This proposal was welcomed by his Indian counterpart S.M. Krishna. In February 2014, Yang as China's Special Representative (SR) paid a visit to India and once again invoked the urgency for the two countries to undertake a maritime dialogue. Indian officials generally welcomed the suggestion but said that the shape, nature, and agenda of the dialogue remain to be determined (Joshi 2014). The Joint Statement between China and India after Chinese President Xi's visit to India in September 2014 also referred to this:

> The two sides decided to hold the first round of maritime cooperation dialogue within this year to exchange views on maritime affairs and security, including anti-piracy, freedom of navigation and cooperation between maritime agencies of both countries. (Ministry of External Affairs 2014)

Unfortunately, as before, nothing concrete has happened since then.

Fifth, from my personal perspective, in order to carry out an effective maritime dialogue, both sides should respect each other's major concerns and core interests and then make maritime cooperation in the MSR into a confidence-builder and catalyst for close collaboration in many other fields. For example, China should realize that the Indian Ocean is correlated with India's national security interests. If necessary, China should inform India of its relevant activities in IOR and take a more cautious stance over sensitive Sino-Pakistani cooperation concerning military technology (such as submarine-launched missiles) in the future. Also, India should understand clearly that the South China Sea, East China Sea, and Diaoyu Islands are China's core interests, and there is no opportunity for compromise by China and no benefit to India to touch on those complicated issues.

As a starting point, the two sides can use maritime dialogue to clarify their misunderstandings on each other's maritime strategies. They can also take the opportunity of the MSR initiative to carry out maritime cooperation on non-sensitive matters. Maritime cooperation actually is much more than just naval exercises which is dealing with common non-traditional security challenges and promoting marine economic development. China's MSR initiative is essentially a maritime cooperation project which includes: port infrastructure construction; capacity building in the law enforcement to safeguard of SLOC; the blue economy; building production bases along the MSR; joint centers for research and development; climate change adaption; pollution prevention and control; even tourism and education; etc. And there is great scope and enormous potential for maritime cooperation between China and India. Whether the Modi government participates in the MSR or not, maritime cooperation between the two countries is the general trend.

References

China Daily USA. 2014. FTZ Key to China's Global Profile, 12 December. http://usa.chinadaily.com.cn/epaper/2014-12/12/content_19074358.htm. Accessed on January 16, 2015.

Gao, Xiang. 2014. Central Bank's First Remarks: AIIB and SRF Will Speed Up the Opening of Capital Account, 26 December. http://news.xinhuanet.com/fortune/2014-12/26/c_127338672.htm. Accessed on January 13, 2015.

Global Times. 2014a. Xi Reiterates Firm Resolve to Advance Practice of One Country, Two Systems, 20 December, http://www.globaltimes.cn/content/897798.shtml. Accessed on January 13, 2015.

Global Times. 2014b. China to Build 18 Naval Bases in Indian Ocean, 21 November. http://mil.huanqiu.com/observation/2014-11/5210569.html. Accessed on January 20, 2015.

Joshi, Manoj. 2014. India is Just Another Stop on China's Silk Route, 19 February. http://www.dailymail.co.uk/indiahome/indianews/article-2563192/THE-BIGGER-PICTURE-India-just-stop-Chinas-silk-route.html#ixzz3PX9nI9KN. Accessed on January 22, 2015.

Liu, Zongyi. 2015. India Still Nervous About China's Growing Strength Despite Economic Ties, 6 January, http://www.globaltimes.cn/content/900129.shtml. Accessed on January 20, 2015.

Ministry of External Affairs. 2014. Joint Statement Between the Republic of India and the People's Republic of China on Building a Closer Developmental Partnership, 19 September. http://www.mea.gov.in/bilateral-documents.htm?dtl/24022/Joint+Statement+between+the+Republic+of+India+and+the+Peoples+Republic+of+China+on+Building+a+Closer+Developmental+Partnership. Accessed on January 22, 2015.

Phoenix TV. 2014. Fang Fenghui: The Rebalancing Strategy of the U.S. Makes the South and East China Sea not So Calm as Before, 16 May. http://news.ifeng.com/a/20140516/403360080.shtml. Accessed on January 12, 2015.

PTI. 2013. India-China Maritime Rivalry not Inevitable: NSA. http://articles.economictimes.indiatimes.com/2013-03-04/news/37437028_1_india-and-china-sino-indian-india-china. Accessed on January 22, 2015.

PTI. 2014. Chinese Media Comments on Narendra Modi's 'Expansionist' Remarks, 2 September. http://articles.economictimes.indiatimes.com/2014-09-02/news/53479794_1_prime-minister-narendra-modi-east-china-sea-senkaku. Accessed on January 20, 2015.

Singh, Sushil K. 2014. Indian Navy Expands to Act East. http://apdforum.com/en_GB/article/rmiap/articles/online/features/2014/12/24/india-navy-policy. Accessed on January 22, 2015.

The Hindu. 2014. Towards an Asian Century of Prosperity, 17 September. http://www.thehindu.com/opinion/op-ed/towards-an-asian-century-of-prosperity/article6416553.ece?homepage=true. Accessed on January 22, 2015.

The Times of India. 2014. Tokyo Declaration for India: Japan Special Strategic and Global Partnership, 1 September. http://www.mofa.go.jp/files/000025064.pdf. Accessed on January 23, 2015.

The White House. 2014. U.S.-India Joint Statement, 30 September. http://www.whitehouse.gov/the-press-office/2014/09/30/us-india-joint-statement. Accessed on January 23, 2015.

Xinhua. 2013. Xi Jinping: Tell Well China's Story Well, Disseminate China's Voice Well, 21 August.

Xinhua. 2014a. Silk Road Initiatives Help Boost Asia Renewal: FM, 8 March. http://www.globaltimes.cn/content/846948.shtml. Accessed on January 12, 2015.

Xinhua. 2014b. 2014 is a Year of Bumper Harvest for China's Diplomacy, FM says, 11 December. http://news.xinhuanet.com/english/china/2014-12/11/c_133848777.htm. Accessed on January 15, 2015.

Xinhua. 2015a. Text: Vision and Actions on Jointly Building Belt and Road, 28 March. http://news.xinhuanet.com/english/china/2015-03/28/c_134105858.htm. Accessed on April 27, 2015.

Xinhua. 2015b. China will be More Proactive in Reinforcing Ties with Neighbors: Diplomat, 1 January. http://en.people.cn/n/2015/0101/c90883-8830445.html. Accessed on January 16, 2015.

Chapter 14
The Clash of Interests: Issues of the US Pivot to Asia and China's Maritime Silk Road

Williams Lawrence S. Prabhakar

China's announcement of the Maritime Silk Road was a direct response to the US re-engagement in the Asia-Pacific. The US had announced its strategic pivot to the Asia-Pacific through the strengthening of the various bilateral relationships and alliances with a robust economic content and the rebalancing and reconfiguration of its forward deployed naval and air force units. The US pivot brings to the fore the essence of forward deployment and economic engagement that would bring US trade and investment into the region as a means to bolster its traditional presence and diplomatic role there. The US-led, trans-regional economic initiative, the Trans Pacific Partnership (TPP), brings into the region US economic resilience, capital, technology, and has been a strong bulwark against China's ascendant rise and its new maritime silk route. China has been busy promoting its new Asian Infrastructure Investment Bank (AIIB) as a rival to the US-supported Asian Development Bank. China has promised to provide US$25 billion, which is half of its $50 billion start-up capital for the bank that would aid the construction of ports, roads, power projects, and other infrastructure across the region.

China's Silk Road fund and Asia Infrastructure Investment Bank pose a direct challenge to the traditional primacy of US-dominated financial and trade institutions in the region, which includes the Bretton Woods system of the International Monetary Fund, World Bank and the Asian Development Bank.

China's Maritime Silk Road thus poses a direct challenge to the traditional US dominance in the region and has been attempting to dent the economic partnerships of the APEC and its bilateral relationships. While the US rebalance has been a traditional military response to China's military rise and aggressiveness, China's maritime silk route diplomacy focuses on the importance of Chinese aided infrastructure diplomacy, credits for developmental projects with the obvious dual-intent of commercial-infrastructure and strategic objectives in the entire region

W.L.S. Prabhakar (✉)
Madras Christian College, Chennai, India
e-mail: lawrence.prabhakar@gmail.com

B.R. Deepak (ed.), *China's Global Rebalancing and the New Silk Road*,
https://doi.org/10.1007/978-981-10-5972-8_14

that provides a swath of China's westward sea movement to the West complimenting its continental axis in the Belt initiative. This unnerves the traditional US framework of economic diplomacy and military partnerships in the region. However, several of the US's traditional allies in Southeast Asia and Asia-Pacific, while welcoming China's economic diplomacy, have been wary of China's intentions had initially refrained from joining its framework of relationships, but have now joined the Belt Road Forum given the unprecedented opportunities that have been accrued in investments, infrastructure and devolopment momentum.

The paper discusses the US initiatives of the pivot and its reenergizing of its economic and strategic relations with the Asia-Pacific. It analyzes the nuances of China's maritime silk route diplomacy and counter responses that could be generated by the US and its allies in the region.

1 Frameworks of the US Pivot and China's Maritime Silk Road

The competing visions and schemes of the US pivot and China's Maritime Silk Road evokes several vistas of great power rivalry and a struggle between a dominant hegemonic power and a rising power with hegemonic ambitions. Two frameworks attribute to the competing visions and schemes of the US pivot and the China's Maritime Silk Road. The Hegemonic Stability Theory characterizes the prevalent dominance of a hegemonic power that would determine all important international rules, agreements, and institutions, through a mixture of diplomacy, persuasion, and military and economic coercion (Kindleberger 1973). The Hegemonic Stability Theory also posits that the hegemons must have unparalleled political and economic strength, which are characteristic of large economies and possessing preponderant strengths in vital technological sectors.

The Hegemonic Stability Theory envisages an activist foreign policy for the dominant power in terms of its role in international affairs. It is expected that hegemonic powers, to protect their status, will commit to defending an concept of an international system, rather than simply serving their own self-interest (Krasner and Pascual 2005). The US, as the dominant hegemonic power, has been defending the post-World War II status quo initially against the Soviet Union and then against China. The US deployed its economic power and military power as the mainstay of the Asia-Pacific through its extensive commitments to the Asian Development Bank and its various bilateral alliance commitments with Japan, South Korea, Australia, and the non-NATO ally status to Thailand and the Philippines, besides the various bilateral and multilateral engagements with ASEAN and its member countries.

Yet another dimension of the Hegemonic Stability Theory envisages that the dominant hegemon creates 'public goods' that are shared by all the states in the system, regional or international (Keohane 2005). Hegemons deploy their resources unilaterally to cater to the stability of the system. The US in the post-World War II invested enormously in the creation of public goods, as well as extensive bilateral and multilateral economic commitments, plus maintained military power that has provided the robust deterrence against revisionist powers. China as an ascendant hegemon aims to initially replicate and eventually replace the US hegemonic role now dominant in the region. The US orchestrated the Marshal Plan at the end of World War-II and provided the framework of extensive aid commitments to the war-ravaged economies of Europe and Asia. The Marshal Plan formed the basis of the US's benign hegemonic role in the global order, its deployment of its military power for the regional military organizations, and the bolstering of the regional allies paved the way for the strategic stability that endured over past 70 years. China's announcement of the Silk Road and Economic Belt is seen as a countermeasure to the US-reinforced presence in the Asia-Pacific. In a grand strategic articulation, China's President Xi Jinping has unfolded the grand strategic design of China's emergent hegemonic order that seeks to expand its soft power into tangible engagement with Europe and Asia much like how the US had engaged the two continents in its post-war period. As the US pivots to Asia, China pivots to Europe with an expanded trans-Asian engagement.

The second framework that could offer perspective is the Power Transition Theory that elucidates the role of the ascendant hegemon and the responses of the declining hegemon. The Power Transition Theory expounds that global politics is a hierarchy of nations with varying degrees of cooperation and competition (Organski and Kugler 1980). The theory differentiates between domestic and international politics by viewing world politics as integrated horizontally and vertically (Kugler 2011). The static picture of structure and rules is complemented by dynamic factors that demonstrate how and why change occurs in the international system (Kugler and Arbetman 1989). Power transition focuses on differential growth rates and their effect on altering relative power between nations, resulting in new relationships among nations and the formation of new political and economic entities (Werner and Kugler 1996). The differential growth among the powers provides the high potential for conflict when a challenger and a preeminent or dominant nation reach the stage of relative equivalence of power, and specifically when the challenger is dissatisfied with the status quo. Power Transition Theory argues that relations within and across the nations are not governed by anarchy; instead, they vary substantially based on satisfaction or its absence (Danilovic and Clare 2007). The most powerful nation atop the global or regional hierarchy is the "dominant" nation, and this dominant or preeminent nation attempts to manage the international system with a coalition of stable, satisfied nations that support the main components of the status quo (Lemke 2004). The Power Transition Theory highlights as dangerous the period of time when a challenging nation approaches the power of a dominant nation. This is called the period of parity and is defined as that time when the challenger reaches 80% of the power of the dominant nation, and it continues until the challenger exceeds 120% (Tammen et al. 2000).

Viewing the two frameworks of Hegemonic Stability and Power Transition, the US and China are locked in the preservation of the dominant status and zestful aspiration of a ascendant power. The US perceives that the era of its long-held hegemonic dominance is waning, given the rising economic and strategic challenges that China offers in the Asia-Pacific region. Hence the reinforcement of the US's presence in the region by way of the US rebalance and the pivot served to reassure US allies and partners of its maintenance of economic engagement and strategic support in the face of China's strategic rise. However, US allies in the region have been in deep economic interdependence with China, as well as the US, while preferring the US military and deterrence umbrella in the face of Chinese military aggressiveness.

The US also perceives a strategic challenge as China asserts itself in the region normatively by the 'Asia for Asians' (an inclusive Asia only approach) policy and strategy that would encompass the Asian countries and elbows out the US. On the other hand, the power transition moment of the challenger in China poses theatre-wide and strategic challenges that lead to anti-access and area-denial strategies blocking the US from intervening in the region for its allies. The US's rebalancing of its air and naval forces thus serves as an enhanced deterrent in the region that intends to counter China's aggressiveness in the South China Sea and East China Seas.

China's response in the Silk Road Economic Belt (SREB) with its emphasis on the 21st Century Maritime Silk Road (MSR) came just as the US militarily rebalances in the region. It is China's economic and investment response to Asia and Europe in the prospect of expanding its influence in Asia and Europe.

China's SREB and the MSR have emerged as China's grand strategic paradigms of consolidating its rise and its westward expansion for a Eurasian and an Asia-Pacific economic domain influence. China has exploited its civilizational roots of its once-famed Silk Road through its western periphery into Central Asia and its Southern coasts to the maritime silk routes to India and East Africa. Chinese contemporary articulation of the silk roads has proved very adept to broaden the influence of its 'belt and road' in contemporary global geopolitics. The 'belt and the road' are the geo-economic and grand strategic constructs of China's Grand Strategy orchestrating its rise as a global power with a Trans-Asian and Eurasian reach. The 'belt and the road' are also inherent constructs for China's hinterland development of China's Westward Development and externalizing its growth through the Central Asian–Russian–Eurasian regions.

China has been able to deploy its massive financial and trade surplus to create the Silk Road Fund and initiation of the Asia Infrastructure Investment Bank (AIIB), inventing an alternative to, with the intent of rivaling, the World Bank, the IMF, and the Asian Development Bank. In fact, the AIIB has seed capital of $US100 billion and with the Asian Development Bank's $US165 billion (Xinhua 2014). The US rebalance and the pivot to Asia preceded the 'belt and road' initiatives. The rebalance and the pivot were aggressive US attempts to contain China in view of China's aggressive posture in the South China Sea and East China Sea and the ramping of tensions with US allies. China had proposed the 'belt and road' initiatives as a means of "Asianizing Asia" that was replete in Xi Jinping's "China Dream" and "Asia for Asians" proposals as the grand themes that have been the counter-narratives for the US rebalance and the pivot and the basis for the 'belt and road' initiatives (South China Morning Post, 14 July 2014).

The Chinese initiatives have been constructed on an economic, infrastructure, and trade development basis with an inclusive integration framework. They provide the much needed economic and infrastructure development for the countries that are covered by its scope. It also brings in the Chinese initiative for free trade in the Asia-Pacific that has a grander inclusive scope for the nations of the Asia-Pacific, outbidding the US-proposed Trans-Pacific Partnership (Denyer 2014). The Belt and Road Initiative (BRI) provides the most alluring economic developmental promises, which come with no-conditionality clauses with regard to environmental restrictions, and it paves way for financial resources for infrastructure development for regimes that do not subscribe to the social and environmental regulations of the Bretton Woods framework. On the other hand, the no-conditionality clauses of the Chinese initiatives further strengthened the US resolve to engage in the Asia-Pacific and also build the geo-economic and strategic momentum for its endurance in the region (Kemp 2014). The announcement of the China One Belt One Road initiative has reinforced the US pivot to Asia that has come by way of economic engagements and the military rebalance in the region.

2 US Pivot's China Focus

The US is in the process of a shift in its global geopolitical dynamism and to sustainably expand its economy and has engaged in the process of building extensive diplomatic, economic, development, people-to-people, and security ties with the Asia-Pacific. The US pivot to the Asia-Pacific and the naval air forces realignment to the Indo–Pacific is the consequence of the increasing economic and strategic gradient of the Asia-Pacific (Campbell 2013a). The assertive rise of China and its military and strategic modernization had driven the US to: (a) engage with the Asia-Pacific closely on economic and commercial terms with a renewed emphasis on multilateral frameworks; and (b) recalibrate US deployment of enhanced military power in the region to counter Chinese strategic and military modernization. The US rebalance is the larger part of the economic and multilateral trade initiative of the Trans-Pacific Partnership to reengage Asia, while the US pivot brings strategic reassurance to US allies and partners in the region. The US pivot also addresses the various means to counter the asymmetric strategies that China, Iran, and North Korea have been adopting and that have been deemed to be threatening to its regional allies.

The Asia-Pacific region is more and more important to the US's economic interests, and China has equally vital interests that are growing with greater economic integration and convergence with the region. The United States on the other hand prefers a dominant hegemonic economic and strategic overlay and prefers to sustain extended deterrence through its forward deployments and works for greater economic integration through various trans-regional economic arrangements like Asia-Pacific Economic Cooperation (APEC), the evolving and now stunted Trans Pacific Partnership (TPP) that reassures US allies and partners of its enduring presence in the region. This presence is buttresed by the reality of US intervention capabilities and its ability to project power through unfettered freedom of navigation in the region. The United States since 1945 perceives that this unfettered acccess is now being constrained and challenged by China, in light of its growing military capabilities and its claims to disputed maritime territory. This dynamic has induced a 'security dilemma' for the United States and its allies with the increasing perception that in the face of growing assertion of Chinese challenges and evident capabilities, the US has been acting with strain and reluctance. This has reinforced the perception among the US allies in Asia-Pacific to doubt the US's commitment to the region, given the fact of the vagaries of the US Defense budget that has undergone various levels of Congressional scrutiny on one hand and sequestration on the other that has been impacting on its orders of battle and sending mixed signals to the Asia-Pacific.

The US, on the other hand, also fears of losing its influence in the Asia-Pacific, and this drives its intents and objectives to counter the political-military challenges thrown up by the Chinese military and strategic modernization. The rebalance and the pivot thus serve to "dissuade" China militarily, while China perceives it as containment and division of the region from China—resulting in Chinese protectionist measures and reluctance to be responsive to US economic interests in the region (Rong 2013).

The US is in the process of shifting its global geopolitical dynamism and to sustainably expanding its economy, by building extensive diplomatic, economic, development, people-to-people, and security ties with the Asia-Pacific.

The strategic contexts of the rebalance come in the context of a "forward deployed diplomacy with a key commitment in its economic assurance and strategic reassurance to US allies and partners in the region. Six priorities feature the strategic contexts of the US rebalance in the Asia-Pacific (Campbell 2013b):

Alliances: strengthen the US alliances that are the foundation of engagement in the region and provide the pillars upon which the region's sustained peace and security rests. In partnership with its allies, the US strives to create a stable security order that builds strategic confidence within the region and provides the context for states to build closer ties with each other.

Improving Relationships with Emerging Powers: The US, while strengthening alliances, is also focused on building new partnerships with emerging powers. One of its toughest challenges has been to build and maintain relations with China, as well as to balance it. Besides China, the US has been building relations with India. The challenge the US faces with regard to India is finding real ways to expand cooperation in economics, development, and security. While India has been developing stronger ties with the US on a variety of fronts, India has been developing strong economic ties with China and has forged strategic ties with the US. The US, while expanding its ties with India, has engaged in a tripartite engagement with Japan for an expanding strategic and economic footprint in the Indo–Pacific. The US is also expanding its engagement with Indonesia, Vietnam, New Zealand, and Singapore.

Economic Statecraft: The core element of US foreign policy is aimed at its economic recovery. Since the 2008 economic crisis, the US has been battling economic woes on the home front and hopes that its engagement with its allies in the Asia-Pacific would serve to boost economic growth of the US and the region. US allies are also keen to invest in the US under a framework of a transparent and predictable legal and investment system. It remains to be seen how the Trump administration is going to compensate for the Trans-Pacific Partnership (TPP) that would have brought together economies from across the Pacific—developed and developing alike—into a single trading community. The US has also launched the Association of Southeast Asian Nations (ASEAN) and the Expanded Economic Engagement (E3) initiative to build capacity in Southeast Asia; Energy diplomacy is also another initiative that the US has initiated with the region. With abundant the resources from its shale oil production, the US hopes to trade with its Southeast Asian allies.

Engaging with Multilateral Institutions: One of the innovative elements of US regional policy has been engagement with the Asia-Pacific's maturing multilateral institutions; these bodies, while relatively young, have the potential to help build and reinforce a system of rules and responsibilities in order to address complex transnational challenges and promote cooperation; US participation in ASEAN Defense Minister's Meeting (ADMM) Plus and the annual Pacific Forum meetings are also ways that are enhancing its engagement with multilateral institutions.

Support for Universal Values: Threaded throughout all US diplomatic engagements in the Asia-Pacific region is steadfast support and advocacy for universal values, including human rights and democracy. The US has provided impetus to political and economic reforms, including the rights to organize and greater freedom of the press. The US has reemphasized the importance of fundamental human rights as the ultimate source of stability and an enabler of national greatness and prosperity.

Increasing the US Military Presence: The US is in the process of developing a geographically dispersed, politically sustainable force posture in the region; announcing new troop deployments to Australia, new naval deployments to Singapore, and new areas for military cooperation with the Philippines—stating that, notwithstanding reductions in overall levels of US defense spending, the US military presence in East Asia will be strengthened. The pivot would bring in a 60/40 distribution ratio of US naval and air forces into the region with a mix and calibration of deployable naval and air power assets between the European-NATO Command and the Asia-Pacific theatre commands. The objective was to enhance the focused deployment in the Asia-Pacific region, enhancing its expeditionary, assault, and amphibious capabilities along with a very substantial US nuclear submarine force in the region.

The six pillars of its strategic rebalance and pivot to the region have been built on existing treaty commitments, value enhancements made to the various bilateral treaties, and creating synergies in the region.

3 China's Maritime Silk Road: Geopolitical, Geo-Economic and Strategic Imperatives

In response, China has engaged the region and the trans-Asian and Eurasian regions building on the sinews of its economic muscle. On one hand, China has been wooing the region, on the other hand its maritime disputes in East China Sea and South China Sea has been persisting (Wang and Ludwig 2015). Notwithstanding, China's Maritime Silk Road has several geopolitical, economic, and strategic imperatives that have impact on the Asian geopolitical order and security architecture. The Belt and the Road expands China's geopolitical profile into Central Asia, Europe, Southern Asia, and the Indian Ocean region. The Belt and Road has the key aspect of fostering the long-term development of the connective infrastructure in the form of high-speed rail lines, roads and highways, and internet networks linking western China with central Asia and, ultimately, with points beyond, such as Iran and Turkey, even going as far as Europe (Clingendael 2015).

The MSR facilitates construction of ports and related facilities that will extend China's maritime reach across the Indian Ocean and, via the Suez Canal, into the Mediterranean basin. Over time, the New Silk Road Economic Belt and the Maritime Silk Road will be interwoven through channels like the projected China–Pakistan Economic Corridor (CPEC), the Bangladesh–China–India–Myanmar Economic Corridor (BCIM), the China Mongolia Russia Economic Corridor, the China Indochina Peninsula Economic Corridor, the Eurasia Land Bridge, and the China Central Asia Economic Corridor etc.

China's multifaceted economic linkages of trade and infrastructure development has a apparent scope of expanding huge volumes of trade with the vast Eurasian market. In geo-economic terms, this would enable currency swaps in cross-border exchange, facilitated by the growing number of currency-swap arrangements between the People's Bank of China and other national central banks, boosting the Renminbi to be a transactional and reserve currency and giving China immense geopolitical and geo-economic leverage. The Belt and Road initiatives have a robust built-in mechanism to improve people-to-people contact and relations. The Belt and the Road covers a demographic swath of contains 4.4 billion people (63% of the world's population), with an aggregate GDP of US$21 trillion (29% of the world's aggregate wealth) (Stokes 2015).

It is this swath of territory and population that energizes the spread and growth of China's preeminence in the region and the world. In terms of strategic rationales, the Belt and the Road opens a comprehensive strategic partnership with Europe and Russia—which are the two major players engaged as stakeholders in China's westward expansion. The Belt and Road initiatives amplifies China's westward development and, all together, the comprehensive development (Chan 2015) that hitherto has been focused eastwards (looking to Japan and the US) shifts westwards to encompass Russia, Central Asia, the Persian Gulf–West Asia, and Europe (Zhiping 2014). While the US–China rapprochement in the 1970s resulted in the shedding of hegemonic intentions by both China and US, it saw China's engagement with the East and Southeast Asia that resulted in the preponderance of its economic growth and development. With China's assertive-rise theory, the US reassertion of its hegemonic intentions by the rebalance and the pivot has resulted in the Chinese assertion of its intentions in the economic sphere shifting its eastward focus from the Pacific to the westward continental movement in trans-Asia and Eurasia and in the Indian Ocean region. As it does so, it seeks to meticulously avoid a military confrontation with the US and harness the economic and infrastructure dividends with Asia and Europe that have been stagnated by economic crisis and slow growth.

The BRI intends to dent the unipolar structure with a greater multipolarity and emerges as a non-military catalyst to the decline of US hegemony. In this ensuing geopolitical calculus, Moscow is also wary of China's engagement in its backyard with its westward expansion in the former Soviet states—the challenge is whether Beijing will be able to maintain its economic and strategic balance. Since Moscow is also building its Eurasian Economic Union that overlaps with China's domain of the Belt (Gallo 2014). The BRI however is the grand strategic balance that Beijing aggressively drives to balance the US's role in the region and would envelop Asia and Europe, while isolating the US as an island between two oceans.

How does the US rebalance and pivot affect the Asia-Pacific region and how does China's use the Maritime Silk Road to counterbalance? These should be analysed in light of their contrasting salience and impacts.

4 The Contrasting Salience of the Pivot and the Maritime Silk Road

The US pivot and China's Maritime Silk Road have contrasting salience and impacts. While the US rebalance and pivot augments economic and strategic instruments of diplomacy and operations to contain China, the Belt and Road initiatives dent the US pivot. The Belt and Road initiatives have emerged as the signs of a victorious power keen to finance trade, infrastructure, and connectivity projects by the Silk Road Fund and the Asia Infrastructure Investment Bank that promises to aid the economic recovery and consolidate China's diplomatic and economic sway. Although China has not won a military conflict since 1979, it does emphasize that the transition of economic power has been gradually inclining in its favor and thus engages in a colossal soft-power engagement with the continental and maritime domains of Asia and Europe.

The US rebalance and pivot significantly lacks the financial element as the US seeks its allies to burden-share economic recovery and military buildup in the region. Conversely, the Silk Road Fund and the AIIB have attracted many European powers, including UK, France, Italy, and Germany who are have signup for membership (Zarolli 2015). While the US is pivoting to Asia, China is leading Asia to pivot to Europe and thus neutralizing Washington's quest to rebalance in Asia. The US refusal to join the AIIB and its strident opposition has been seen as a sign of weakness of the US in the face of several US European allies like UK, Germany, France and Italy joining the AIIB (Kuo and Tang 2015).

However, the US rebalance and pivot was declaratory that the US was back in the Asia-Pacific, when, in the first instance, they had never left the Asia-Pacific, and the focus of the US pivot has been China. The BRI is the subtlest maneuver to focus on engaging Eurasia and the West Asia–Persian Gulf, indirectly playing into areas of US strengths and signaling Washington DC that any US trans-regional economic initiative like the TPP would not be successful without engaging China. The US had launched the strategic rebalance at the dawn of the 2008 financial crisis; the fallout of the 2008 financial crisis has ensured that it does not have sufficient resources to finance the rebalance, whereas China, flush with its US$4 trillion reserves is able to expend US$40 billion on the Silk Road fund and the AIIB (Ren and Ng 2015).

China's Belt and Road Initiatives stress the "Three Nos": non-interference in the internal affairs of the countries; not to seek "spheres of influence"; and not to strive for hegemony (Deepak 2014). The US pivot draws strong military operational elements that would neutralize China's rising military power, while engaging in the democratic norm as the basis for containing China.

The US pivot has the following military dimensions:

Reinforcing naval access and basing strategies has been a prominent military transformation development that has resulted in robust forward basing of naval and air assets, including unmanned aerial vehicles and other surveillance equipment. The US rebalancing has resulted in new deployments of naval and air assets in Singapore, South Korea, and Japan, which have enhanced the efficacy of air naval expeditionary capabilities. Joint exercises have increased the interoperability of the forward based forces with the regional powers (Denmark et al. 2013).

Ramping up of naval and air expeditionary capabilities has resulted in the investments made in the order of battle of the Southeast Asian states, South Korea, Japan, and Australia. The emphasis on naval and air expeditionary capabilities reflect the nature of future wars that would in operate the air-sea domains even as the maritime disputes in the region seem to move into highly contested states. The US has been transferring military hardware to Southeast Asia, as well as transferring relevant technology to its allied partners that create and enhance new capabilities (Tellis 2014).

Development of anti-access and area-denial capabilities (A2AD) and counter-measures has resulted in the response and counter-responses in the technologies that have lead to the development of anti-access and area-denial capabilities. The US–China arms competition has evidenced the slew of new missile technologies that are being unleashed by both sides even as they battle in area dominance and denial operations. The development of anti-access and area denial capabilities are in tune with the regional and theater military strategies of the US and China (Holmes 2012).

Air-sea, Cyberspace architectures would form the operational framework constitute the main operational framework of the emerging capabilities, even as the US and China build the capabilities to contend and neutralize the other. The US-led initiatives have now been built into the allied capabilities of Japan, Australia, and South Korea that constitutes the strategic interdependence of the US and its allies in the region. Chinese responses to the new architectures have been robust and have continued with increasing investments into the frontier area of technologies (Callaway 2014).

Forward basing and strengthening of regional alliances have been achieved by the US, bringing in renewed US troop presence in Darwin, Australia, as well as the stationing of unmanned aerial assets in the region to maintain surveillance over the South China Sea. US rebalancing efforts have increased the efficacy of its forward deployed forces throughout the region and have been able to surge its naval and air assets during the recent Korean flashpoint crisis with North Korea (Schreer 2013).

New thresholds of sea-based nuclear forces—nuclear ballistic and cruise missile deployments have been the accents by which the US, China, and India are now investing and building sea-based assets in the form of nuclear-propelled platforms, as well as nuclear-tipped ballistic and cruise missiles (Mohan 2012).

Deployments of the nuclear ballistic and cruise missiles and their platforms raise the threshold of the strategic competition. The US however has the predominance in terms of the two classes of nuclear-tipped missiles and in the number of platforms that operate in the Pacific Command. Sea-based nuclear forces have their scope and purpose in coercion and compellance missions and also aid in the extended nuclear deterrence of the allied partners.

Sea-based missile defenses have proven their increasing relevance in the age of ballistic and cruise-missile proliferation. The US, Japan, and South Korea have increased the numbers of the cruisers and destroyers that deploy sea-based ballistic missiles which have been deployed to counter the North Korean ballistic-missile threat (Rourke 2008).

Thus a variety of military transformations are in effect in the region, even as the region posits the prospect of economic growth as well as strategic competition. The Indo-Pacific's seamless maritime space thus presents the scope for the re-energized alliance dynamics based on maritime partnerships of trade and security that the US has spawned in the region as a synergy of economic and military responses to China's rise and its continued economic engagement.

5 Conclusion

Thus, a variety of military transformations are in effect in the region even as the region posits the prospect of economic growth, as well as strategic competition. The Indo–Pacific's seamless maritime space thus presents the scope for the re-energized alliance dynamics based on maritime partnerships of trade and security that the US has spawned in the region as a synergy of economic and military responses to China's rise and its continued economic engagement.

The 'Belt and Road' Initiative and the US rebalance and pivot constitute the competitive rivaling strategies of China and US, even as the two powers act as rivals in Asia and Europe; China moves westward even as the US pivots into Asia. China's Belt and Road Initiative has subtle strategic imperatives glossed over by a strong economic, trade, infrastructure, and connectivity dynamics, while the US Asia pivot has largely military and strategic overtones of policy and strategy in its content and direction.

The contrasting salience of the 'Belt and Road Initiative' and the pivot reveal the strong accents of power transition even as China emerges to orchestrate a 'Marshall Plan' of soft-power engagement, while the US relies on military dynamics to contain China.

US allies in Asia, while militarily aligned with the pivot, are engaging economically with China which reflects the balance of regional and global geo-economic and geostrategic priorities. The US and China are in a hegemonic struggle for mastery over Asia and the world; it remains to be seen how values, economic statecraft, and power hegemony work out.

References

Callaway, John. 2014. The Operational Art of Air-Sea Battle. *The International Relations and Security Network.* Accessed at http://www.isn.ethz.ch/Digital-Library/Articles/Detail/?id=182171 on April 30, 2015.

Campbell, Kurt. 2013a. The Obama Administration's Pivot to Asia. *The Foreign Policy Initiative*. The Brookings Institution. Accessed at http://www.foreignpolicyi.org/content/obama-administrations-pivot-asia on April 30, 2015.

Campbell, Kurt. 2013b. Explaining the US "Pivot" to Asia. London, United Kingdom: The Asia Group Chatham House. Accessed at www.chathamhouse.org/sites/files/…/Americas/0813pp_pivottoasia.pdf on April 30, 2015.

Chan, Irene. 2015. China's Maritime Silk Road: Emerging Domestic Debates. *RSIS Commentary* 053, March 13, 2015. Singapore: S. Rajaratnam School of International Studies, Nanyang Technological University. Accessed at www.rsis.edu.sg/wp-content/uploads/2015/03/CO15053.pdf on April 30, 2015.

Clingendael Report. 2015. *China, Europe and the Maritime Silk Road.* Accessed at http://www.clingendael.nl/publication/china-europe-and-maritime-silk-road on April 30, 2015.

Danilovic, Vesna, and Joe Clare. 2007. Global Power Transitions and Regional Interests. *International Interactions* 33 (3): 289–304.

Deepak, B.R. 2014. "One Belt One Road": China at the Center of Global Geopolitics and Geo-economics? Paper 5838, Guest Column. *South Asia Analysis Group,* December 4. Accessed at http://www.southasiaanalysis.org/node/1672 on April 30, 2015.

Denmark, Abraham et al. 2013. Regional Perspectives of US Strategic Rebalancing. *Round Table,* Asia Policy No. 15, January. Accessed at www.nbr.org/publications/asia_policy/…/AP15_B_Asia_balanceRt.pdf on April 30, 2015.

Denyer, Simon. 2014. China promotes 'Asia-Pacific dream' to counter US 'Pivot'. *The Washington Post,* November 11, 2014. Accessed at http://www.washingtonpost.com/world/chinas-promotes-asia-pacific-dream-to-counter-us-pivot/2014/11/11/1d9e05a4-1e8e-4026-ad5a-5919f8c0de8a_story.html on April 30, 2015.

Gallo, Ernesto. 2014. Eurasian Union versus Silk Road Economic Belt? *Policy Brief 159,* Institute for Security and Development Policy August 29. Accessed at http://mercury.ethz.ch/serviceengine/Files/ISN/184909/ipublicationdocument_singledocument/334863b1-bcb6-4938-

b698-b66bd0eb2233/en/2014-gallo-eurasian-union-versus-silk-road-economic-belt.pdf on April 30, 2015.

Holmes, James A. 2012. US Confronts an Anti-access World. *The Diplomat,* March 9. Accessed at http://thediplomat.com/2012/03/u-s-confronts-an-anti-access-world/ on April 30, 2015.

Kemp, John. 2014. China's Silk Road Challenges US Dominance in Asia. *Reuters* November 10. Accessed at http://www.reuters.com/article/2014/11/10/china-apec-silkroad-idUSL6N0T03CY 20141110 on April 30, 2015.

Keohane, Robert. 2005. *After Hegemony: Cooperation and Discord in the World Political Economy*. Princeton: Princeton University Press.

Kindleberger, Charles P. 1973. *The World in Depression 1929–1939*. California: University of California Press.

Krasner, Stephen, and Carlos Pascual. 2005. Addressing State Failure. *Foreign Affairs* 84 (4): 153.

Kugler, Jacek, and Marina Arbetman. 1989. Choosing among Measures of Power. *Power in World Politics,* ed. Richard Stoll and Michael Ward, 49–78. Boulder: Lynne Rienner.

Kugler, Jacek, ed. 2011. Special Issue: Power Transitions. *International Interactions* 38 (5).

Kuo, Mercy A., and A.O. Tang. 2015. China's AIIB and the US Reputation Risk. *The Diplomat.* Accessed at http://thediplomat.com/2015/04/chinas-aiib-and-the-us-reputation-risk/ on April 30, 2015.

Lemke, Douglas. 2004. Great Powers in the Post-Cold War World: A Power Transition Perspective. *Balance of Power: Theory and Practice in the 21st Century*, ed. Paul T.V., James Wirtz, and Michel Fortmann, 52–75. Stanford, CA: Stanford University Press.

Organski, A.F.K., and Kugler, Jacek Organski. 1980. *The War Ledger*. Chicago: University of Chicago Press.

Raja Mohan, C. 2012. *Samudra Manthan: Sino-Indian Rivalry in the Indo-Pacific*. Washington DC: Carnegie Endowment for International Peace.

Ren, Daniel, and Ng Teddy. 2015. China's Silk Road Dream falls into place with US $40b fund. *South China Morning Post,* February 17, 2015. Accessed at http://www.scmp.com/news/china/article/1715764/chinas-silk-road-dream-falls-place-us40-billion-fund on April 30, 2015.

Rong, Chen. 2013. A Critical Analysis of the US "Pivot" to the Asia-Pacific: How Realistic is Neorealism? *Connections*: *The Quarterly Journal* 12(3): 39–62. Accessed at http://connections-qj.org/article/critical-analysis-us-pivot-toward-asia-pacific-how-realistic-neo-realism on April 30, 2015.

Rourke, R.O'. 2008. Sea-Based Ballistic Missile Defense—Background and Issues for the Congress. CRS Report for Congress November 21. Accessed at fpc.state.gov/documents/organization/115955.pdf on April 30, 2015.

Schreer, Benjamin. 2013. Pivot 2.0. *The Strategist,* Australia: Australian Strategic Policy Institute, January 18. Accessed at http://www.aspistrategist.org.au/pivot-2-0/ on April 30, 2015.

South China Morning Post. 2014. Xi Jinping's 'Asia for Asians' mantra evokes Imperial Japan. *South China Morning Post,* July 14, 2014. Accessed at http://www.scmp.com/comment/insight-opinion/article/1553414/xi-jinpings-asia-asians-mantra-evokes-imperial-japan. Accessed on April 30, 2015.

Stokes, Jacob. 2015. China's Road Rules Beijing Looks towards Eurasian Integration. *Foreign Affairs,* April 19. Accessed at https://www.foreignaffairs.com/articles/asia/2015-04-19/chinas-road-rules on April 30, 2015.

Tammen, Ronald, Jacek Kugler, Douglas Lemke, et al. 2000. *Power Transitions: Strategies for the 21st Century*. New York: Chatham House.

Tellis, Ashley J. 2014. Balancing without Containment: An American Strategy for Managing China. Washington D.C.: Carnegie Endowment for International Peace. Accessed at carnegieendowment.org/files/balancing_without_containment.pdf on April 30, 2015.

Wang, Zheng, and Ludwig Andrew. 2015. China's Maritime Silk Road and South China Sea Tensions: HYSY 981 in Action. *China & US Focus.* Accessed at http://www.chinausfocus.com/peace-security/chinas-maritime-silk-road-and-south-china-sea-tensions-hysy-981-in-action/ on April 30, 2015.

Werner, Suzanne, and Jacek Kugler. 1996. Power Transitions and Military Buildups: Resolving the Relationship between Arms Buildups and War. *Parity and War: Evaluations and Extensions of the War Ledger*, ed. Jacek, Kugler and Douglas Lemke, 187–208. Ann Arbor: University of Michigan Press.

Xinhua. 2010. AIIB authorized capital amounts $100 billion. October 24, 2014.

Zarolli, Jim. 2015. New Asian Development Bank Seen as China's Growing Influence. April 16 NPR. Accessed at http://www.npr.org/2015/04/16/400178364/finance-officials-to-discuss-asian-development-bank-at-spring-meetings on April 30, 2015.

Zhiping, Pan. 2014. Silk Road Economic Belt: A Dynamic New Concept for Geopolitics in Central Asia. Shanghai: China Institute of International Studies, September 18. Accessed at http://www.ciis.org.cn/english/2014-09/18/content_7243440.htm on April 30, 2015.

Chapter 15
'One Belt, One Road': China, US and the Emerging Hegemonic Struggle in Asia

Chintamani Mahapatra

Ever since Chinese President Xi Jinping made proposals for a "Silk Road Economic Belt" and a "twenty first century Maritime Silk Route" in 2013,[1] Asia specialists in various parts of the globe have been engaged in a detailed discussion on various dimensions of these two Chinese initiatives. The "New Silk Road" is a land-based, infrastructure-connectivity project and the "Maritime Silk Route" is an oceanic version of the same. The two put together are often referred to as the "One Belt, One Road" initiative.

Strategic analysts and policy scholars have examined the Chinese "One Belt, One Road" initiative from many diverse perspectives which are useful to understand this initiative. However, an important dimension of this development that necessitates careful scrutiny is the emergence of such ideas in the context of the current transition in global governance and power structure. Any attempt to explain this innovative Chinese scheme without factoring in the current transition that the international system is undergoing would be ill-considered.

[1]In September 2013, about six months after becoming China's new President for a ten year tenure, Xi Jinping, while delivering a speech at Kazakhstan's Nazrbayev University, proposed the establishment of a Silk Road Economic Belt. A month later, while speaking to the Indonesia's Parliament, he proposed the creation of a twenty first Century Maritime Silk Route.

C. Mahapatra (✉)
Centre for Canadian, US and Latin American Studies, Jawaharlal Nehru University, New Delhi, India
e-mail: Prof.chintamanimahapatra@gmail.com

B.R. Deepak (ed.), *China's Global Rebalancing and the New Silk Road*,
https://doi.org/10.1007/978-981-10-5972-8_15

1 Global Power Transition

Theorists of international relations often seek to explain patterns of relations between small and big, rich and poor, weak and strong nations in terms of a hegemonic structure where the most powerful country sets the broad rules and norms of international behavior. While conflict and cooperation are perennially inherent aspects of international relations, global peace is managed by the hegemon. The US has been the global hegemon for decades, so the global economic system, political norms, and broader rules of behavior have been regulated or influenced by it.

During the Cold War, the former Soviet Union posed the greatest challenge to Pax Americana, but the collapse of the Soviet System in early 1990s further strengthened the hold of the US over global governance. The unipolar international system, however, has come under renewed challenge by a rapidly rising superpower —the People's Republic of China. China's miraculous economic growth and wealth creation has been accompanied by the concomitant loss of American influence in various parts of the globe. The US inability to eliminate the Taliban in Afghanistan, its failure to restore stability in Iraq—despite its success in overthrowing the regime of Saddam Hussein—the rise of the Islamic State of Iraq and Syria (ISIS) and the creation of a Caliphate by Non-State-Actors, cracks in the Trans-Atlantic Ties, the potential implosion of the major US ally in the global war on terror, i.e., Pakistan, the relative weaknesses in the US economy since the Great Recession, the inability of the US to rescue the EU from its persistent economic problem, fissures in US–Israel alliance, the loss of bipartisanship in US foreign-policy—making process, growing domestic political polarization, explosion of the US national debt, downsizing of the US defense budget, and several other developments clearly demonstrate the mounting weakness of the current global hegemon.

Concurrently, the swift augmentation of China's influence in various parts of the globe has been truly an astonishing development. China has replaced the US as the number one manufacturer, importer, and exporter of goods in the world. Beijing has become the number one banker to the US by dint of its holding the greatest value of US Treasury Bonds by any single country. China also possesses the largest foreign-exchange reserves in the world. What is striking, nonetheless, is China's ability to replace the US as the largest trading partner of many Asian countries who have for decades maintained the closest of alliance relationships with Washington.

At one time, the US was proud of its soft power in almost every nook and corner of the globe. But US soft power has been eroding swiftly in various parts of the globe, while China's has been ascending rapidly. The foreign-assistance policy that brought lots of leverage to the US policy makers in the recipient countries has come under question. Unlike the US, China doles out economic assistance today without imposing political conditions. The Washington consensus is viewed with suspicion by a rising number of countries due to the economic downturn in the US and Europe, while the Chinese model of growth has come to be admired in various capitals in the Afro-Asian and Latin American regions. While the US is apprehensive of losing its economic interests in the sub-regions of dynamic economic growth in Asia (China's backyard), China has made impressive economic inroads into America's backyard (Latin America) in a big way.

While China has announced creation of new international banks with partner countries, such as the BRICS Bank, Asian Infrastructure and Investment Bank, and the New Silk Road Fund, the US is in no position to come up with grand economic or financial projects and rather appears preoccupied in safeguarding the international system that it erected in the post-Second World War period. Last, but not least, the US has been preoccupied with foreign wars from the very beginning of the twenty first century, whereas China has successfully extended its influence across the globe.

2 Contest for Hegemony

America's relative decline and China's credible rise as a new global power clearly create the picture of a budding international power transition, although it would be premature to forecast the outcome. Will the US lose its top position in the hierarchical power structure of the world? Will China occupy the US position? Will there be a new kind of a bipolar international system resulting from the current contest for global influence between the US and China? Will the US prove to be an enduring superpower that could constrain China's rise beyond a point? Will there be a new condominium in global governance shared by Washington and Beijing?

These questions cannot be satisfactorily addressed at the moment. But there is no denying that a new contest between the established superpower and the aspiring superpower for hegemonic control over the Eurasian space has started. In the wake of the Obama administration's decision to end US military occupation of Iraq and draw down troops from Afghanistan, it was expected that US policymakers would turn their focus to the rapidly expanding Chinese influence around the globe in general, but more particularly in the Asia–Pacific. Growth in China's military strength commensurate with its large economic footsteps in the Asia–Pacific raised the possibility of the US losing its power and influence in this dynamic region. Before it was too late, the US sought to convey the message that it continues to be an Asia power and that the region was crucial to its economic and security interests.

To more intensely project US interests and maintain its role in the region, in 2011, the Obama Administration announced a New Silk Road Project that would aim at economically linking the Central Asian republics with South Asian countries.[2] It sought to promote a north-south economic corridor that would not only address the regional conflicts under US guidance but also allow US businesses to

[2]Secretary of the State Hillary Rodham Clinton stated that the US-backed New Silk Road would bolster economic development and cross-border trading in Central and Southern Asia and beyond. See Ekaterina Blinova, "Chinese Initiative to Diminish US's Role," *Pioneer*, 9 February 2015.

enter into this neglected region.[3] In the same year, President Obama also declared a new "pivot to Asia" strategy that would include strengthening existing US alliance networks and building up the new strategic partnerships with countries, such as India and Vietnam. A third projection involved creating a new geo-political construct. The Pentagon began to articulate a strategy that would combine the area surrounding the Indian Ocean with that of the Pacific Rim in Asia and thus a new concept, the Indo–Pacific, was born.

China was in for a domestic political transition when the Obama administration vowed to refocus its energy on the Indo–Pacific region. Only six months after becoming the new President of China, Xi Jinping was ready to counter the US diplomatic and economic offensive. In 2013, Xi proposed the creation of a New Silk Road Economic Belt and then a 21st Century Maritime Silk Road. The geographical area that encompasses the New Silk Road and the Maritime Route is huge, similar in scope to the one envisaged by the US in its Indo–Pacific construct.

Moreover, as the US proposed to re-energize its security architecture in the region, China began to suggest creation of a new Asian security architecture that would seek to resolve Asian security issues by the Asian countries and, by implication, sought to keep the extra-regional powers, such as the US, out of it.

In the economic sphere, as the US joined the TPP and began to lead negotiations for establishing a Trans-Pacific Partnership, China began to play a more proactive role in Regional Comprehensive Economic Partnership (Umut 2014).[4] Subsequently, China proposed an Asia Pacific Free Trade Area that spanned a much larger canvas of economic connectivity than the TPP. All these developments put together symbolize a fierce competition between the US and China for occupying the political space in Asia.

However, it must be pointed out that such a diplomatic tug of war is far from the Cold War struggle that the US and the Soviet Union were deeply engaged in. Announcements of mega projects, declarations of big initiatives, and the larger-than-life diplomatic postures of President Barack Obama and President Xi Jinping to woo the Asian leaders through frequent summits did not allow the bilateral economic cooperation between the two countries to deteriorate. But, simultaneously, the US–China political and diplomatic rivalry posed a dilemma for many Asian countries.

---

[3]For details on Washington's New Silk Road initiative, see "National Security Priorities in the Fiscal Year 2015, International Affairs Budget," Hearings, US Senate Foreign Relations Committee, 113th Congress, 8 April 2014.

[4]Umut (2014).

3 Implications for "One Belt, One Road" Initiative

China's "One Belt, One Road" initiative will gradually enter the operational stage, and, without a doubt, China has created a fund to implement this proposal. But regional complexities, the levels of cooperation from all the stakeholders, China's own economic trajectory, and the need to address the perception of a potential threat from China need to be addressed before this proposal succeeds. And all this will take a long time.

First of all, several countries that would become stakeholders in this initiative are poor and backward with little resources to contribute. Secondly, some of them would continue to be close partners of the US, including alliance partners, and may have suspicions about China's main intention. Thirdly, unless the regional heavy-weights make common cause with China, implementation of such a grand project will be far from easy.

The struggle between the US and China, the former seeking to maintain the current order and the latter trying to reset the order with new norms, already threatens to delay the Chinese initiatives.

The US and its allies and strategic partners already read Chinese "strategic motivations" in Xi Jinping's proposal (Leverrett 2015). There are apprehensions that Beijing harbors the ambition to emerge as the hegemon in this large region, and there is little to suggest that implementation of the New Silk Road project will necessarily be a win-win situation, as argued by the Chinese (Kaczmarski 2015). Some analysts argue that China's "One Road, One Belt" initiative is nothing but a Chinese "Monroe Doctrine" where China intends to play the dominant role to the exclusion of extra-regional powers. Others express the view that what the US sought to do with the Marshall Plan—bringing Western Europe under US economic leverage—is China's goal as it seeks to create a regional economic system where Chinese companies and currencies would play the dominant role.

Both these views have been dismissed by China. In this age of globalization, a Monroe Doctrine anywhere will simply not work. It no longer works in Latin America, where the US intended to keep all extra-regional powers out of this region. In fact, the Chinese economic presence in Latin America has been expanding to a degree where the US would increasingly find it difficult to implement the Monroe Doctrine. In more recent times, even Russia has been trying to enhance its foothold in Latin America.

How can China implement an Asian Monroe Doctrine where the US, Russian, and European presence is very strong? China has also refuted the view that the "One Belt, One Road" proposal is similar to the Marshall Plan.[5] In fact, it was the

[5]When asked to comment on comparisons between China's "Belt-and-Road" plan and the Marshall Plan—through which the US delivered billions of dollars of aid to Europe in the aftermath of the Second World War—Chinese Foreign Minister Wang Yi replied: "It ['Belt and Road'] is a product of inclusive cooperation, not a tool of geopolitics, and must not be viewed with the outdated Cold War mentality." See, "Beijing Calls for New Silk Road Between China and

war-devastated economies of Europe that necessitated a Marshall Plan from the US. It was aimed at European economic recovery and simultaneously it sought to check the spread of Soviet influence in Western Europe. Moscow similarly did not allow Marshall Plan aid to Eastern Europe where its political control was robust. China's proposal does not involve massive economic assistance to prop up the economies of regional countries. China seems to be interested in contributing the large sums of money, but expects the participating countries to join and make it a win-win project for all. Moreover, China does not bar any country from joining this initiative.[6]

Drawing parallels to the Monroe Doctrine/Marshall Plan is certainly flawed logic. But, at the same time, the fear of China dominating the region by dint of its massive economic clout appears to be running uppermost in the minds of regional leaders. China counters by saying that its initiatives have the elements neither of the Monroe Doctrine nor the Marshall Plan.

A critical mass of political and business elites in China argue that the "One Belt, One Road" idea seeks to promote geographically balanced growth across all of China—jump-starting economic modernization in western China

Others outside China read in this a grand Chinese plan to extend its influence across South, Central, and West Asia all the way up to Europe.

4 India's Dilemma

Diverse perceptions of the Chinese "One Belt, One Road" initiative are mirrored in scholarly analyses, and it this a natural phenomenon. Had the Chinese economy not grown to the extent it has, had Chinese military modernization not reached the point it has, had China's rise not attracted concerns in the American political and intellectual circles, and had China not been seen as flexing its military muscles in its maritime and land neighborhood, the critical perceptions on its "One Belt, One Road" proposal would not have cropped up.

Beijing's explanations that the goal is only regional economic cooperation would have carried more weight. But widespread belief that China is an emerging superpower has led even neutral observers to conclude that, by floating the concept of the New Silk Road and 21st Century Maritime Silk Road, China has taken a significant step towards creating a new regional order under its leadership.

(Footnote 5 continued)

Europe," 10 March 2015, http://www.euractiv.com/sections/trade-society/beijing-calls-new-silk-road-between-china-and-europe-312748.

[6]A Xinhua commentary contended that "The Marshall Plan was part of U.S. attempts to contain the expansion of Soviet Union, excluding all Communist countries. The Cold War mentality and bipolar structure, however, have found no resonance in China's "One Belt and One Road" initiatives, which are open to all countries and aim to achieve win-win situations rather than regional hegemony. China is by no means organizing alliances to confront any other country." See Xinhua (2015).

Many in India believe that, at the moment, China's "One Belt, One Road" initiative is little more than consolidating Chinese leadership in the region,[7] particularly in opposition to the primacy of the US. Given the pattern of Sino–Indian interactions since the 1962 War and India's reading of the Chinese policy towards other Asian countries, India remains unconvinced that China's intentions are plain and simple altruistic (Jacob 2015).[8] Some analysts in India do not place too much faith in China's invitation to India to join this initiative. Still others are proponents of an Indian policy in the region that would make India an autonomous and important player, rather than make it play second fiddle to another major power.

Then there are some in India who positively view the "one belt, one road" economic project of China. These analysts are not only critical of the US, but also by and large supportive towards China. There are, of course, many others who distrust China and invariably oppose Chinese initiatives and read Chinese conspiracy in the project that would ultimately encircle India. The serious differences on security issues between India and China come in handy to for them to push their arguments.

In the present author's view, China and India need to reach a major deal. This diplomatic bargain is necessary in view of the adversarial relations between the two countries in the past and the huge gap in trust level between the two countries that still exists. India cannot be on board grand Chinese initiatives, unless there is a quid pro quo on certain critical and core areas of Indian strategic sensitivities. For example, China's willingness to incur massive investment in the Pakistan-occupied Kashmir as part of the New Silk Road project can never be acceptable to India. Significantly, China does this even as it complains about exploration of oil by Indian companies in the disputed waters of the South China Sea. Moreover, China's position on Arunachal Pradesh, the so-called South Tibet, has the potential to force India to alter its position on Tibet. Unless there is a desire to resolve such critical and strategically sensitive issues, Sino–Indian cooperation in mega projects on regional connectivity will remain just a dream.

[7]Brahma Chellaney argues that "Simply put, the Silk Road initiative is designed to make China the hub of a new order in Asia and the Indian Ocean region. Indeed, by working to establish its dominance along major trade arteries, while instigating territorial and maritime disputes with several neighbors, China is attempting to redraw Asia's geopolitical map." In "A Silk Glove for China's Iron Fist," Chellaney further argues that "The strategic dimension of the maritime Silk Road is underscored by the fact that the People's Liberation Army has led the debate on the subject. The PLA National Defense University's Major General Ji Mingkui argues that the initiative can help China to craft a "new image" and "win influence," especially as the US "pivot" to Asia "loses momentum." http://www.project-syndicate.org/commentary/china-silk-road-dominance-by-brahma-chellaney-2015-03.

[8]Jacob (2015).

5 Conclusion

China's proposal for a New Silk Road Economic Belt and a 21st Century Maritime Silk Road is certainly not the only new initiative for regional connectivity. The US itself is trying to shape a new order in Asia through its initiatives on North-South Corridor and its Asia Rebalancing strategy. India has floated the idea of "Project Mausam". Indonesia seeks to create a new "Maritime Fulcrum" around itself.

But there is a little doubt, ultimately that two powers are competing for political space and influence in Asia through economic and strategic policies, and the powers are the established superpower (the USA) and aspiring superpower (China). Washington's Asia rebalancing strategy involves all its strategic alliance partners, such as the Philippines, South Korea, Australia and Japan, and none of them is likely to abandon the US for China, despite their tremendous economic ties with China. Washington's new strategic partners, such as Vietnam, India, and Myanmar are unlikely to take sides with either the US or China in a situation where they may be expected to choose one. Unless the US military power diminishes vis-à-vis China or the Chinese government will have the ability to achieve economic supremacy to a point where they would be the de facto hegemon, the current power transition will not have a definite outcome.

What has already started and is likely to continue is a 'Cold Confrontation' between the US and China. This is an inevitable phenomenon inherent in the nature of a superpower seeking to preserve the international order and an aspiring superpower seeking larger space for itself in the existing order. Such a situation brings more complications for a country like India. India traditionally is a believer in non-alignment. Even when India established close security ties with the former Soviet Union, it did not abandon the principle of non-alignment. As and when the strains manifest themselves in US–China relations, New Delhi will most likely adopt a non-aligned stand.

India will not shy away from building cooperative economic ties with China that would be productive for itself. If India decides to join the "One Belt, One Road" economic project, it will not mean that it is siding with China against the US. If India stays away from it, it will not be because of its policy towards the US. In other words, India's dilemma would likely arise from perceptions that China's Silk Road and Maritime Silk Route initiatives are attempts at challenging US supremacy in Asian affairs. Can India convince the Chinese that India–US defense cooperation is not aimed against China? Can India assure the US that its cooperation with China in BRICS, on the Asian Investment and Infrastructure Bank or in "One Belt, One Road" project would not mean challenging US policy towards Asia?

It is comforting for India when US officials point out rather repeatedly that Washington has no policy for containment of China. It is equally welcomed in India when Chinese leaders express the view that Beijing does not want to alter a global order that helped it grow. But can such statements be accepted on their face values? India neither completely agrees with the US assurances nor the Chinese ones.

India is aware that the American discourse on the 'China threat" is disconcerting for China, and Chinese perceptions of a US-led containment strategy is perhaps perplexing for the US as well.[9] The distrust between the US and China is partially responsible for the Sino–US cold confrontation, and countries like India are expected to take a position. India actually needs to improve its ties with both the powers. But the Indian dilemma makes it harder to do so.

Last, but not least, this project is still at the project level. It will take a long time to succeed. One of the important determinants of the success of this project is undoubtedly the sustenance of Chinese economic stability and growth. There are signs now of a slowdown in Chinese economic growth. Chinese leaders have begun to talk about a "new normal" in Chinese economic growth. Recently, Chinese Premier Li Keqiang told the World Economic Forum that the Chinese economy has entered a "new normal" stage where its economic growth rate may be somewhere between 5 and 7%. To counter any perception abroad of potential adverse consequences of Chinese economic slowdown, Li sought to emphasize that, even at this level of growth, the absolute growth would be remarkable.[10]

However, observers have been noting the rebound of the American growth rate. The Great Recession appears to have ended, and the US economy looks quite resilient. In addition, the shale-gas revolution in the US has made the country more energy independent. This has happened at a time when China is increasingly becoming energy dependent on foreign sources. The emerging cold conflict in US–China relations thus will face more difficult times ahead, and, by implication, it is premature to forecast the outcome of the "One Belt, One Road" project.

References

Beijing Calls for New Silk Road Between China and Europe. 10 March 2015. http://www.euractiv.com/sections/trade-society/beijing-calls-new-silk-road-between-china-and-europe-312748.

Jacob, Jabin T. 2015. Pothole Potentials on China's Silk Road. http://www.atimes.com/atimes/China/CHIN-02-130315.html.

Kaczmarski, Marcin. 2015. The New Silk Road: A Versatile Instrument in China's Policy. http://www.osw.waw.pl/en/publikacje/osw-commentary/2015-02-10.

Leverett, Flynt, Hillary Mann Leverett, and Wu Bingbing. 2015. China Looks West: What is at Stake in Beijing's "New Silk Road" Project. *World Financial Review*, January 25, 2015.

[9]"American experts stress that China's infrastructure initiative was started as a response to the challenge of the US strategy of maintaining its influence in Asia". Indeed, in 2011 Washington announced the idea of developing a New Silk Road project in order to create a "new North-South transit and trade routes that complement vibrant East-West connection across Eurasia," the US Department of State official press release read. http://sputniknews.com/analysis/20150203/1017731544.html#ixzz3TUOKyEdj.

[10]*The Hindu, 23 January 2015.*

Umut, Ergunsu. 2014. China's New Silk Road Initiative Attracts Turkey's Attention. http://www.hurriyetdailynews.com/chinas-new-silk-road-initiative-attracts-turkeys-attention.aspx?pageID=238&nID=78523&NewsCatID=396.
Xinhua. 2015. China's Silk Road Proposals Not Marshall Plan. http://news.xinhuanet.com/english/china/2015-01/29/c_133956612.htm.

Chapter 16
Interrogating Competing Claims in South East Asia: The South China Sea or the West Philippine Sea

Reena Marwah

1 Introduction

Throughout China's long history, Chinese rulers showed little interest in the seas—with some exceptions, such as Zheng He's voyages in the fifteenth century (Kotani 2012). Protection of sea routes was never considered a priority; in fact under Mao Zedong, China was an insular country, with a weak navy. However, the situation underwent a sea change as China grew into an Asian economic giant propelling the engines of growth of other countries dependent on it.

According to official records, China maintains business and foreign trade with 163 countries around the world. It has signed ten free-trade-zone agreements and 80 bilateral investment treaties, in addition to other trading arrangements. Thus, at the same time, China's interconnectedness with all continents grew and sea routes became increasingly used. Moreover, with secure land borders, China's policy direction shifted to the maritime domain, and it is evident that China's land borders are not under threat at the present (Kaplan 2014).

The policy shift is manifest as follows: China is creating a wider strategic buffer in the western Pacific vis-à-vis the US Seventh Fleet. Chinese strategy conceives two "island chains" as its maritime defense barrier. The "first island chains", along the Ryukyus, Taiwan, the Philippines, and Borneo is more than 400 nautical miles from the Chinese coast, and China has enhanced anti-access/area-denial (A2/AD) capability in the "first island chains by purchasing from Russia Su-30 ground-attack aircraft, Kilo-class attack submarines, and Sovermmeny-class destroyers with SS-N-22 missiles—all of which the Soviet Union had developed to target US

R. Marwah (✉)
Senior Fellow, Indian Council of Social Science Research, New Delhi, India
e-mail: rmarwahicssr@gmail.com

B.R. Deepak (ed.), *China's Global Rebalancing and the New Silk Road*,
https://doi.org/10.1007/978-981-10-5972-8_16

carrier strike groups—spending some billion dollars annually. China is also introducing Shang-class ultra-quiet, nuclear-powered attack submarines. The Chinese Navy has also expanded operational areas into the high seas toward the "second island chain" running along the Bonins and Marianas (Kotani 2012). Moreover, according to statistics gathered by Michael McDevitt, a retired rear-admiral at America's Center for Naval Analyses (The Economist 2014): China is now the world's largest shipbuilder; has the third-largest merchant marine and by far the largest number of vessels flying its own flag; and boasts a 695,000-strong fishing fleet. It accounts for about a quarter of the world's container-ship trade.

While providing the rationale for China seeking to secure sea lanes for economic reasons, the quest for energy and marine resources cannot be overlooked. The South China Sea, also referred to by Kaplan as the throat of the Western Pacific and Indian Oceans, is where the global sea routes converge, and it is rich in oil and natural gas resources, in addition to deep- sea mineral resources, so hence it is of strategic importance. In addition to its strategic location, the sea has proven oil reserves of seven billion barrels and an estimated 900 trillion ft^3 of natural gas (Kaplan 2014: 9–10). China is in need of energy to fuel its economic growth. However, along with its maritime strength, China's maritime assertiveness is displayed in no uncertain terms. China claims almost 90% of the South China Sea, much to the chagrin of the other littoral states, especially the Philippines, which claims part of the SCS as the West Philippine Sea.

There are other contenders and stakeholders in the waters of the SCS. The US, along with other nations, have declared that the Global Commons, which are not limited to maritime waters but extend to air-space and outer space, are the common heritage of all peoples as they provide the connective tissue for communications, and no single state can declare sovereignty over them. During the ASEAN Regional Forum (ARF) meeting in July 2010, Hillary Clinton stated that the US "has national interest in freedom of navigation, open access to Asia's maritime commons and respect for international law in the South China Sea". Appraisal of the intentions of the US and China in the region indicates strategic confrontation between the two in the twenty first century, particularly in the Southeast Asian region. However, much as China would like to see the exit of the US from Southeast Asia, this is unlikely to take place. On the contrary, the US seems to be intent on getting embedded more deeply in the Asia–Pacific (Katoch 2012). According to Kaplan, the US now deliberately operates a strategy to contain China with the support of regional nations in Asia, thus developing strategic partnerships with countries in South and Southeast Asia.

This study discusses competing claims by the Philippines and China for shoals and reefs in the Spratly Islands. The bilateral dispute cannot be studied in isolation, especially without bringing in ASEAN and the US, critical stakeholders in the South China Sea. China claims most of the area, with overlapping claims from the Philippines, Vietnam, Malaysia, Brunei, and Taiwan.

2 China's Assertiveness in the Maritime Domain and ASEAN

China's economic muscle has translated into an enhancement of its military capacities, especially its maritime capabilities propelled by its determination to safeguard its economic or core interests. China has declared the South China Sea as her core concern which implies that China is prepared even to go to war to ensure this declared sovereignty. Many of the ASEAN member countries have competing claims on islands and reefs with China in the South China Sea, and thus there are several bilateral disputes as well. ASEAN leaders do not speak in one voice at ASEAN meetings, because the South China Sea remains a contentious issue. While, prior to July 2010, ASEAN-China relations were excellent, the level of ASEAN–China mutual trust has been significantly reduced due to the SCS issue. This is despite the fact that China is a major trading and investment partner for all countries of ASEAN.

2.1 ASEAN's Diverse Views on the South China Sea

It is not surprising then that, at the ASEAN Summit meetings held in recent years, the issue of the South China Sea has usually not been discussed. However, when the issue was brought up by an affected member country during its chairmanship of ASEAN in July 2012, there was stiff resistance from Cambodia. This is because it has very strong relations with China and was hence unwilling to permit contentious bilateral issues to be discussed. It was for the first time in the group's 45-year history that the customary communiqué was not issued.

As stated earlier, China's relations are better understood through the bilateral, rather than the multilateral, lens. While China does engage with ASEAN as a regional group, it prefers to engage bilaterally with each country. The One China policy[1] has been easier to manage on the part of China's Southeast Asian neighbors, including the Philippines. However, it is the issue of the SCS that continues to engage strategic thinkers in these countries.

Ahead of the ASEAN Summit meeting (with Malaysia as Chair of ASEAN), in April 2015, Philippines President Benigno Aquino asked leaders of the Association of Southeast Asian Nations to issue a collective statement condemning China's reclamation of the disputed waters at the end of their Kuala Lumpur meeting. It is the Philippines and Vietnam who have been the most vocal critics of China's reclamation steps in the South China Sea. In fact, satellite images clearly point out

[1]The One China policy holds that there is but one China and that Taiwan is part of China. For details see: http://www.slate.com/articles/news_and_politics/explainer/2000/05/what_is_the_onechina_policy.html.

that China has made rapid progress in building an airstrip suitable for military use in the South China Sea's Spratly Islands, and there could be another in the near future.

However, the ASEAN summit host Malaysia, which has close economic ties with China, has traditionally downplayed tensions in the South China Sea. An advance copy of Najib's statement, as of April 16, 2015, made no mention of China's reclamation work in the area. It emphasizes the importance of "creating, maintaining and enhancing mutual trust and confidence and exercising self-restraint in the conduct of activities". A draft copy of the statement by Malaysian Prime Minister Najib Razak includes two paragraphs about the tensions in the South China Sea, but does not take sides in the matter.[2]

China's actions, delineated later, in the South China Sea have created a deep divide between the ten ASEAN members, four of which have competing claims over the disputed territory. According to Baviera, the ASEAN member countries of Malaysia, Philippines, and Vietnam have adopted different strategies to manage China, even as they assert their territorial claims, yet cannot shrug off their economic dependence on China.

For the Philippines, dependence on the US and institutionalism has been the preferred strategies in contrast to non-alignment for Malaysia and internal balancing for Vietnam. These strategies according to Baviera differ, depending on the degree of threat perception or historical conditions.[3]

3 Spat Over the Spratlys

The islands of the South China Sea are generally classified under four major groups namely, Paracels, Spratlys, Pratas, and the Macclesfield Bank, and the various islands have been occupied by different powers. The *Spratlys* are more than 600 nautical miles from *Hainan* Island (China), and Scarborough Shoal is 500 nautical miles. However, maps in the Philippines show that Chinese territory extends only to Hainan.

It is also important here to understand that the Philippines archipelago comprises almost 7,100 islands, with a coastline of about 22,000 miles within three island groups, and these had little in common when they were colonized by the Spanish. Luzon is in the north and is inhabited by those who speak Tagalog, formerly from south East Asia. In the south are Mindanao and the Sulu archipelago, occupied by Muslim Moros who are better connected with Malaysia and Indonesia than with those on Luzon. The Philippines had been a colony of the US and was host to US troops in Subic Bay and Clark Airfield until 1992.

[2]Menon and Manuel (2015).

[3]Aileen Baviera, Personal Interview to Reena Marwah; 22 November, 2014.

The Spratlys constitute around 150 features, with about only 40 above sea level at all times of the day, and have been claimed by Philippines only since the 1950s. Located about 123 miles west of Subic Bay and 137 miles east of its nearest landmass, Palauig in the province of Zambales, Scarborough Shoal (Bajo de Masinloc), located just north of the Spratlys, is a disputed territory and is claimed by both China and the Philippines. The Shoal's status is often discussed in conjunction with other territorial disputes in the South China Sea such as those involving the Spratly Islands or the Paracel Islands. Bajo de Masinloc's (Scarborough Shoal), a chain of reefs and rocks, is about 124 nautical miles from the nearest coast of Luzon but at a distance of nearly 472 nautical miles from the nearest coast of China.[4] Since the Shoal is within 200 nautical miles of the Philippines, it regularly conducts scientific, topographic, and marine studies in the shoal. Moreover, Filipino fishermen have also been fishing in this area.

To put the issue into context, it is important to discuss here the origin of the SCS issue, commencing from 1992. Chinese maritime expansion began with the encircling of the resource-rich South China Sea. This was soon after the Philippines kicked out the US Navy from Subic Bay in 1991. It was then that Beijing reasserted territorial claims over the Paracel and Spratly archipelagos. Later, in 1995, China seized Mischief Reef in the Spratlys (Kotani 2012).

All the disputed territories fall within what China calls its nine-dash line, which covers virtually all of the South China Sea and more than half of its neighbors' own EEZs. Since it took over Mischief Reef in 1995, China has quarreled with Vietnam over the Spratly Islands and installed garrisons there. It also occupied Scarborough Shoals after a stand-off with the Philippines in 2012. Since the 2012 Scarborough Shoal standoff, access to the territory has been restricted by China.

In present times, China is continuously sending small coast-guard ships and fishing vessels to demonstrate its sea power to the Philippines. The Philippines Navy, which is no match to even the small Chinese vessels, is struggling to cope with Chinese dominance over waters in its immediate surroundings. As a Filipino political scientist mentioned during an interview, "The internal conflicts have occupied most of our forces, so there has been very little strategic thinking as far as securing the sea is concerned."

3.1 China's Claim and Response

China claims about four-fifths of the South China Sea, which comprises the world's busiest shipping lanes, under a China termed nine-dash line drawn on a 1940s map. Vietnam, the Philippines, Taiwan, Malaysia, and Brunei also claim territory in

[4]Is a ring-shaped coral reef, which has several rocks encircling a lagoon. About five of these rocks are above water during high tide. Of these five rocks, some are about 3 m above water level. The rest of the rocks and reefs are below water during high tide http://www.gov.ph/2012/04/18/philippine-position-on-bajo-de-masinloc-and-the-waters-within-its-vicinity/.

the waters. In 1992, China issued a new law concerning its territorial sea, claiming the Spratlys and the Paracels. In response, the ASEAN Foreign Ministers (of the six original members, as Vietnam had not yet joined ASEAN) issued, through an initiative taken by The Philippines, the Manila Declaration on the South China Sea. The Declaration called on parties of the dispute to exercise self-restraint. China agreed that there were "positive elements" in the declaration but asserted that it would continue to have indisputable sovereignty over the area. In 1994, the UN Convention on the Law of the Sea (UNCLOS) came into force, providing coastal states sovereign rights over waters and resources formerly not under their control. In 1996, China issued a Baselines Declaration which reiterated its sovereignty over the Paracels and the Spratlys, enclosing the former within baselines while seeming to defer action on the latter (Beckman et al. 2013: 60).

When the Philippines took its opposition to China's maritime claims to UNCLOS in March 2013, China refused to accept the arbitration. It has also sought to stop American naval and air-force vessels operating in its exclusive economic zone (EEZ), 200 nautical miles from its shoreline, which America and many of its allies consider a violation of UNCLOS. In August 2014, a Chinese fighter plane intercepted an American Navy P-8 maritime patrol in international airspace about 135 miles off Hainan Island, which was considered a serious issue in the US. The US's policy of rebalancing has implied that it is supporting its ally in the Philippines.

It is interesting to note that within China, the Philippines is being viewed as a country that is trying to bully China. In fact, the Chinese believe that the Philippines, together with Vietnam and Japan, are driving tensions in the Asia–Pacific region by taking sides with an external power (alluding to the US).

China further blamed the Philippines, Vietnam, and Japan for "reneging on their claims of a shared commitment to peace and the peaceful resolution of the disputes through their words and deeds".[5]

Since 2014, China has undertaken reclamation work at seven disputed reefs that the Philippines also claim in the Spratly Islands. The main concerns for Manila are the two reefs that are closest to their occupied areas. Reclamation work by China started on Mischief Reef, which is very near Second Thomas Shoal, where a small Philippine contingent is based. An airstrip appears to be taking shape at the other, Subi Reef, which is about 75 km from Thitu Island, where 150 Philippine civilians live.[6]

Defending the reclamation work, Beijing has said this is not targeted at any country. It further clarified that it was well within its rights to build on its own territory and that the work was meant for civilian needs, as well as being required for "necessary military defense." Irritated with the interference of the US in its

[5]Charly (2014).

[6]"Philippine, US Open Joint Military Exercises Amid China Concerns, Accessed on 7 March 2015, URL: http://www.voanews.com/content/philippine-us-open-joint-military-exercises-amid-china-concerns/2726553.html.

South China Sea dispute with the Philippines, China's Deputy Foreign Minister Liu Zhenmin stated that the South China Sea dispute should be resolved through bilateral negotiations involving the countries directly concerned and that intervention by outsiders would only complicate the situation.[7]

3.2 The US's Response

The US pivot to Asia strategy announced by Hillary Clinton in 2010, also referred to as rebalancing, is based on the recognition that the Asia–Pacific Region's importance has scaled a new peak in the twenty first century. Although the US visualizes the strategy in terms of greater economic cooperation and people-to-people contacts, there are misgivings about its real intentions, especially in China. The Philippines, a former colony of the US, is embarking on a phase of military modernization and capability building (including more exercises and training for inter-operability with the US forces) to face the country's myriad maritime security challenges, but no doubt with one eye on a scenario of potential conflict with China. Locklear, head of the US Pacific Command, said the U.S. has reinvigorated its alliance with the Philippines and is looking at helping its government improve its minimum defense.[8] The US entered into an Enhanced Defense Cooperation Agreement (EDCA) with the Philippines in 2014. To help improve security in the region, the US, Locklear underlined, had also developed partnerships with nations that may not have been considered possible over the past two decades. The reference was to Vietnam, Malaysia, and Indonesia.

Although the Philippines closed Subic Bay, the major US naval station in 1992, as well as Clark Airfield in the same year, the Philippines has not been able to reduce its dependence on the US for military support. At the time the US bases were closed, China was not a threat in its waters. It is also worthwhile to note that, during the time that the Clark and Subic facilities were permanent American bases, the Philippines received US$200 million annually in military assistance from Washington. After the bases were closed, the amount was reduced to zero. However, with the Chinese threat surging in the 1990s, the year 1999 was witness to the signing of a new status of forces agreement which awarded US$35 million annually (Kaplan 2014: 133).

The Philippines' policy towards China has also not been consistent as various regimes have engaged China differently—bilaterally or multilaterally—but the focus on regional cooperation was never lost. Moreover, China is the Philippines' third largest trading partner and is host to a large ethnic Chinese population. The US has always been an ally of the Philippines, but this relationship too has gone

[7]"In tiny Brunei, India makes inroads into ASEAN", http://www.rediff.com/news/report/in-tiny-brunei-india-seeks-to-make-inroads-into-asean/20131009.html, accessed on 15 January 2015.

[8]Tweed (2015).

through phases. As stated above, the US viewed the Philippines as a significant partner in anti-terrorist operations after 9/11, and the Philippines hoped for the big power to be a support to counter the threat from China. In addition, US strategists have been advising their government to recognize its ally's strategic location and importance to the US's own military power.

Ronald O'Rourke, a naval analyst for the United States Congressional Research Service, says Chinese officials have a "cabbage strategy" to encircle the shoals and reefs. The islands are wrapped, cabbage-like, in successive layers of protection formed by fishing boats, Chinese coast guard ships, and finally naval vessels. On Mischief Reef, also located in the Spratlys, China has constructed a three-storey building and five octagonal concrete structures, all for military use. Even on the shoals, China has constructed helipads (Kaplan 2014: 13).

In its island disputes, security analysts believe that China is picking fights with US allies to test the US's commitment to upholding the law by proxy, in steps small enough to make retaliation difficult. But in the process, it is gradually establishing "facts on the ground" in its own back pond. Euan Graham of the Singapore-based S. Rajaratnam School of International Studies says that eventually these could enable it to thicken its EEZ into a robust coastal buffer.[9]

The congressional US–China Economic and Security Review Commission stated: "As a result of China's comprehensive and rapid military modernization, the regional balance of power between China on the one hand and United States and its allies and associates on the other is shifting in China's direction".[10]

The solicitor General of the Philippines also stated that there is no guarantee, even if the EDCA is declared as constitutional, that the US under its EDCA will defend the Philippines from foreign invasion or territorial disputes. However the EDCA will help the Philippines in improving barracks, facilities, and ports and in matters relating to training exercises in the Philippines.

Whatever the level of US engagement, the Philippines would do well to leverage the power of its ally for its advantage while understanding that the US will not be a panacea for all its ills.

4 Managing an Asymmetric Relationship

The Philippines has tried to manage the asymmetric relations with China in the SCS through two primary means: reliance on institutions and norms (ASEAN, ARF, Law of the Sea); and external soft-balancing strategies invoking its mutual defense treaty and close security ties with a countervailing power, i.e., the United States.

---

[9]"Your rules or mine", in *The Economist*, 15 November, 2014, Accessed on 11 March 2015, URL: http://www.economist.com/news/special-report/21631792-trade-depends-order-sea-keeping-it-far-straightforward-your-rules-ormine.

[10]AieBalagtas See, SolGen: EDCA no guarantee US will aid Phl versus China, The Philippine Star, November 26, 2014, Page 8.

The same emphasis on an institutionalist approach, i.e., peaceful, diplomatic norms and rules-based solutions for the disputes, may be observed in many previous initiatives of the Philippines, whether bilateral or multilateral.

These include:

1. The 1992 Manila Declaration on the South China Sea by the ASEAN ministers of foreign affairs. The Declaration called for self-restraint and peaceful settlement of disputes.
2. In 1995, shortly after the Philippine's discovery of Chinese occupation of Mischief Reef, it signed with China a bilateral agreement on "principles for a code of conduct", seeking to move forward even without a satisfactory resolution to Chinese occupation of Mischief Reef.
3. The two parties set up working groups for confidence-building measures, fisheries, and marine environment protection—with a provision indicating possible expansion of such agreement into a multilateral arrangement, with either other claimants or the whole of ASEAN in mind. A similar Philippines-Vietnam bilateral agreement was signed in 1997.
4. Manila also played an active role in persuading ASEAN and China to negotiate a code of conduct (COC), resulting in the 2002 Declaration of Conduct of Parties in the South China Sea (DOC), and it insisted on moving the agreement forward from the DOC into a legally binding COC.
5. The Philippines paved the way for the state-owned oil companies—originally its own Philippine National Oil Company and China's China National Offshore Oil Corporation, but later joined by PetroVietnam—to hold a Joint Marine Seismic Undertaking (JMSU) involving pre-exploration[11] research possibly leading to joint development of disputed areas. The agreement was signed on the premise that it was without prejudice to the respective positions and sovereignty claims of the countries. However, this agreement was allowed to lapse after it became entangled in domestic Philippine politics.
6. The Philippines also proposed to ASEAN to turn the South China Sea into a Zone of Peace, Freedom, Friendship and Cooperation (ZOPFFC), a proposal that has yet to find traction with the other littoral states, including member states of ASEAN. It has also challenged China to allow the international court to decide on the merits of the claims.
7. The Philippines also continued to engage China economically and on other fronts, with the two countries even launching an ambitious program of multi-dimensional exchanges billed "Years of Friendship and Cooperation" covering 2012 and 2013. These were complimentary and simultaneous strategies.
8. Another means by which the Philippines has been seeking to address asymmetry with China was its filing of an arbitration case under the International Tribunal of the Law of the Sea. Citing the unlawfulness of Chinese actions under the UNCLOS (Notification and Statement of Claim on West Philippine

[11]Romero (2008).

Sea 2013), the Aquino government asked the panel to comment on: Whether China can lawfully make any maritime claim based on its nine-dash line, either to sovereignty over the waters or to sovereign rights to the natural resources within the waters; whether the "islands" occupied by China can claim more than twelve-nm territorial sea, or are even legitimately subject of sovereignty claims; and whether China can be commanded to refrain from preventing Philippine vessels from exploiting the living resources in the disputed waters (Beckman et al. 2013).

9. The Philippines is also in a process of garnering support for its islands and reefs. A travelling exhibition titled Historical Truths and Lies: Scarborough Shoal in Ancient Maps is a cartographic exhibit that includes copies of 60 ancient maps of China and the Philippines, relating to both countries' disputed claims in the West Philippine Sea are being displayed for the international community.[12] The exhibition authenticates that the Chinese territorial claims are unjustified. This exhibition (with maps defining the territorial boundaries of China from 1136 to 1933) was presented initially by Supreme Court Senior Associate Justice Antonio Carpio. Carpio, who led the launching of the cartographic exhibit at the University of the Philippines Diliman, explained that none of the maps indicates that the disputed Kalyaan (Spratlys) Islands and the part of the South China Sea (West Philippine Sea) claimed by the Philippines have been covered by the Asian giant's sovereignty "since time immemorial," Carpio said.
10. With the US, the Philippines has reinvigorated its defense and strategic relations. The Enhanced Defense Cooperation Agreement (signed by the two countries on 28 April 2014) commits the US to defend the Philippines from foreign invasion or territorial disputes.[13] President Obama, in answer to a question about the EDCA, stated:

> With respect to the new Defense Cooperation Agreement that's been signed, the goal here is wide-ranging. We've had decades of alliance with the Philippines, but obviously in the 21st century we have to continue to update that. And the goal for this agreement is to build Philippine capacity, to engage in training, to engage in coordination – not simply to deal with issues of maritime security. But also to enhance our capabilities so that if there's a natural disaster that takes place, we're able to potentially respond more quickly; if there are additional threats that may arise, that we are able to work in a cooperative fashion. With the signing of a new military pact between the United States and the Philippines, this is possibly testimony to America's "ironclad" commitment to defend the Southeast Asian nation.[14]

[12]Institute for Maritime and Oceans Affairs and Maritime Law Association of the Philippines launched a Cartographic Exhibit on "Historical Truths and Lies: Scarborough Shoal in Ancient Maps displaying copies of 60 ancient maps of China".

[13]Carl Thayer, *The Diplomat*. May 2, 2014.

[14]Thayer (2014) .

11. Other partner countries of the Philippines have also responded to the assertiveness of China in the South China Sea in different ways. Japan (as of June 2014) provided $3.63-million worth of official development assistance, representing the largest share or 28.6% of the Philippines total ODA portfolio and is donating ten patrol boats to the Philippines. Moreover, the UK Ambassador to the Philippines Asif A. Ahmed stated that: "The Maritime Silk Road does not require sentries or toll gate[15] operator".

Despite the employment of several soft balancing measures, as well as the invocation of international legal recourse, the situation is far from being resolved. China has refused to participate in any arbitral proceedings, citing its indisputable sovereignty as well as preference for bilateral dialogue and consultations. It remains to be seen whether international law will, as the Philippines hopes, help level the playing field. The fact that the Philippines filed the case unilaterally and without seeking China's consent has led China to see this as a hostile and confrontational act. In fact, in December 2014, Vietnam sided with the Philippines and accused China of undermining UNCLOS.

Since the Scarborough Shoal standoff of April–June 2012 and indications of an aggressive push by China to alter the status quo in its favor (including blocking off the shoal from Filipino fishermen, sending military escorts with their own fishing fleets into the Kalayaan Islands, and in May 2013 surrounding Philippine-occupied Ayungin Shoal), the Philippines has decidedly been moving towards the direction of hard balancing. A bilateral strategic dialogue process with the US has resulted in an agreement to host an increased rotational military presence by the US.

The US and the Philippines annual ten-day military exercises—called Balikatan, or "Shoulder to Shoulder"—in 2015 doubled in size compared with 2014, with more than 6,600 US forces and 5,000 Philippine personnel, as well as 61 Australian troops. According to the US Army, this higher level of US commitment to Balikatan is part of the US military's "Pacific Pathways" strategy.[16]

5 Conclusion

First, the dispute over how to address the increasingly assertive role of China—an ally of several ASEAN states—in the strategic waters of the South China Sea makes the issue clearly Southeast Asia's most critical military flash point. China says it has a right to carry out construction work on its sovereign territory in the South China Sea. Moreover, efforts by the Association of Southeast Asian Nations to work with China to develop a code of conduct in the South China Sea have not helped. On the other hand, the US's rebalancing strategy has implies that its alliance with the

[15]Alexis Romero, UK: Asia Silk Road needs no toll operator, The Philippine Star, November 28, 2014, Page 6.
[16]Moss (2015).

Philippines has intensified, and it is looking at helping its government improve its minimum defenses.[17] To help improve security in the region, the US had also developed partnerships with other ASEAN countries such as Vietnam, Malaysia, and Indonesia. The US policy of "rebalancing" or the "US pivot to Asia" implies that certain ASEAN members can rely on the new posture of the US to hedge and leverage vis-a-vis China. The Philippines is at the forefront here, but to a lesser extent also are Vietnam, Malaysia, and Brunei. In other words, current internal ASEAN rifts are attributable not just to China's assertive rise but also to the vigorous re-engagement of the US. However, as also articulated by Kaplan (2014), it is not in the US interest for China to dominate the SCS. But neither is it in the US interest to be dragged into a conflict with China (Kaplan 2014: 134).

Second, another source of tension is the parties' contrasting conceptions of rules. For China and other parts of Asia, the idea that Western rules on issues like freedom of the seas, democracy and human rights are set in stone is anathema, says Wang Gungwu, chairman of Singapore's Lee Kuan Yew School of Public Policy. "Nothing is absolute, everything is negotiable." Thus, whether or not the Philippines is able to obtain a favorable outcome on the legal questions, unless the Philippines finds some way to persuade China that its intentions are not unfriendly, this act has potentially aggravating effects on the asymmetrical ties. UNCLOS, evidently in an effort to provide guidelines for the management of shared ocean spaces and resources, according to Baviera, appears to have, on the contrary, managed to sharpen the competition for resources.[18]

Third, the EEZ dispute could have profound implications for the stability of trans-Pacific sea routes, overseen for generations by the US Navy. "It may sound arcane," writes Bill Hayton, author of "South China Sea: The Struggle for Power in Asia (2014)", "but the legal debate over what one country's military vessels can do in another country's [EEZ] has already brought the United States and China to the edge of conflict. It's a battle between American demands for access to the 'global commons' and China's search for security. It's a struggle that will define the future of Asia and possibly beyond." Wang Gungwu says China is particularly irritated by the US's sense of the immutability of its superpower status, especially in a region that China has historically considered its own sphere of influence. "The idea of the status quo forever and ever is so alien to the Chinese way of thinking. Throughout their history the only norm is change."

Fourth, China is building an anti-navy navy, designed to push US sea and air forces away from the East Asian coastline. It is the combination of the two impulses, of China's rising air and naval forces and its enhanced Asian trading patterns, that threaten the independence of other Asian states, particularly those in the South China Sea (Kaplan 2014: 38–40)

[17]Tweed (2015).

[18]Baviera (2013).

For the Philippines, sheltering under the deterrence effect as long as it lasts, seems to be the only option.[19] Other opinions are not so optimistic. John Mearsheimer in his book *The Tragedy of Great Power Politics* seems to believe that war is inevitable because the dominant power, the US, will simply not accept the rise of a new power or willingly yield its supremacy. At the same time, China will not give up its ambition to become a super power even in the face of opposition from a dominant power. Kaplan writes: "An increasingly powerful China is likely to push the US out of Asia, just the way the US pushed out the European powers out of the western hemisphere." He further declares that the long-term strategy of China is to have the US out of Asia (Kaplan 2014: 44).

Thus, while it can be stated with certainty that there is no stopping China in its maritime ambitions, it is equally certain that the US cannot be a guardian of either its former ally, the Philippines, or other countries involved in disputes around the SCS. Instead, China must be constructively engaged through the tools of dialogue and diplomacy. The US as a responsible power cannot afford to isolate or ignore China or expect that China could accept the role of the US as a mediator in the SCS. In the same vein, China must understand that it is not in its own interest to be branded as a country with extra-territorial ambitions within the comity of its neighbors. As global interdependence only intensifies, China's unchecked assertiveness and aggressiveness in foreign policy could well compromise its growth trajectory. The Philippines too must understand that China, not the US, is its neighbor and thus cannot be wished away. The Philippines must engage China bilaterally for shared prosperity in the SCS.

References

Baviera, Aileen S.P. 2013. China-ASEAN Conflict and Cooperation in the South China Sea: Managing Power Asymmetry. *The Study of National Security at Fifty: Re-awakenings*. http://www.ndcp.edu.ph/for%20NDCP%20website/BAVIERA_China-ASEAN%20Conflict%20and%20Cooperation%20in%20the%20South%20China%20Sea%20Managing%20Power%20Asymmetry.pdfBaviera. Accessed on 15 Mar 2015.

Beckman, Robert C., Ian Townsend- Gault, Clive Schofield, Tara Davenport, and Leonardo Bernard. 2013. *Beyond Territorial Disputes in the South China Sea: Legal Frameworks for the Joint Development of Hydrocarbon Resources*. Padstow, Great Britain: T.J. International Ltd.

Charly. 2014. Can the Philippines Really Bully China? https://cbholganzablog.wordpress.com/tag/hainan/. Accessed on 7 Mar 2015.

Kaplan, Robert D. 2014. *Asia's Cauldron, The South China Sea and the End of a Stable Pacific*. New York: Random House.

Kotani, Tetsuo. 2012. Geopolitical Change in Asia and Legal Warfare at Sea: Maritime Asia. In *Peace and Stability in Asia Pacific Region: Assessment of the Security Architecture*, ed. Maj Gen Y.K. Gera. New Delhi: Vij Books India Pvt. Ltd.

[19]Bauzon; Interview with Reena Marwah. Personal interview. Manila, November 28, 2014.

Menon, Praveen, and Mogato Manuel. 2015. Host Malaysia Avoids Chinese Ire Over Disputed Sea at ASEAN Summit. *Reuters*. http://www.reuters.com/article/2015/04/23/us-asean-summit-philippines-idUSKBN0NE0TL20150423. Accessed on 26 Apr 2015

Moss, Trefor. 2015. U.S., Philippines Add Muscle to Military Drills.http://www.wsj.com/articles/u-s-philippines-add-muscle-to-military-drills-1429511920. Accessed on 22 Apr 2015

Romero, Paolo. 2008. RP may scrap Spratly joint study with China. The Philippine Star. http://www.philstar.com/headlines/49267/rp-may-scrap-spratly-joint-study-china. Accessed on 10 Mar 2015

Thayer, Carl. 2014. Analyzing the US-Philippines Enhanced Defense Cooperation Agreement. *The Diplomat*. http://thediplomat.com/2014/05/analyzing-the-us-philippines-enhanced-defense-cooperation-agreement/. Accessed on 10 Mar 2015.

The Economist. 2014. Your Rules or Mine, November 15, 2014. http://www.economist.com/news/special-report/21631792-trade-depends-order-sea-keeping-it-far-straightforward-your-rules-ormine. Accessed on 11 Mar 2015

Tweed, David. 2015. China May Gain Control of South China Sea, U.S. Navy Says.http://www.bloomberg.com/news/articles/2015-04-17/china-may-control-south-china-sea-with-new-isles-u-s-navy-says. Accessed on 20 Apr 2015

Part IV
Risks Along the 'Belt and Road' and China's Role in the Emerging Global Order

Chapter 17
Dealing with the Risks of the Belt and Road Initiative

Yiwei Wang

French historian Alexis de Tocqueville (1996: 181) once made a penetrating analysis of the differences between big and small countries. Insightfully, he noted that "the goal of small countries is to create a free, wealthy and happy life for their nationals, but big ones are destined to create what is great and eternal, while taking responsibility and pain." Great undertakings are always at risk. The five factors of connectivity, namely 'policy communication, infrastructure connectivity, unimpeded trade, monetary circulation and understanding between peoples', envisaged by the 'Belt and Road Initiative' (BRI) blue print, are likely to integrate China with the world in terms of development and connectivity unprecedented in the entire history of China. Why will the BRI encounter risks? And, what are the risks? Let's examine them in the following treatment.

1 Political Risks

On 28 March 2015, the Chinese National Development and Reform Commission, Ministry of Foreign Affairs, and the Ministry of Commerce jointly released an official document titled "Vision and Actions on Jointly Building the Silk Road Economic Belt and the twenty first-Century Maritime Silk Road," which extended the geographical coverage of the Belt and Road throughout the Eurasian continent, closely linking Europe, Asia, and Africa together. Since most of the projects concerning the BRI are big infrastructure ones, with lengthy investment periods and large amounts of capital, their operation and maintenance will not be easy. Some of the infrastructure projects already in the public domain include:

Y. Wang (✉)
Chongyang Institute for Financial Studies, Renmin University, Beijing, China
e-mail: yiweiwang@ruc.edu.cn

B.R. Deepak (ed.), *China's Global Rebalancing and the New Silk Road*,
https://doi.org/10.1007/978-981-10-5972-8_17

Fields	Projects under planning or implementation
Cross-border high-speed rails	• Eurasian high-speed Rail (starting from London, passing through Paris, Berlin, Warsaw, Kiev, and divided into two branches after passing Moscow: one enters Kazakhstan, and the other extends to the Russian Far East, and then enters China's Manchuria) • Central Asia high-speed Rail (starting from Urumqi in China, passing through Uzbekistan, Turkmenistan, Iran, Turkey, and arriving in Germany) • Pan-Asia high-speed rail (starting from Kunming, Yunnan, in China to Myanmar. The main line runs through Laos, Vietnam, Cambodia, Malaysia, and reaches Singapore; the other branch reaches Thailand)
Infrastructure	• Building Line D of China–Central Asia natural-gas pipeline • Renovation and upgrading of Indian railway • Promoting the construction and operation of Sri Lankan ports and the development and construction of industrial parks around the public parks
Overland cross-border oil and gas pipelines	• Lines 3, 4, and 5 of the West-East Natural Gas Transmission Projects • Line D of the Central Asia gas pipeline • Eastern Line and Western Line of China–Russia gas pipeline
Communication and power	• Unfinished cross-border communication lines between China and Myanmar, China and Tajikistan, and China and Pakistan • The submarine optical-fiber cable project under planning in the direction of Southeast Asia • Planning, upgradation, and renovation of the Southwest PLC information channel and China–Russia PLC information channel

It is undeniable that various political risks are inevitable if the initiative is to be implemented over such a vast area. Political risks can be divided into two categories: domestic political risks of various countries and geopolitical risks. How do we deal with these risks?

I suggest we adopt 'two accommodations,' 'two divisions,' and a 'double track" approach. In terms of 'two accommodations,' first, the initiative should accommodate the existing local cooperation frameworks and try not to establish new ones; second, the initiative should accommodate actors outside the region and never seek to exclude powers such as Russia, the US, the EU, and Japan. The US's comparative advantage is its military alliance system, while China's are personnel, skills, experience, and geography. Therefore, the initiative can refer to the cooperation model of NATO, and the EU–NATO guarantees the hard security of Europe, while the EU provides soft security services to avoid overlapping and competition. The so-called 'two divisions' refer to the proper division of work and responsibility. Financial investment cannot be all on the Chinese banks, and security risks cannot be all on the Chinese army. It is imperative that local stakeholders and social forces cooperate and turn the idea of 'China guarantees security' to that of 'various countries guarantee their own security,' so as to share the risk. As regards the 'double track', it refers to simultaneously promoting the following three aspects:

First, the double track of security and economy: Disputes over territorial waters with relevant countries should be addressed through bilateral negotiations. It should be emphasized that the Maritime Silk Road is highly valuable for advancing regional cooperation initiatives and global public goods and that it should not be interfered with by historical and current conflicts. Countries should avoid viewing it as a unilateral strategy of China. In addition to the shared spirit with the overland Silk Road, the Maritime Silk Road (MSR) attaches more importance to the principles of openness, inclusiveness, and transparency. If the MSR cooperation becomes a new highlight of China's relations with other countries, then all parties' concerns should be accommodated. Second, the double track of bilateral and multilateral cooperation: Bilateral cooperation with countries along the Belt and Road is important, including the free-trade zones, negotiations on investment agreements, and so on. Multilateral economic corridors are also important, such as the Bangladesh–China–India–Myanmar Economic Corridor (BCIMEC), which is nodal in linking maritime and overland Silk Roads. They complement each other, reinforce each other, and together explore a new model of mutually beneficial economic cooperation with win-win results. Third, the double track of the South China Sea and the Indian Ocean: The South China Sea is the first station on the MSR, while the Indian Ocean is the terminal of the MSR. Being two ends that echo each other, these stations are highly important for connecting Asia, Africa, and Europe and are vital to reach the terminal of Europe by sea. In terms of making progress in the double track of the South China Sea and the Indian Ocean, it is a feasible measure to steer clear of the Malacca Strait and go through the Gwadar Port and the Kra Canal. Of course, a double track is only a form, rather than an aim. In the final analysis, the two tracks should integrate and be promoted as one.

Externally, the US still plays a prominent role, and the thought of circumventing the US must be abandoned; Russia, the Gulf Cooperation Council, India, Iran, and Turkey are key points; and the European Union is a handle to rely on. As the terminal is Europe, it needs the western end to take the initiative to dock with the eastern end's efforts. In particular, Europe can play a significant role in managing the tripartite relationship among China, the US, and Russia. China should further encourage the EU to join the Shanghai Cooperation Organization (SCO) and to carry out cooperation with European countries in operating the markets of Central Asia, the Middle East, West Asia, and North Africa. China should strive to have a bigger voice in the global governance of the Internet; and join hands with Europe in promoting democratization, taking a chance that the US 'gives up' the plan to offer private companies the right to internet domain names. The China–EU maritime cooperation, third-party cooperation, and internet cooperation should be promoted through the China–EU new style of comprehensive strategic partnership.

2 Security Risks

Covering a wide area, the BRI involves various kinds of interests in related regions. The variety of geopolitical risks it faces is closely associated with security risks. In the process of the construction of the Belt and Road, great importance should be attached to all kinds of security problems and preparation should be made for possible risks so that the implementation of the initiative can go ahead smoothly.

2.1 Traditional Security and Non-traditional Security

Traditional security mainly refers to security in the fields of the military, politics, and diplomacy. Today, when China is seeking a peaceful rise, it will never be provoked to launch military actions against countries along the Belt and Road. But in certain hotspots such as the Middle East; but there is the possibility that their domestic armed conflicts will threaten those countries and slow down the construction of the Belt and Road. However, in the real construction process, there will be more non-traditional security threats, including the threat of terrorism, ecological pollution, information security, and resource security, the coverage of which is wide. Specifically, non-traditional security risks during the building of the Belt and Road mainly include the following, as described in the next sections.

2.1.1 Natural Risks

The building of the Belt and Road has to overcome difficulties brought about by nature in the first place. The diverse geographical characteristics bring about diverse natural risks, such as mud-rock flows, landslides, etc., which are unpredictable and abrupt and will affect the progress, quality, and builders' safety, as well as the operation and maintenance once these programs have been completed. These problems will not only cause loss of wealth, but also damage the reputation of the initiative. For this type of risk, monitoring and early warning mechanisms should be strengthened.

2.1.2 Environmental Risks

China's official document has innovatively put forward the development thinking for a 'green Silk Road,' implying that, in the process of the Belt-and-Road building, we should attach importance to environmental protection, develop reasonably and appropriately, and respond to environmental threats by means of science and technology. A number of countries along the Belt and Road suffer from a fragile ecology and environment, and the technological and human invasion of these areas could lead to air, water, and air pollution causing widespread damage and imbalance to the ecosystem. Hence, it requires the countries along the routes to enhance coordination, set up environmental standards, and strictly adhere to those standards.

It should be noted in particular that natural risks could lead to political risks. For example, the pollution of some rivers flowing through several countries may lead to trans-national problems. Again, the overuse of water and over-fishing in some areas of Central Asia has further deteriorated the already serious problem of water shortages. In order to avoid damaging the unity of countries along the Belt and Road, we should establish, in the process of development, community awareness that "we are bound together for prosperity or losses."

2.1.3 Threat of Extremist Forces

There are a great number of extremist forces along the Belt and Road, some of which have considerable strength and combat experience, such as the Islamic State (IS) currently active in the Middle East. The rapid rise of the IS in Syria and Iraq has further lead to a "spillover effect" that poses a challenge to regional and global security. The construction of the Belt and Road is also highly likely to be slowed down due to the influence of IS (Dong 2014).

For now, the danger of Central Asia, Africa, and Southeast Asia becoming the next Middle East is increasing. Extremist groups are varied in terms of ideology and strength. Members of many extremist groups in Central Asia and other places have obtained experience in warfare due to long-term combat with various government troops, gaining diverse military tactics and skills, which suggest their strong capability of survival. Is the construction of the Belt and Road destined to be attacked by extremist forces?

The answer is a YES. Firstly, in terms of ideology, the Belt and Road Initiative is in conflict with extremist forces. The initiative is aimed to achieve regional prosperity and wealth-sharing, while various extremist groups' purpose is to attack existing governments and realize their own dictatorships. It goes without saying that the objectives of the initiative and the extremist groups collide with each other. It should also be taken into account that China needs to enhance its cooperation with regional governments in the process of the Belt-and-Road building. However, as conflicts exist between extremist groups and regional governments, the former is likely to shift their targets of attack to the Belt and Road.

Secondly, in terms of the effects of the Belt and Road, this initiative is not in line with the interests of the extremist groups and can therefore be the target of their attacks. This inclusive way of development will help promote the common prosperity of countries, enhance exchanges and mutual understanding among them, mitigate intraregional ethnic, historical, and even political disputes, and improve the overall environment of the region. As it hardly will be easy for extremist groups to realize sustained development, the possibility of their conducting cross-border incursions will be reduced. When the BRI drives the economy toward prosperity, and the people's well-being improves continuously, the extremist groups will find it difficult to recruit people, which will threaten the foundation of their existence, and gradually corrode their social influence.

2.1.4 Threat of Non-governmental Organizations

During the construction of the BRI, there are possible risks in which non-governmental organizations (NGOs), mainly those from the West, could mobilize the masses to protest either under the garb of 'China Threat' rhetoric or blemishing China for plundering resources of related countries and damaging the ecological environment. In countries where political stability is not achieved, it is possible that they may even attract all kinds of forces to get involved, and further escalate the situation into large-scale unrest and color revolutions. The impact could be two-fold: First, protests will lead to suspension of projects—China is inexperienced in this, and no feasible plan has been worked out; second, this kind of activity could also be exploited by extremist forces.

The BRI construction should encourage the active participation of the local population, and, in the process, create an understanding among the locals, especially the young as regards its goals and prospects, so that they can take up the initiative as their own road to pursue.

2.1.5 Maritime Security Risks

As the 21st Century MSR passes through a great number of world-famous straits, risks exist with regard to maritime security. The piracy problem may well exemplify this. In recent years, countries have been working together to deal with the threat of pirates, but they have failed to achieve satisfying results. As the BRI is carried out, we should establish effective monitoring mechanisms and address the problem of staffing of security forces on ships. Moreover, while in pirate-infested waters, we should carry out anti-piracy activities and enhance cooperation with countries in the region to jointly cope with the risks of piracy. China and Europe's cooperation on countering pirates in Somalia may serve as a good case of responding to such threats.

3 Economic Risks

Looking at the global economic figures, the growth rate of the global economy in 2015 hovered around 2.6% (WESP 2015). GDP-growth rates in most economies was apparently lower than the figures before the global financial crisis. With the slowdown in global economic growth, the widening gap between developed and developing countries, and weak global economic recovery, the new economic situation is complicated. Most of the countries along the Belt and Road are developing countries with weak financial structures and capital monitoring, and they are prone to be affected by monetary policies of the developed economies; other countries like Indonesia, Russia, and Turkey (SIF 2015: 5) are facing serious problems, such as current account deficits, excessive expansion of credit, too much participation of foreign investors in local bond markets, and poor comprehensive ability to guard against external risks. An unexpected change of monetary policy of developed economies is likely to cause great losses for the capital markets of countries along the Belt and Road and even pose risks to cross-border capital flow. As the largest emerging economy, as well as the country that proposes and implements the BRI, China must guard against the risks of differences among global monetary policies in the short term, and, in the medium and long term, the risks in the future global economic restructuring.

In addition, under the influence of different monetary policies in major countries, global foreign-exchange markets have shown varied trends, with a number of countries along the Belt and Road becoming the worst-hit areas of currency devaluation. If enterprises are to invest in and trade with Russia and other countries along the routes, they may face huge exchange losses. In theory, we can use hedging instruments to manage risks. However, Russia and most of the countries along the routes exercise capital control and do not have adequate financial tools, which makes it hard for enterprises to have access to hedging instruments. In the future, exchange rates of countries, influenced by their different monetary policies, will fluctuate in the markets. And, in the building of the Belt and Road, we should be more vigilant in dealing with exchange-rate risks resulting from the different global monetary policies to avoid losses caused by exchange-rate fluctuations.

It can be expected that the economic structures of both developed and developing economies will enter an era of in-depth readjustment, which will to some extent cause uncertainty for the outlook of the global economy. In particular, after the financial crisis, for both developed and developing countries, the economic structures of most economies can no longer support their rapid growth before the crisis, which leads to a risk of lower potential growth rates. For example, after the outbreak of the European debt crisis, facing huge debt pressure, the Greek government had no choice but to accept the reform prescriptions centering around "financial retrenchment" given by the "Troika,"[1] which has seen that country sink into the vicious cycle of financial retrenchment and economic recession.

Financial integration is an important support for the BRI. There is a huge financing gap in the infrastructure construction of countries along the Belt and Road. According to the estimate of the Asian Development Bank, before 2020, the need for investment on infrastructure was up to US$730 billion every year in Asia. However, existing multilateral institutions could not provide such a huge sum of money. Currently, the major source of capital supporting the BRI includes the Asian Infrastructure Investment Bank (AIIB), the Silk Road Fund, the BRICS

---

[1]Here the "Troika" refers to the European Commission, European Central Bank, and IMF.

Development Bank, the SCO Development Bank, and the financing platform of the Belt and Road Initiative. China has made a commitment to support the efforts of governments of the countries along the Belt and Road and their companies and financial institutions with good credit ratings to issue Renminbi bonds in China. Qualified Chinese financial institutions and companies are also encouraged to issue bonds in both Renminbi and foreign currencies outside China and use the funds thus collected in countries along the Belt and Road. Financial integration efforts also include strengthening cooperation in financial supervision, promoting the signing of the memorandum of understanding on bilateral supervision cooperation, and gradually establishing efficient supervision and coordination mechanisms within the region. Besides, efforts will also be made to improve risk response and crisis-management systems, build regional financial risk early-warning systems, and establish exchange and cooperation mechanisms to deal with cross-border risks and crisis management. The cross-border exchanges and cooperation among credit-investigation bureaus, credit-investigation agencies and rating organizations will be strengthened.

If China, as an engine of future economic growth in Asia and the world, is to share the fruits of economic development through win-win cooperation and common development, it must in the first place consider the macroeconomic risks of regions and countries along the routes. At the outset, as a fund-provider, China may face the risk of not being able to recover the funds. If political upheaval occurs on the fund-receivers' part, the way to recover the funds is a realistic question to be analyzed beforehand. Therefore, China should strengthen policy coordination with developed countries, in particular, about how the role of export-credit insurance should be enhanced. China should also actively participate in the international coordination and cooperation of the "Paris Club" and the International Union of Credit and Investment Insurers, as well as other related institutions, and, according to the requirements of a public document, make the cooperation cake bigger, and more importantly, better. Second, both the country and the enterprises may face the risk of insufficient motivation for technological innovation. Even though China will transfer its own industries abroad, this does not mean that China's industrial mechanism is perfect. Rather, more innovation is needed on China's part to satisfy the specific needs of various regions. Meanwhile, with the Belt and Road construction gaining momentum, the market for Chinese products will be larger. The rise of company profits is likely to be accompanied by slower paces of scientific and technological innovation, leading to an insufficient driving force for innovation. In addition, with the Chinese people' lack of taxpayer consciousness, supervision, and restraint mechanisms, a headlong rush into the Belt and Road construction could see the danger of new debt emerging. It is fair to say that 15 years ago, debtors in China were mainly state-owned enterprises, and those today are mainly local governments. So, if risk management is not improved now, most of the China's debtors 15 years later are highly likely to be foreign governments and enterprises. Should this become a reality, how will China resolve debt risks? (Wei 2015).

3.1 Macro Risks

The accelerated integration of economic globalization is the biggest trend of the global economy since we entered the twenty first century. The Belt and Road Initiative marks a major transition from China's "bringing-in" to the combination of "bringing-in" and "going global." It is also an important process for China and other countries along the routes to deepen cooperation and influence each other. Opening up to the outside world and integrating into the global economy is the only option, but a negative impact is too much exposure to risks of fluctuation and shock of foreign economy for Chinese economy. In this context, countries' economic systems, economic operation institutions, economic quality, level of openness, level of regulation, conformity of their economy with the international standards system, economic stability, and things such as macroeconomic factors, become must-be-considered issues for the Belt and Road construction.

It becomes even more complicated when it comes to programs involving multilateral cooperation. In particular, due to the small land size, population, and economic volume, as well as their worry about economic autonomy, many countries along the Belt and Road may be concerned about China, a giant economy. As one of China's innovations, the AIIB, during its operation, will face a number of challenges concerning economic issues. For example, after European countries get involved, it is certain that they will attempt to obtain more controlling interest for themselves. And it will test China's wisdom to balance the share structure of the AIIB with various groups. Another challenge is that the development level of the Asian members of the AIIB, with their weak infrastructure, are relatively backward compared with Western countries, and the rate of return for the AIIB also becomes a major concern faced by China. Meanwhile, economic problems between China and the US, as well as China and Japan, may arise as the emergence of the AIIB will inevitably affect the interests of the US and Japan, and challenge the hegemony of the dollar. Therefore, during the construction of the AIIB, China needs to unite various countries and use its masterly diplomatic skills to maximize cooperation among countries, so as to ensure the smooth construction of the AIIB and promote the in-depth development of the Belt and Road construction.

During the Informal Meeting of the APEC Leaders on 8 November 2014, Xi Jinping delivered a speech titled "Connectivity Spearheads Development and Partnership Enables Cooperation," announcing that China would offer US$40 billion to establish the Silk Road Fund, with a view to ensure that the BRI could be carried out smoothly. In the same vein, the Silk Road Fund is of great significance in addressing financial conundrums, but it will also face economic problems. At the same time, in terms of management experience of the Silk Road Fund, although there have been similar programs, such as the China-Africa Development Fund, China is still lacking guidance in real economic operations, and economic problems are likely to occur in the spending and use of funds, budget setting, financial examination and approval, and such processes.

3.2 Industrial Risks

The BRI is both a national initiative of China and an initiative for world development. The Belt and Road construction shoulders not only the responsibility of the problems concerning the overcapacity of China and its industries "going global," but also that of achieving industrial improvement and common economic development for countries along the routes. Therefore, the building of the Belt and Road should fully take into consideration the industrial structure, market size, trend of industrial upgrading, and future market changes of countries along the routes.

Economic development cannot live without balanced economic structure, which requires the common development of agriculture, industry, and commerce. In particular, local advantageous industries and traditional industries should be revived. The question of how to achieve the coordinated development of manufacturing, agriculture, industry, and commerce will be a test for China. Agriculture is the foundation of a country, which can ensure jobs and stability. This is the conclusion drawn from the history of China and the world, which will always stand the test of time. It is important that the Belt and Road Initiative helps the comprehensive development of agriculture, industry, and commerce of countries along the routes, their traditional and most advantageous industries in particular. This is directly related to the question of whether the BRI can be distinguished from among others, as an assistance plan, finance plan, annexation plan, or Marshall Plan.

In terms of the model of economic development, if Chinese companies only exploit local resources, sell them back to China or sell them locally after processing, these countries' economic volume might grow, but the majority of local people will not stand to benefit, with only those in the manufacturing industry seeing their profits grow. If low income is still relied on, rather than a proper increase in efficiency, it will be hard for locals to benefit from economic development, which will lead to the lack of these countries' own economic vitality, and the development of manufacturing will have no option but to depend on the sustained investment from China. Therefore, investments and other economic activities should be carried out in such a way that not only the industries but domestic development should be promoted.

In addition, it is also necessary to optimize the labor division and layout of the industrial chain, promote the coordinated development of upstream and downstream of the chain and related industries, encourage the establishment of R&D, production, and marketing systems, and improve regional industrial supporting capacity and comprehensive competitiveness. The proposal to build a "green Silk Road" has demonstrated China's commitment to both its domestic "ecological construction", shouldering global responsibility, and promoting global governance.

3.3 Lack of Risk Response Mechanisms

If China is to deepen its reform in an all-around way, it needs to release capacity and further expose its economic factors to foreign markets, capital in particular. In the past, China needed to bring in foreign capital, and now it is time for the capital of China to go beyond its borders (Huang 2014). The process of Chinese enterprises' "going global" efforts are affected by their limited global vision and knowledge of international laws and management, as well as a talent pool with global competitiveness. Moreover, China is also lacking in-depth understanding of countries along the Belt and Road. All these lead to the absence of enough awareness about the risks of global operation, and it is even harder to establish related risk-response mechanisms.

3.4 Lack of Supporting Facilities for the Modern Service Industry

The modern service industry is an important part of economic globalization, and its comparative advantages in competition are more and more prominent. Commercial management, advisory services, and accounting and auditing consultancy which are familiar with international management, Western accounting systems, and taxation systems are indispensable for the "going global" of the modern service industry. However, the international comparative advantages of China's modern service industry are not prominent, which is mainly reflected in the following: The level of foreign funds utilization is low, with the focus mainly on traditional tourism and labor exports, while knowledge-intensive and technology-intensive services make up a small share. There is a rather wide gap between Chinese and overseas service enterprises in terms of management, marketing, and scale. In Chinese enterprises' "going global" efforts, professional service with high international standards are necessary in helping them become familiar with international conventions and adjust themselves to international operations.

4 Legal Risks

Laws can play an important constraining role in the actions of two sides. In the construction of the Belt and Road, it is of great significance to regulate the actors within a legal framework. During 2017 Belt and Road Forum in Beijing, China signed 56 major projects and signed trade-cooperation agreements with 30 countries along the routes. But the implementation of these documents requires all parties to abide by laws and carry out cooperation in accordance with laws.

The BRI involves a great diversity of areas, including strategic cooperation, transport connectivity, international trade, energy cooperation, and financial cooperation between China and countries along the routes. China's overseas investment has been on the rise over the recent years hitting three-trillion Yuan in 2014, however, due to complex political situations outside China, particularly countries along the Belt and Road, further aggravated by global financial crisis and debt crisis, China is facing various legal risks and challenges over its overseas investments. Firstly, the BRI involves more than 60 countries with different legal systems, which will give rise to the risk of asymmetric legal information. The legal systems of these countries mainly fall into the European continental legal system, Anglo-American legal system, and Islamic legal system, while China has adopted a unique socialist legal system.

In addition, the legislation of some countries is not sophisticated enough with frequent amendments. In terms of law enforcement, these countries discriminate against foreign or foreign-funded enterprises, sometimes even issuing targeted legal regulations, to some degree, on certain transnational companies to benefit their domestic, political, and economic situations. In today's world, trade protectionism has re-emerged in some regions, where economic development lacks vitality. Therefore, if China fails to pay enough attention to legal issues, be unfamiliar with laws of various countries, blindly trust international conventions, or lack specific legal personnel, all these can lead to the inadvertent violation of local laws and regulations. These are the legal risks faced by construction of the Belt and Road. According to the content, area, and how the risk occurs, the legal risks of the BRI can be generally divided into six categories:

4.1 Legal Risks Due to Investment

Overseas investment is a key link in the realization of connectivity for the building of the Belt and Road, the process of which will encounter legal risks. As the interests of China and other countries along the routes do not match exactly, local investment by Chinese enterprises may face the risk of limited market access. Differing systems may result in limitations in the scope and share of investment, independence of overseas joint ventures, disputes over intellectual property rights, difficulty of transnational mergers and acquisitions, etc. In addition, out of ideological national interests and security concerns, some countries usually set limitations on foreign investment in some key industries, such as special restrictions on holding a stake in petrochemical, national defense, infrastructure, and like industries. For instance, the "Rules on the Regulation of Asset Acquisition, Merger and Takeover" by Malaysia in 1974 stipulates that acquisition, merger, or takeover of assets or any equity to be discussed, must directly or indirectly make the Malaysians obtain ownership and control more equity, and should not exert a negative impact on national policies of national defense, environmental protection, or regional development, etc. Singapore has strict limitations on and even forbids foreign capital in some sensitive industries. For example, foreign capital is forbidden in public service, including transport, communications, electrical equipment, and news media; and foreign capital should be subject to prior government approval in the financial and insurance industries. Another example is that of PetroChina's acquisition of Petro-Kazakhstan in 2005: the House of Commons of Kazakhstan unanimously adopted a bill on 5 October 2005, which allowed the government to intervene in the sale of shares by domestic oil companies to foreign companies. On 15 October 2005, Kazakhstan President Nursultan Nazarbayev signed a bill which granted the government the priority to purchase all the strategic resources of the country, as well as the right to cancel all deals violating that bill. Eventually, PetroChina was forced to sign an agreement and sold the 33% share it purchased to a Kazakhstan's state-owned oil company, called Kazmunanigaz, for US$1.4 billion. Only thereafter did the government of Kazakhstan approve the merger and acquisition. In the acquisition of Netherlands' Borg by China International Marine Containers (Group) Ltd. (CIMC), the biggest obstacle came from the antitrust investigation conducted by the antitrust authority of the European Commission. The European Commission once vetoed this acquisition, giving the reason that CIMC's market share in the sub-product of global tank containers had exceeded 50%. Yet another example would be the alleged violation of Company Law by China in The Democratic Republic of the Congo, when the Congolese Government announced that the agreement on the Zijin Mining Group's acquisition of Platinum Congo was invalid.

4.2 Legal Risks Due to Labor Issues

In view of the overseas business coverage of the Belt and Road Initiative, attention should be paid to the legal risks concerning employment relationships. First of all, if enterprises carry out unequal employment in host countries and ignore their specific ethnic and gender issues, then they are prone to violate laws related to equal opportunity and anti-discrimination and face penalties. Besides, if enterprises fail to be aware of the legal rights of labor unions in host countries, for example, if they do not build a good relationship with local workers and labor unions, then there is a possible risk of strikes and violent protests; in terms of staff entitlements and benefits, transnational companies can also easily violate the labor laws of host countries and face the risk of penalties, lawsuits, and even failed merger and acquisitions. Last but not least, when enterprises downsize or reassign staff in the acquired companies, they should pay special attention to the host countries' laws concerning the permitted scale of staff reduction and compensation for retrenched staff.

4.3 Legal Risks Due to Environmental Issues

In the face of stringent environmental laws, countries around the world have enacted protective laws to restrict or prohibit foreigners' investment in enterprise programs that will undermine resources and pollute the environment. For example, Shell, which is based in the UK and the Netherlands, was fined US$1.5 billion by the local government due to the pollution it caused in the Niger Delta. Overseas projects of the BRI face similar legal risks concerning the environment. On the one hand, companies need to comply with the environmental standards set by local laws, which may drive their costs up; on the other hand, if companies do not comply with the environmental standards and violate environmental laws, they will face legal action and will even be forced to close down. For instance, Sri Lanka suspended China's construction program in the port city of Colombo, which is the largest investment by China in the country, at US$1.5 billion. Some Sri Lankan politicians claimed that the program should be stopped, as it would threaten the environment (Chen and Shasha 2015). Therefore, enterprises should follow the idea of a "green Silk Road," strive to adapt to the environmental standards abroad, and reduce legal disputes caused by ecological and environmental problems.

4.4 Legal Risks Due to Poor Management

Weak legal awareness is not uncommon among Chinese enterprises, which are likely to face legal risks due to their ignorance of related laws in the management of companies. These risks fall mainly into the following categories:

First, if enterprises have no knowledge of, pay little attention to, or do not conduct in-depth research on related laws of the host countries, then it is easy for them to violate those laws in their day-to-day operations and management. Second, enterprise management may face commercial corruption and other related legal risks. Once a company is found to have problems, such as bribery and corruption, its reputation could be destroyed overnight, and it will face huge risks of litigation and sanction at the same time. Also, corruption is rampant in the political systems of some less-developed countries in Asia and Africa, which brings about risks as Chinese enterprises try to promote related programs. Third, taxation laws and policies vary in different countries, and various sovereign states will collect taxes from the same taxpayers according to their legal provisions.

4.5 Legal Risks Due to Imperfect Laws

The BRI involves a great many countries, some of which have the problem of inefficient legal structures. In their overseas business, there is a great possibility that

Chinese enterprises will find no laws to follow. In addition, in the case where no relevant legal provisions are available, once Chinese enterprises conflict with law enforcement authorities in host countries, the latter are likely to cause losses to the Chinese enterprises out of their own interests, which also constitutes a risk. Some legal provisions related to enterprise operation in host countries may conflict with the international law or laws of China, which leaves Chinese enterprises operating abroad in the dilemma of choosing between violating the international law or laws of China and violating laws of the host countries.

4.6 Legal Risks Due to Trade

The key to the Belt and Road cooperation lies in unimpeded trade. Legal risks, however, also exist in the practice of international trade. In terms of the differences of the standards of goods in international trade, the access standards for goods set by trading partners involved in the BRI are often different from those of China, and the standards for commodities such as food, set by the EU, are particularly strict. Therefore, when goods that meet Chinese standards enter other countries, there is a risk that they are not in line with local standards. In terms of trade barriers, out of their consideration to protect their own national economy, trading partners in the BRI will usually adopt strict laws to implement trade protection policies. These legal restrictions are mainly reflected in such aspects as tariffs and their management, customs procedures, technical barriers, anti-dumping policies, and the cancellation of preferential tariff treatment.

5 Moral Risks

Moral risks faced by the BRI take place on three levels: national, enterprise, and individual.

5.1 Moral Risks at the National Level

The building of the Belt and Road assumes that countries are the main implementing actors, and the initiative is promoted in a coordinated manner through cooperation at the government level among various countries. In this context, whether countries along the routes can honor their promises and keep good credit is of paramount importance to the building of the Belt and Road, because this is related to the operation of all other branches of the Belt and Road. Only good credit and government support can ensure the smooth building of the Belt and Road on other levels and can seek policy support to solve all kinds of problems, deepening the Belt and Road cooperation as various governments enhance mutual political trust.

In terms of Central Asia and the Middle East, Central Asian states have adopted a "balanced diplomacy," which aims at maximizing their own interests by bargaining with various countries outside the region. Although China's Belt and Road construction can bring tremendous development opportunities to Central Asia, improve the infrastructure and people's livelihood in Central Asia, and promote mutual benefit in the region, while sharing China's development bonus, Central Asian countries will face strategic temptation from the US, Japan, and Europe. If the former side with the latter and fail to honor their promises, then it will harm the Belt and Road construction. The same goes for the Middle East.

In addition, Southeast Asia has now created a situation where it depends on the US politically and China economically. Southeast Asian countries may be subject to US influence and put pressure on China, affecting the Belt and Road construction. As an important part of China's peripheral diplomacy, the good credit of Southeast Asia can provide a stable auxiliary environment for the Belt and Road construction and be a positive example.

In addition, as African countries enter an important period of strategic opportunities, all major countries around the world are enhancing contacts with African countries. In particular, Europe even regards Africa as its important strategic hinterland. From a historical perspective, African countries have cultivated a fraternal friendship with China, and China has promoted the progress of Africa through interest-free loans. Despite this deep friendship between China and Africa, the developing Africa, under the influence of Western values, is very likely to witness reduced support from some of its countries for the BRI due to their own self interests.

5.2 *Moral Risks at the Enterprise Level*

During the Belt and Road construction, China has invested large amounts of capital in macro-control, with a view to ensure the smooth construction of the initiative. Meanwhile, at the early stage of construction, infrastructure is the priority. As enterprises undertake the tasks, they will also face a great many moral risks, mainly including market moral risks and social moral risks.

As regards the market moral risks, if Chinese enterprises overseas do not comply with the spirit of the contract, frequently default, and even conduct contract fraud, they are causing moral risks for themselves, as seen in the China Holding Limited case, where the company was fined 2.5 billion yuan and which seriously affected Chinese enterprises' image abroad. Secondly, overseas business usually needs financing in host countries and even requires the enterprises to be listed there. If Chinese enterprises obtain large loans or capital through illegal means, but fail to pay the debt because of bankruptcy, then they will cause significant losses for banks, financial institutions, and other creditors in host countries, creating corresponding moral risks. For example, China Aviation Oil's bankruptcy in Singapore caused US$550 million worth of losses for its trading in oil derivatives. Thirdly, the issue of dumping and trade subsidies has also dented the image of Chinese enterprises abroad. For example, on 18 October 2011, the US branch of the German company SolarWorld united six other producers to formally apply to the US Department of Commerce for an antidumping and countervailing investigation targeted at China's PV products. These companies claimed that Chinese PV companies illegally dumped polycrystalline-silicon photovoltaic cells on the US market and that the Chinese Government provided Chinese manufacturers with illegal subsidies, including supply-chain subsidies and setting of trade barriers. They asked the federal government to impose tariffs of more than US$1 billion on PV products from China.

As regards social moral risks, these arise due to resource consumption and environmental pollution cause by the projects along the Belt and Road countries, thus damaging the capacity of sustainable development of the host countries. For example, on 30 September 2011, Myanmar's President Thein Sein suddenly and unilaterally declared that during his tenure, he would suspend the Myitsone Hydropower Plant Project, which was a joint venture with investment from the Burmese Ministry of Electric Power, the Chinese State Power Investment Corporation, and the Burmese Asia World Group. This action was taken out of concern that the project may affect the local ecological balance and undermine the local environment. Another example is China–Myanmar Letpadaung Copper Mine Project that invited the fury of the locals owing to the low compensation the displaced workers had received. Secondly, these risks may also arise due to cultural differences. Other risks may include insensitivity to local cultural traditions and customs, thus inviting the wrath of the local populace.

5.3 Moral Risks at the Individual Level

With the development of the Chinese economy, the number of China's outbound tourists is growing. As individuals travelling beyond the Chinese borders, these tourists have become important ambassadors of China. And China's tourism policy also identifies enhancing tourism cooperation and expanding the scale of tourism as an important task, with a view to promoting understanding between peoples. At the same time, Chinese citizens touring other countries should project a positive image; builders of the Belt and road abroad should respect the local customs and traditions and work in the right way. Three distinct entities could illustrate the moral risks at the individual level.

The business entities, out of their pursuit of self-interests, may distort national policies and make the Belt and Road a tool for raking in profits. Such acts in violation of laws can leave an enormous impact on the Belt and Road construction, and China's image as a nation will be damaged. Secondly, a great number of business people who do not have much business experience will hope to take the chance to come and look for opportunities in China, or trade with China in their own countries. However, these people might not speak the language or have very little knowledge of China, which can very easily cause misunderstandings and tarnish China's image. Therefore, China should pay more attention to foreigners operating in China. Efforts should be made to offer them more help as they go through formalities, apply for loans, and carry out marketing work, so as to improve China's image while doing business with foreigners. Thirdly, studying in China has become one of the important ways for ordinary people to know more about the country. For now, foreign students from countries along the Belt and Road are, more often than not, students from well-off families, or those funded by both governments. However, despite their important role as ambassadors of Chinese culture, often, they are unable to integrate fully with the people or the culture, hence failing to truly understanding the Chinese culture; also, at times, some already have preset impressions about China and are influenced by the "China threat" rhetoric. In response, China has noted in its official documents that it will expand the scale of student exchanges with major countries around the world, carry out joint education, and 10,000 government scholarships will be offered by China to countries along the Belt and Road on an annual basis. This move, as an effort and attempt to enhance understanding between peoples, reflects the importance China attaches to young talent. At the same time, foreign students should not be limited to those studying in universities and colleges, and their coverage should be expanded. For instance, we should introduce foreign workers and farmers to learn techniques in China. Once the exchanges between ordinary workers of two countries are enhanced, understanding between peoples can be greatly promoted, and so can the development of countries along the Belt and Road.

Efforts should be made in the following two aspects to cope with the moral risks on the individual level.

First, overseas Chinese in regions along the routes should play a positive role, and the Confucius Institutes should promote understanding between individuals. The positive role of overseas Chinese should never be underestimated. And, though not intended for the Belt and Road, Confucius Institutes have virtually laid the foundation for understanding between peoples of countries along the routes. In the new era, Confucius Institutes and the Belt and Road can work together and complement each other. Confucius Institutes are a reflection of the revival of the Chinese civilization in the modern era, bringing insight into the charms of the culture. The BRI stresses the philosophy of wide consultation, joint contribution, and shared benefits, which are in line with that of the Confucius Institutes. Efforts to carry forward the Silk Road spirit of peace, cooperation, openness, inclusiveness, mutual learning, mutual benefits, and win-win results will also inject a new driving force for the future development of the Confucius Institutes, facilitate mutual understanding on the individual level, and avoid the moral problems of individuals to some extent.

Second, the moral risks of the Belt and Road originate from China itself. It is therefore necessary for us to pay closer attention to the communication with our own people during the Belt and Road construction, open even wider to the outside world, promote domestic reform, deepen the understanding toward China by neighboring countries and those along the routes, enhance understanding between peoples with great sincerity, and deal with the moral risks emerging in the construction process with a responsible attitude. As noted in the official documents of China, efforts should be made to inherit and carry forward the friendly and cooperative spirit of the Silk Road and carry out extensive cultural, academic and personnel exchanges and cooperation, media cooperation, and exchanges of young people and females, as well as volunteer services, so as to lay a solid foundation of public opinion for the in-depth bilateral cooperation, and, through these measures, dissolve moral risks in a step-by-step manner, thus achieving real understanding between peoples.

6 Conclusion

It can be discerned that the five factors of connectivity enshrined in the BRI have their corresponding risks. The grandiose initiative undoubtedly will face a multitude of risks. The political risks will threaten policy communication and may impinge on the bilateral as well as multilateral engagement of China in some cases. Infrastructure connectivity needs to respond to varied security risks; unimpeded trade and monetary circulation are full of economic risks; and without an understating between peoples, the Belt and Road initiative will be trapped in moral risks.

China needs to be extremely careful while executing the BRI. It should accommodate the existing local cooperation frameworks on the one hand and be accommodating to actors outside the region, be it the US, Russia, Europe, or Japan. Financial and security risks cannot be all on the Chinese side; rather, these need to be shared collectively by the participating countries. The BRI should not be seen as a grand strategy of China, rather it is an initiative based on principles of openness, inclusiveness, and transparency.

References

Chen, Chen, and Yang Shasha. 2015. Sri Lanka Suspended Chinese-funded Port City Program: Transitional Governments Often Express Contradictions. *Global Times*, March 6, 2015.

Dong, Manyuan. 2014. The Influence and Prospects of the Islamic State's Rise. *International Studies* 5.

Huang, Ao. 2014. Belt and Road: China Takes the Initiative to Reshape the Political and Economic Landscape of Asia. *Dongfang Daily*, May 19, 2014.

SIF. 2015. *Studies of International Finance*, vol. 1, 5.

Tocqueville, Alexis de. 1996. *Democracy in America*, vol. 1. The Commercial Press, 181.

Wei, Jianing. 2015. *Watch Out for the Potential Risks of the Belt and Road Initiative*. 21st Century Economic Report, March 11, 2015.

WESP. 2015. *World Economic Situation and Prospects 2015*, the United Nations.

Chapter 18
Emerging International Order and China's Role

Honggang Wang

Many scholars around the world have studied how our international order evolved. This scholarship is also important for informing China on strategy. This paper attempts to answer the questions: How has our current international order become what it is today? And, how should we better understand the transition it is undergoing? It takes a long-term historical perspective and views the international order as a constantly changing organism. It also stresses the anatomy of key issues in the current international order, predicts where it is going, and discusses what role China should take in this process. How should China's own modernization play a part in the modernization of the international order?

1 Theoretical Framework

The international order describes how countries relate to each other at the global level and is a product of each nation's development. Starting with the Renaissance, and then especially with the Enlightenment, scholars and statesmen in Europe began to formulate concepts and rules to govern nations and their relations. Over the ages, even though the world experienced dramatic changes, these concepts and rules endured and complemented each other. Together they laid the foundation for today's international order. Generally speaking, the following principles were accepted in building an international order.

Honggang Wang is a research professor and executive director of the Institute of World Politics, CICIR. He specializes in the global strategic situation, China-US relations, and peripheral security issues.

H. Wang (✉)
Institute of World Politics, CICIR, Beijing, China
e-mail: wanghonggang@cicir.ac.cn

B.R. Deepak (ed.), *China's Global Rebalancing and the New Silk Road*,
https://doi.org/10.1007/978-981-10-5972-8_18

1.1 The Concept of Sovereign Equality

In the sixteenth century, French scholar Jean Bodin came up with the concept of national sovereignty as a way to enhance the position of the King and to prevent religious disputes and keep the peace. Later, Thomas Hobbes posited a "state of nature" leading to a "war of all against all". In such a state, the people form a social contract in establishing a society—and all individuals in that society cede some of their rights in exchange for the protection of a sovereign authority (the king in those times). These ideas supported the necessity of sovereignty (Kissinger 2015: 27).[1] The German philosopher Christian Wolff argued that sovereign states must respect the independence of, and equality among, nations and the primary rights and obligations of a nation stemmed from international agreements and their role as members of an international society. A priori, the transcendental nature of sovereignty is equality that, together with the right to self-determination, are inalienable (Chen 2013: 18–19).[2] Influenced by this, Swiss philosopher Emer de Vattel said sovereign states are equal and have the right to self-determination, which means that no foreign power could dominate any part of any other nation. No state shall interfere with the body politic of any other state (Chen 2013: 20).[3] In his *Perpetual Peace*, Immanuel Kant wrote that: "No state shall by force interfere with the constitution or government of another state (Kant 2006: 9)".[4] These epoch-making propositions on the independence and equality of all states are at the heart of today's international order.

---

[1]This is the main idea Thomas Hobbes pursues in *Leviathan* published in 1651. This paper uses translations from Henry Kissinger, *World Order*, trans. Hu Liping, Lin Hua and Cao Aiju, Beijing: China CITIC Press, 2015, p. 27.

[2]Wolff, Christian, *The Law of Nations Treated according to the Scientific Method* (1749). This paper uses translations found in Chen Yifeng, *Lundangdaiguojifashang de bugansheyuanze* [Principle of Non-Intervention in International Law] (Beijing: Peking University Press, 2013), pp. 18–19.

[3]Vattel, Emer De, *The Law of Nations or the Principles of Natural Law* (1758). This paper uses translations found in Chen (2013).

[4]Immanuel Kant described the steps that should be taken immediately, or with all deliberate speed, in *Perpetual Peace* published in 1758. Please see Immanuel Kant, *Perpetual* Peace (Trans.) He Zhaowu, Shanghai: Shanghai People's Press.

1.2 *The Primacy of National Interests*

If sovereign equality was the prerequisite for states to establish formal relations, then the primacy of national interests is the rule that governs foreign relations. Hobbes believed that the national interests of one state by nature ran counter to that of another state, and each state had the right to pursue its own national interests (Bull 2015: 25). Armand Jean du Plessis de Richelieu, the French Chief Minister from 1624 to 1642, was even more explicit. He said that a country does not act on the king's personality, family interests, or the desire to spread a religion but rather on its national interests (Kissinger 2015: 16). These ideas had a great influence on Europe, the "Paris Paradigm" was contagious, and it spread to newly emerging nations across the continent (Cormona 1994: 819). In the nineteenth century, British politician Lord Palmerstone once said: "We have no eternal allies, and we have no perpetual enemies. Our interests are eternal and perpetual." (Kissinger 2015: 25) When it comes to competition, nations usually form alliances, and, in the extreme case, resort to warfare. Some people view this as just causing chaos, but others see it as a way to drive the international order forward when it serves the objective of striking a balance among nations.

1.3 *The Rule of International Law*

Anarchy leads to nations craving security, and this leads to competition, but also inevitably it gave birth to the rule of international law. International law is a basic code of conduct for all states; it governs how they relate to each other and it acts to neutralize the extreme pursuit of self-interests by providing stability and predictability (Hsiung 2001: 243–245). Hugo Grotius laid the foundations of international law. In his *De Mari Libero* (Freedom of the Sea), he argued that the dispute between the Netherlands and Portugal over navigation rights should be settled with laws known to all. That is, everyone enjoys the right of free navigation in accordance with international law. He argued that international law came from God, and thus it became one of the key foundations for building an international order (Zhang 2010: 109–116). The emergence of international organizations embodied the precedence of international law and helped to sustain international cooperation and order. According to the same thinking, British scholar Bayless suggested European states meet annually to discuss laws to maintain international peace. In 1717, French priest St-Pierre said an eternal alliance should be set up which should enforce international law. German philosopher Immanuel Kant said nations should give up their militaries and instead create a loose alliance to protect human rights and enforce international law. British philosopher Jeremy Bentham agreed, arguing for disarmament, freeing colonies, establishing an international Court of Justice, and creating a collective legislature for European states. Despite the utopianism of these ideas, they have had a significant impact by helping to establish a number of international organizations (Rao et al. 2013: 43–44).

1.4 Great Power Leadership

Great powers are those countries with the most military and economic strength, so that they tend to have a stronger voice in the international arena and wield the most global influence. Of course, the equality of nations doesn't mean that every nation has equal influence. Irrespective of whether a great power is active or passive, smaller countries tend to follow. This could be viewed as controversial, yet it has been the de facto situation as we undergo a transition in the international order. The behavior of these great powers has a huge impact on whether we enjoy international peace. That is why great power relations are seen as the basic architecture of a complex world (Bull 2015: 174). Of course, great powers are not unscrupulous enough to do whatever they please; they assume a special obligation to be the guardian of international peace. They satisfy their national interests often through the use of reform or transformations in the order, usually in a prudent manner (Bull 2015: 191).

1.5 Respect for Human Rights

The rudimentary concept of popular sovereignty or sovereignty of the people began in ancient Greece. It was explicitly or implicitly evident in the Draconian Constitution of the early sixth Century BC, in the Reforms of Solon. The Reforms of Pericles underlay the idea that civil rights and the people's will must be respected, that is, the idea of popular sovereignty or sovereignty of the people. After the Middle Ages, as the modern nation state developed, the idea that human rights should be respected grew more popular, and it became a part the definition of international order. John Locke maintained that the state is based on a social contract, and thus sovereignty belongs to the people. He also advocated the separation of powers into legislative, executive, and federative. The legislative right should be given to Parliament, members of which were the deputies of the people. The people had the right to dissolve Parliament and overthrow the rule of a tyrant by force (Wang 1998: 201–202). Rousseau argued that the sovereignty of a state was built on the basis of a social contract that belonged to the people, and the people's will is the soul of a nation (Yang 2006: 18). The ideas behind respecting the human rights and sovereignty of people were later further developed. There are individual rights, which stand opposite to the national authority, and also the right of national self-determination, which put the nation beyond the control of any foreign power. In practical use, they are used to support people overthrowing a dictator and fighting for freedom, as well as independence movements against a colonizing power such as in Asia, Africa, and Latin America. They safeguard the right of survival and the right to develop.

Scholars have argued that these five principles contradict each other. For example, sovereignty conflicts with human rights, the equality of nations, great powers, the primacy of national interests, and international law. Others have argued that international law and human rights are unnecessary or just wishful thinking. History shows us that nations have met setbacks in holding on to these principles. However, despite such conflicts, the principles have survived. Although, some of them appear idealistic and are often abused, they are aimed at preserving peace, prosperity, and the common development of the world—surely a goal of everyone on this planet. They are aligned with the fundamental interests of all mankind and must be respected even during a transition of the international order. This contradictory relationship over the long-term keeps this organic process of transition alive.

2 Shaping and Reshaping of the International Order

It took several hundred years for Europe and the rest of the world to unshackle itself from religion, feudalism, and foreign control, and to become independent sovereign states. Generally, they evolved into what we recognize today as modern countries, and this has made the new transnational order possible. This was also the time during which concepts and rules about international order were solidified and made mainstream. The power of individual states has waxed and waned over the centuries, locked in competition and cooperation and sometimes even endless warfare. But these rules and concepts did not fundamentally change, and they have held up the international order.

Today's international order began properly with the Westphalian system. After a series of upheavals, a new system of state governance was established (Gaillard et al. 2000: 285), which laid the foundations for the modern nation state. The Thirty Years' War raged in Europe and acted as an external factor in consuming belligerent states and forcing leaders to pursue peaceful and rational means to conduct relations with each other. The signing of the Treaty of Westphalia set out a series of key norms to guide international relations. It confirmed the sovereignty of all the vassal states of Germany, the Netherlands, Switzerland, and others. Following this, sovereign states began to spring up all over Europe, symbolizing the emergence of the new international relationship, a precursor to the modern international order. It gave legal legitimacy to the idea of national sovereignty that began in the Renaissance, smashing the arrogance of Rome's ideology of world sovereignty (Fu et al. 2009: 53). The Treaty of Westphalia ruled that a state enjoyed supreme authority over its territory, made sovereign states the key players in the international order, stated that all states were equal, at least nominally, and were free to pursue their own interests. This allowed states to compete with each other in an orderly manner with checks and balances, embodying the cardinal principles of sovereign equality, the primacy of national interests, and the rule of international law.

Sovereignty has proved a powerful concept. The framework of the international order shaped by the Treaty of Westphalia paved the way for more sovereign states to appear, which in turn supported the international order. New states emerged after each major war. We even saw this as a result of the Cold War. The framework also managed relations among European countries, and most countries around the world have signed on to this framework. US statesman Henry Kissinger once said that although European countries did not extend the concept of sovereignty to their colonies, the people in their colonies used it to pursue independence (Kissinger 2015: 14–15). The cardinal principles that emerged out of the Treaty of Westphalia, and are described here, were invaluable tools for the people in these colonies to fight for their independence. After WWII, national liberation movements in Asia, Africa, and Latin America broke out, heralding a spectacular expansion of the international order.

The primacy of national interests has taken a leading role in shaping the modern international order. Even before the Thirty Years' War, the goals of European rulers were often the prosperity and progress of their "countries", and they pursued this through enhancing their military, expanding their colonies, forming alliances, or adopting a belligerent stance. In the Thirty Years' War, almost all European "countries" sought to expand their territory (Fu et al. 2009: 44). As the idea of building the nation state spread, the pursuit of national interests became dominant and the key factor determining national policy. Over the next few hundred years, competition between nations and between the US and Europe to scramble for colonies, enhance their overseas interests, build regional hegemonies, and control strategic ocean and land routes did not dissipate. War helped the construction of the international order across the globe, driven by national interests. War also built powers up and destroyed others such as WWI, WWII, and even the Cold War. Competition of this kind helps build national identity and governance, and drove the growth of sovereign states. Meanwhile, as many Asian, African and Latin American countries won their independence, we saw an increase in the number of non-Western countries participating in global competition, also pursuing their own national interests, safeguarding their own rights, and growing their own influence. Although, international competition is often accompanied by brutal conflict and war, it is an enduring feature of an international-order transition that drives the modernization of sovereign states.

The Vienna System established the idea of great powers leading the order. In the post-Napoleon era, no European country was keen to wage war for material gain, rather they wanted to establish a balance between nations. The stronger countries—the UK, Russia, Prussia, and Austria—developed this idea and set up a system of joint governance that was set out in the Final Protocol at the Congress of Vienna in 1815. Proposed by Klemens Wenzel von Metternich, the then Austrian Empire's Foreign Minister, the mechanism of leadership by great powers was a dispute-settlement system. To protect this system and better manage European affairs, Russia led Prussia and Austria in signing the Treaty of Holy Alliance. Later on, other countries, except for the UK, the Vatican, and Turkey, joined this Alliance. Not long after, the UK, Prussia, Russia and Austria formed the Quadruple Alliance. Worrying that France would feel isolated and that would create trouble later on, they brought France into the Holy Alliance, turning the Concert of Four Nations into a Concert of Five Nations. Even though the Holy Alliance was split by conflict, it did succeed in building a new balance of great powers and safeguarding regional peace. Because these groupings encouraged collusion and power politics, they can be considered regressive, however they can also be considered epoch-making. With the League of Nations and then the United Nations, this idea has become ever more established and is an important guarantee and driving force of the international order.

The Rule of International Law started off quite weak, but developed rapidly through international cooperation and international-dispute settlement. The Peace Treaty of Westphalia started the practice of requiring all members to abide by its rules, and in the event of an infringement the aggrieved party could file a case or adopt regular judicial proceedings (GTJ 1994: 31–32). In effect, sovereign states were obliged to follow international law. The Treaty also introduced the diplomatic system. The Vienna System took the rule of international law a step further with founding international organizations, the key one being the Central Commission for Navigation on the Rhine (1816), the first international organization that resolved technical issues to do with interstate navigation and taxation. Later on, the Danube Commission (1856), the International Telecommunication Union (1865), the Universal Postal Union (1874), the International Institute of Agriculture (founded in Rome in 1905), the International Office of Public Health (1907), and many other international organizations were established. The Congress of Vienna developed the diplomatic service by dividing it into three levels—ambassadorial, minister plenipotentiary, and agents and their precedence subject to their Date of Arrival (Wang 1995: 3–14). An international arbitration system was also established. In 1794, the UK and the US signed the Treaty of Amity, Commerce, and Navigation, also known as Jay's Treaty, which ruled that territorial and civil disputes between the two nations and its citizens shall be resolved through arbitration (Rao 2013: 42). Later, the Permanent Court of Arbitration was set up by the Hague Convention for the peaceful settlement of international disputes in 1900. This was the first international tribunal to resolve disputes between member states, international organizations, or private parties arising from international agreements. International law was even drawn up to rule how countries could behave with each other during war. On the understanding that war is inevitable, European countries twice convened peace conferences at the Hague before WWII to create conventions and declarations that governed war-time conduct. These are now widely recognized international laws (Wang 1995: 364–366). Even during WWII, nations complied with these laws covering neutral nations and prisoners of war. During the Cold War, the US and the then USSR also abided by them (Bull 2015: 39–40).

Respect for human rights underwent a similar progression from immaturity to maturity. In the American War of Independence, emphasis was intentionally put on human rights—that is respect for individual human rights and resisting UK rule. The Declaration of Independence explicitly stated that all men are created equal; it also talked about the right to self-determination. It severed the US's ties to British Royalty. Its Bill of Rights pledged to protect the freedoms of religion, speech, and the press (Zhang 2002: 18, 43). France made its Declaration on the Rights of Man and of the Citizen in August 1789, for the first time declaring that freedom and equality would be upheld through the law. It was a further development to human rights as laid out in the US's Declaration of Independence. This encouraged nationalism and national movements in many European countries, spurring a social transformation, usurping European feudalism and paving the way for democracy and the right to self-determination to take root (Fu et al. 2009: 96). The American War of Independence and the French Revolution encouraged the colonies of France, Spain, and Portugal in Latin America to pursue independence themselves. In the early twentieth century, Lenin used the Marx's right to self-determination to call for all oppressed peoples to rid themselves of foreign domination and to create their own independent nation (CCTV 1995: 369–402). After WWI, US President Woodrow Wilson also said colonies had the right to choose their own governments. However, he failed to get this written into the Covenant of the League of Nations. Since then, the right to national self-determination has travelled far and wide.

The key events in the transition of the international order are the birth of the United Nations and the establishment of global governance. The principles we addressed earlier are enshrined in both of these events, and they continue to be shaped today. The UN has solidified the idea behind the equality of sovereign nations. In October 1943, at a preparatory meeting about the UN held in Moscow, China, the then USSR, the US, and the UK made the Declaration of the Four Nations on General Security, which recognized the need to establish an international organization (which became the UN), based on the principle of sovereign equality of all peace-loving states. It should be open to membership to all such states, large and small, for the maintenance of international peace and security (Yang 2006: 71). Proposals at the Dumbarton Oaks Conference embodied these ideas; at the San Francisco Convention, sovereign equality was made the top principle in the UN Charter, which was again stressed in the Declaration on the Inadmissibility of Intervention in the Domestic Affairs of States and the Protection of Their Independence and Sovereignty (1965) passed by the UN General Assembly, the Declaration on Principles of International Law concerning Friendly Relations and Co-operation among States in Accordance with the Charter of the United Nations (1970), the Declaration on the Establishment of a New International Economic Order (1974), and the Charter of Economic Rights and Duties of States among others.

Second, the principle of great power leadership was reflected in the founding of the UN itself. The process was led by US President Roosevelt, carried out by the US and the UK, coordinated by the US, the UK, and the USSR, and launched through the collaboration of the US, the UK, USSR, China, and France. Thus, the framework and operational mechanisms of the United Nations took shape (Zi 1995: 18–27). The UN General Assembly also embodies this principle. The UN Charter conferred the obligation to safeguard international peace on the Security Council and gave permanent seats to China, France, the USSR, the UK, and the US. To preserve its effectiveness, the holders of these five permanent seats have extra rights compared with other UN members.

Third, the UN Charter prioritizes global peace and security and tries to prevent war caused by competition based on national interests. There are two measures to achieve this: collective security and the settlement of international disputes. A series of resolutions was adopted, and a special committee was formed to clarify the conditions of the "non-use of force" (Xu 1998: 39–43). To encourage members to seek peaceful means of settling international disputes, in 1982, the UN passed the Manila Declaration on the Peaceful Settlement of International Disputes. The UN also promotes international cooperation based on common interests, creating opportunities, and establishing international mechanisms and bodies.

Fourth, it enriched the meaning of respect for human rights and created human-rights protections. The aims of the UN Charter mention respect for the principle of equal rights and self-determination of peoples. The Universal Declaration of Human Rights was passed in 1948, and, in 1950, the UN General Assembly adopted a new resolution that confirmed self-determination was a human right. This principle was written into the International Covenant on Civil and Political Rights and the International Covenant on Economic, Social, and Cultural Rights. In 1952, the UN adopted the Right of Peoples and Nations to Self-determination; the Declaration on the Granting of Independence to Colonial Countries and Peoples in 1960, and the Declaration on Principles of International Law concerning Friendly Relations and Co-operation among States in accordance with the Charter of the United Nations in 1970 (Xu 1998: 17–21). To protect the rights and interests of certain groups inside a country, the UN General Assembly adopted resolutions on women's rights and against segregation and human trafficking and set up the Commission on Human Rights and, later, the United Nations Human Rights Council to overlook the implementation of human rights in member countries (Xu 1998: 24). Under the framework of the UN, developing countries have increasingly argued that the right to development is a human-rights issue. In 1986, the UN passed the Declaration on the Right to Development. Developing countries formed the Group of 77, asked for a South-North Dialogue, and sought a South-South Cooperation. These were measures aimed at proactively fighting for their right to development and equal participation in the global economic system.

Fifth, international cooperation that has been encouraged by international law has become popular, and this has improved global governance. The UN, the International Court of Justice, and other organizations are the embodiments of the principle of the rule of international law. Driven by the UN, the concept of international law gave birth to more international treaties, more effective international organizations, and more regularized international cooperation. And together these have built a framework of global governance. There are now a great number of professional governmental and non-governmental organizations and mechanisms around the world in the fields of economics, politics, security, society, and culture. They complement the work of states by mobilizing resources, coordinating national interests, and promoting international cooperation. If cooperation in the early years of the international order following the Thirty Years' War could be characterized by a minimum level of enthusiasm derived solely from security concerns, then the levels of international cooperation and enthusiasm in the twenty first century are at an all-time high.

3 Who Will Dictate International Order?

It is possible to view our contemporary international order from an historical perspective that looks at how it has developed over the past few hundred years and uses the lens of dialectical materialism. In this way, we can view international politics as a natural and gradual unity of opposites rather than viewing regions in isolation, an approach that could be seen as bigoted. This approach stresses the efforts of all parties to contribute to the modernization of the international order over hundreds of years, including all nations into this period of human development.[5]

This approach is helpful on many counts. First, it helps to answer the question of where did the current international order come from? There is a theory that international orders have followed the pattern of colonial order, post-war order, Cold-War order, and post-Cold-War order. This definition, *sensustricto,* inevitably leads to a fragmented understanding about international orders, and it gives the impression that the development of the international order has been very volatile. There is an alternative theory that the current international order is a combination of all these stages and that they overlap with each other. But this is too general, as it does not tell us anything about their differences nor does it help to explain how they have co-existed. Our approach has laid a more logical foundation and explains the transition over the long-term in a more complete way.

Second, this perspective embraces the above-mentioned methodologies. Scholars of the international order use Hobbesian, Kantianism, and the Grotius doctrine, and while these have their merits, they cannot by themselves offer a complete explanation. Thus, China has strictly followed the theories of Marx, which emphasizes the cruelty of international competition, the nobility of human nature, and the vagaries of history. It also stresses the necessity of international law. Dialectical materialism can integrate these different parts. Its perspective on our contemporary international order complies with Chinese tradition and mainstream thinking, helps to express China's vision about the international order to the world, and also gives theoretical and moral support to China's foreign policy.

Third, it recognizes Europe's role, but it is not Eurocentric. The contemporary international order did originate from Europe and in the early years European countries had the biggest influence in shaping the international order and its subsequent transition, but it has spread across the globe, in the same way as the industrial revolution. It is no longer the exclusive possession of Europe (or the Western world). It has spread to other cultures in later times.

Fourth, it has universal applicability. Since today's international order resulted over a long period of time and is the product of nations around the world working together like an integrated organism, then the role of any individual nation is

[5]For a study on the global modernization process please see Qian Chengdan et al. (1997) *Shijiexiandaihuajincheng* (Global Modernization History), Nanjing: Nanking University Press, pp. 1–13.

important yet limited. This means that it does not support zero-sum games or the logic that one country's rise means another's fall, thus negating the possibility of a Thucydides' Trap. Particularly since the international order is well suited to promote equilibrium, it has helped to integrate developing countries into its fold. All nations—not just in Europe or the US—have worked hard to develop the international order, modernize it, and create benefits for all parties.

There are a number of crucial issues that we need to study in order to better understand disputes in the international order. There can only be one international order at any one time. If there is any discontent, rather than expressing that through violence, it would be channeled into the pursuit of modernization through cooperation with others. So, in changing the international economic or political order, there is a process, and it should not be seen as disruptive, but rather as a driver of progress. The principles, organizations, and mechanisms we have discussed are powerful instruments that can be used to modernize the international order. China upholds this perspective and considers it important. It doesn't consider this to be revisionism. It is a perspective that supports its engagement in international and UN affairs. In the future, as we become more engaged on the international stage, we will be in a stronger position to require other international players to respect the international order, its concepts, and rules.

The contemporary international order is very different from world order. Contemporary international order prioritizes sovereignty and equality of states. The prerequisites for an international order are respect for other sovereign nation's cultures and traditions, systems, governance, policy, and so on. We have an international order because nations govern themselves and the principles of international order may not be disregarded. World order, on the other hand, is about the pursuit of a global society that is not diverse. We cannot insist that all countries must follow exactly the same model in managing their domestic affairs, nor can we simply take for granted that could be achieved overnight. If a world order is to be realized, it can only happen naturally and not by force.

International order at its heart is a force for good. As part of the transition of the international order, European countries became more integrated from the starting point of war; many developing countries emerged on the global stage, with vibrant growing economies and rising influence to stem the suppression by Western countries, and to exert a greater push for peace and development; the bullying and violence of warlords have been rejected by the international community. The contemporary international order will surely exert a positive influence on mankind, promoting enduring prosperity, eternal peace, and common progress. But this will not necessarily lead to a substantial reduction in transnational rivalry. It would be too utopian to define the contemporary international order as free from war and conflict. As long as there are borders, the principle of the primacy of national interests will remain for all nations, and international competition will be an enduring element in the international order.

Lastly, no single country can control the international order. The emergence of an international order was inevitable, but it was not the creation of an individual country. Even though major powers do wield more influence and play a bigger role in leading a transition, only those that follow international law and global rules are able to gain the upper hand in transnational competition. Further, this influence is not permanently bestowed, and those who try to oppose the international order will end up paying a high price. The wheel of history protects those who work for the well-being and evolution of the whole system, pushing the international order forward. The UK, France, Germany, and the former USSR all had their heyday, taking a dominant role on the international stage, but no country lasted forever. The US played an unparalleled role in setting up the UN and was the major driver that powered the transition of the international order. It has dominated the UN and even was a world superpower at one point. However, as developing countries emerged, the US lost its advantages within the UN framework. The best example of the US's waning power was its decision to declare war after the 9/11 terrorist attacks without the backing of the UN and its push to influence democratic reform and color revolutions in other countries, thus violating their sovereignty. It has seen its own soft power and hard power shrink drastically as a result.

4 Riders to International Order

After answering where does the international order come from, we naturally turn to the question, where is the international order going? A hundred years after the Treaty of Westphalia, and with the establishment of the UN and a framework of global governance, and the acceptance of the principles mentioned above, the international order has taken today's shape, representing a major step forward for mankind. The current international order certainly needs to be improved for it to bring eternal peace, enduring prosperity, and common progress. Because the principles that are at the heart of the international order both complement and contradict each other and because of globalization and the dawn of the Information Age, the transition of the current international order has stalled. To kick start the next modernization round, there are five key challenges to be overcome.

The most obvious challenge is to find a way to effectively improve the modern governance of nations once they have obtained independence and equality. Nations in Asia, Latin America, Africa, and elsewhere now have independence and equality, if even only nominally, after hundreds of years of struggle. For the foreseeable future, sovereign states will still be the fundamental and primary unit of the international order. At the end of the Cold War, sovereignty was eroded and transferred, but this proved to be quite limited. The recent Brexit referendum and a surge in nationalism symbolizes the very strong will in the public to defend their sovereignty. But a new round of modernization of the international order must occur with a corresponding improvement in governance. Modernization is not being held back by the seemingly outdated sovereignty concept or from over-powerful nation states, but from under-development and lack of capability. Our current international order would not be possible without the existence of real sovereign states that are able to exercise their sovereignty internally and externally.

Likewise, the common modernization of all nation states is essential to maintaining the international order. Currently, European countries and the US are struggling with governance issues because economic growth is sluggish, their politics are polarized, and their societies have become unstable.[6] Emerging and developing countries in Asia, Africa, and Latin America also are struggling with poorly structured economies, problematic political systems, unhealthy social development, and other huge problems holding back their modernization. In particular, the least economically developed and the least politically stable countries face brutal terrorist attacks, illegal immigration, disease, famine, insufficient levels of primary education, and gross violations of basic human rights, among others. There is a very obvious global deficit of good governance. That is why, in this latest round of modernization, the focus has been on finding the right kind of modernization to suit the local circumstances and in that way erasing the imbalance between countries' governance capabilities.

Another equally prominent challenge is in how to better manage rivalries and expand cooperation as nations became more interdependent. The principle of the primacy of national interests is the basis for a sovereign state to survive and thrive, and has driven international order so far and will continue to drive it. Over the past several hundred years, all sovereign states have engaged in fierce competition; competition is the driving force behind the international order. History has always guided nations to pursue their own interests behind the scenes, while externally these behaviors have powered the forward direction of the international order. Competition is necessary and rational. However, as human society has entered into an age when everyone must take responsibility for global governance and global issues that threaten all of mankind become more numerous, these issues cannot be tackled if any one nation focuses too much on its national interests. Clearly, less competition would help solve these issues, where everyone respects common interests and learns to cooperate. Nations must be aware of overflow and backwash effects, become more self-controlled, better manage competition, and improve cooperation by making it more active and strategic. How well countries do on these accounts will act as an important benchmark in evaluating this new round of modernization.

Another challenge is preventing strategic conflict. Competition between major powers is not exceptional; it is a permanent feature of a transition in the international order. However, if not handled properly, cooperation and conflict can drag the world into war. Fortunately, each new order established after the end of a major war was an improvement, which has helped to propel the international order forward (Ikenberry 2008). Many scholars saw the competition between the US and the

[6]"*Conundrum of modern countries governance*" and its discussion please see Honggang Wang, "American Disease of the twenty first Century: Basic analysis on conundrum of modern countries governance of America," *Xiandaiguojiguanxi* (Contemporary International Relations), No. 7 (2015): pp. 1–9; Honggang Wang, "Conundrum of Modern Countries Governance in Modern Western Countries," *Xiandaiguojiguanxi* (Contemporary International Relations), No. 8 (2016): pp. 3–5.

USSR during the Cold War, as opposed to a hot war, as a positive driver. However, in the two decades following the end of the Cold War, hostilities and frictions between major powers have risen because of changes to national strengths, strategic expectations, and adjusted deployments. Their stances on key issues have diverged, and there is mounting anxiety stemming from internal adversity and external changes following the global financial crisis. Change generates opportunities and deep unease, causing countries to sometimes take defensive actions, which are then seen as aggressive and the situation may descend into a security dilemma. This is illustrated by tensions experienced currently between the US and Russia, China and the US, and China and Japan. Any individual country can ramp security dilemmas up, but, where communication mechanisms are in place, these tensions seem manageable. But if internal issues are not resolved, then hostilities will rise. If risk-management mechanisms lose their effectiveness, conflict between major powers could erupt. People today have never been so interconnected and interdependent, but nations also have the power to completely destroy the planet, so world peace is extremely fragile. A global war would destroy all peace and prosperity. The international order cannot be modernized through war. Rather it can only be achieved if nations improve their strategic coordination to prevent a major-powers conflict.

Another challenge will be to improve the rule of international law and the effectiveness of international mechanisms. In an anarchical world with no international government, modernizing the international order should be aimed at helping to govern trans-border issues, and make international governance more effective. This requires improvement in the rule of international law and international mechanisms. Indeed, decades of efforts by many countries has improved the rule of international law, with specific frameworks and processes established to address individual issues. Countries must now focus on the details, put theory into practice, and create tangible instruments. So far, most international treaties are still vague rules with very general stipulations, others are intentionally ambiguous on key issues, which makes them ill-suited to restraining countries. By focusing on the details and clarifying ambiguities, this will improve the effectiveness of international treaties. There are a great number of international treaties and documents, and many of them are not working because of this reason. In putting theory into practice, I refer to improving the implementation of international treaties and obligations. Transforming institutions into tangible instruments requires making international laws and treaties into strictly enforceable instruments, and taking action against those who violate them (He 2013: 238–78), particularly major powers who often regard themselves as above the law. We should set up a system to punish those who blatantly violate international law. We should encourage wider participation, complete coordination and full discussion, and common consent to achieve the above and avoid the phenomenon of having just a small number of countries dominating decisions. We should also establish systems of mutual monitoring to foster common understanding and to gradually push forward progress in such organizations, including the UN, as well as establishing and strengthening other auxiliary and governing organizations and mechanisms.

The final challenge is in ensuring the right to development for all nations, safeguarding the momentum of international development, and finding solutions to solve common global issues. The right to development is founded on material resources and is also a powerful engine of the international order transition. The right to development is also considered a key human right and foundation of human progress. Without development, the modernization of a sovereign state would not be possible, and, if sovereign states cannot modernize, then neither can the international order. A key challenge today for the modernization of the international order is assisting all countries to develop. There are a number of very underdeveloped countries whose problems have crossed borders to hamper the development and security of other countries. Many countries also suffer from a poor development model and are under motivated to develop. In particular, they have not shared wealth equitably. This impacts their development, common development, and the quality of development. Other obstacles to development are global problems including climate change, environmental degradation, cyber threats, financial-system weaknesses, and the widening wealth gap (Goldin 2013: 10–46). Development has been a global focus since the end of the Cold War. In 2000, the UN published its *Millennium Development Goals* to address hunger and poverty, and it proved to be effective. In 2015, the UN published *Transforming Our World: The 2030 Agenda for Sustainable Development*, with the objectives of eradicating extreme poverty and safeguarding the right to development and the common development of all nations.[7] Development issues are at the root of the well-being of mankind, and thus they are the backbone of modernizing the international order.

5 China's Opportunity to Shape the International Order

These five challenges have lingered, impeding progress on the transition of the international order. Currently, most nations are struggling to cope with their domestic affairs and challenges, before they can focus on reaching a consensus on the big global issues, something that requires joint action. If nations could get together to face these challenges as one, a new round of modernization of the international order would lift mankind to a higher dimension. There is an urgent need for a new power who will dare to take on these challenges, share its knowledge and experience in addressing governance issues, and play a pioneering role in bringing peace, cooperation and benefits to all. What is needed is an overall perspective on how to bring countries in conflict to see their mutual interests, for this new power to provide for the public good in terms of ideas, platforms, and tangible materials to bring common development to all.

[7]United Nations, *Transforming the World: The 2030 Agenda for Sustainable Development*, accessed October 20, 2016, https://sustainabledevelopment.un.org/content/documents/21252030%20Agenda%20for%20Sustainable%20Development%20web.pdf.

There are few countries that fit this bill; but people are increasingly looking to China to take on this role. European countries are too preoccupied with their own flagging economies, social instabilities, and fractured public opinion. European nations will follow instead of taking the lead in the future; it will be hard to recapture their glory years of the eighteenth and nineteenth centuries. The US is in a relatively better position; it is a strong major power, and it had played a key role in shaping today's international order. However, the polarization in domestic politics and rising nationalism are diverting its power inwards. Some argue it now plays a negative role in the international order. Russia is still recovering from the dissolution of the Soviet Union and suffers from an underdeveloped economic structure, fragile political system, and geopolitical problems, thus weakening its ability to rise to be a middle power. If military power is not backed up by a strong economy, then it cannot exert much influence. Japan is shouldering a heavy historical burden and a stagnant economy and is overly dependent on its alliance with the US, so it is far from being qualified to lead the international-order transition. Brazil and South Africa are not strong enough—they are regional powers, not global powers. While India does show potential and is growing rapidly, it does yet have the capability. The part it will play in shaping the international order will in the end depend on its vision. Today, only China is widely recognized as a dynamic element and an important part of the system. This is not just wishful thinking. Over the past decade or so, China's rise has been a topic discussed everywhere, and ideas have proliferated about how the world can benefit from this development. When global issues surface, everyone is watching how China responds. Whether we are talking about criticisms or requests, every global issue is connected to China, a reflection of its special weight today.

It is no accident that China is now seen in this light. After the Opium War, China was thrown into the formidable whirl of an international-order transition because of colonization. This started an independence movement. Stepping through the delicate period of the Cold War and boldly launching its reform and opening-up, China transformed itself into the most noticeable developing country from an impoverished Third-World nation. China is a success story (Hsü 2008), an example of the inclusiveness of the international order, and a good example for other developing countries to learn from. China's strengths and influence have attracted wide attention, and its GDP is now only second to that of the US. China is now the world's biggest engine of economic growth, and it's expected to contribute 39% to global economic growth this year (Roch 2016). As one of the five permanent members of the UN Security Council, China plays a significant role in global affairs. China's every move is also felt by its neighbors. Since the Asia–Pacific is now the strategic focus worldwide, China's geopolitical advantage of being at its center is amplified. And many believe China hides much more untapped potential. While China is still a developing country, others see it as a "superpower" (or at least a quasi-superpower). When China makes further improvements to its political system and governance, upgrades the economy, adjusts the economic structure and taps domestic demand, its potential will be further unleashed, and it will become an even better role model. Importantly, China is diverse—a combination of its time-honored culture and its status as an emerging country, a developing country with developed regions, an example of Eastern culture and a nation that embraces cultures of the globe, and a socialist country with a market economy. Such diversity means that all nations can find a piece of themselves in China. This is why China is now facing a responsibility to shoulder the push for a transition of the international order. It is quite possible that China will play the part that European countries did in the eighteenth and nineteenth centuries and the US did in the twentieth century in leading the international order. It will lead improvements in the national governance of all states, coordinate divisive interests, prevent major power conflicts, promote the rule of international law, and push the common development of all nations, becoming the backbone of this new round of modernization in the twenty first century.

This is an historical opportunity for China. China's key objective is the great rejuvenation of the Chinese nation for which the country must modernize its governance. To achieve a great rejuvenation, China must change how it deals with the rest of the world, and it must face up to greater uncertainty in doing so. China must establish a permanent mechanism to achieve domestic stability and to adapt and change with the adaptation and changes of the international order. This will require China to use its power as the two of them modernize in step and mutually drive each other. China has enjoyed a strategic window in the past few decades, a time that has been largely peaceful and stable, with good development momentum and improvements in the rule of international law. In decades to come, that could change and there may well be more strategic resources and better strategic space ahead.

Does this all mean that China can do whatever it wants? Of course not, and there are at least three reasons why it can't. First, the US is playing an important role in the established international order and also has enormous vested interests in it. It finds it difficult to stop thinking in terms of a zero-sum game. The US will not want China to lead globally because it fears China will use its position against the US. So, while the US recognizes China's rise and says it expects China to be a more responsible global player, it also spreads the idea that China is a threat and that it is inevitable there will be a conflict between the rising power and the hegemonic power. It also acts to keep contain China. So, China is patient and careful when it deals with the West. Secondly, many non-Western countries are now thriving in the international order. They have given China a warm welcome to play a more proactive role, and expect China to share the benefits of development with them. However, some are looking for China to become powerful enough to balance the West, and in that way, they can take advantage of the situation. They also worry that China is a neo-colonialist and that they will become too reliant on China just after they have liberated themselves from the old colonizers of the West. China must respect these countries and be careful of appearing arrogant. Thirdly, the external environment is changing. As sovereign states become aware of equality and the need to act now, it is inevitable that power will be distributed among a greater number of stakeholders. If we can label the past several hundred years as hierarchical, this new round of modernization in the international order is likely to be characterized by more equality and less chances for superpower status. Global leaders will still exist, but they cannot have any privileges. A subtle checking mechanism will emerge to balance strategic motives against the development momentum. All players, including China, will need to respect this when operating on the international stage.

The Way Forward

Today's international order has been developing for several hundred years, and China is keenly aware of the historical opportunity that now faces it. China must clarify its vision and work towards a win-win result of common development. This paper would like to offer some thoughts on the way forward.

First, China should use its position to tell its own story and shape domestic and international opinion. China's story is one that describes the country's current reality and also expresses its vision and ideas. It is a story with a domestic and international audience. A modern outlook should emphasize logic and dialecticism; we can call it a Marxist outlook, and it places China correctly in its historical and future paths. This will prevent any disparity between what is said domestically and globally and stays true to the real China. Our story is one that will provoke thought. We must have a clear mind when dealing with the world, guide the public into properly understanding the international situation and global issues to curb any extremism, and encourage a progressive outlook. In this way, China can also find its correct global role, reach a consensus in how to modernize the country and how to modernize the international order, how to boost morale, and how to unify China's international presence. We should promote our modern outlook to assuage global anxiety and lead elites and the public into taking a long-term and progressive view of global development. We must work to combine the efforts of all nations to play a part in the modernization of the international order and to change the idea that it should only be dominated by a small number of countries. We should encourage them to see they also must play a part and that they should also feel confident and find value in this.

Second, China must establish a strong architecture to support its responsibilities in the twenty first century upon which it can develop larger national interests. The call for China to take a more responsible global role has grown louder. We can use this momentum. China should match its national interests with the needs of the international-order transition by clarifying the right responsibilities and rejecting unreasonable demands. This will put us in a fairer position in which to assume obligations, to play our part as a major power, and to shape a more favorable international environment. China must work more closely with other nations on governance, sharing best practices, improving coordination on national micro policies, and jointly seeking common development, especially in helping latecomers stand firm against foreign intervention and preventing color revolutions and social upheaval. China should also break the West's monopoly of international influence, reject the argument that political rights are the same as human rights, and say no to the double standards on human rights. So, China should promote the right to survival and the right to development, protect latecomers' values on human rights, and promote development under the framework of *Transforming Our World: The 2030 Agenda for Sustainable Development.* China must defend and promote the rule of international law and regulations and prevent powerful countries from trying to avoid complying and push for wide participation, equal negotiations, and discussions to support the rule of international law and global governance. China must safeguard the five permanent seats of the UN Security Council. It also must offer a set of values that offer heritage, inclusiveness, and progress towards global modernization and support for co-existence in the twenty first century.

China must also become sophisticated, mature, and bold and bridge gaps between nations. We must be resolute and plan ahead for the one-hundred-year anniversary of Opening Up and Reform. We must also face up to possible adversity. The country needs to have a better understanding of itself; recognize its responsibilities; get rid of our victim mentality; defend our rights and interests; and handle our foreign relations well. We must present an image of China that is humble, austere, composed, prudent, and down-to-earth. This requires the Chinese Communist Party to remain modest, prudent, humble, and steadfast both at home and abroad. That means that although China may well become a global leader, it should be careful in describing its role as "leading the world" or viewing itself as a "world leader". China should be a link between the past and the present; it should balance the East and the West, the South and the North, while holding on to its own identity and character and in this way build global consensus. China should improve its consultative democracy, connect cultures, development paths, governance strategies, and regulations with other nations in the name of common development. Gradually, we can promote the transition of the international order. We can also hold on to our traditional values in order to achieve the great rejuvenation of the nation.

Last, we should make full preparations domestically. That means the country should improve systems and foster talents. From our export-oriented economy, we need to make our social and political systems more transparent and ordered, collect ideas from everyone, engage in global governance, and become passionate about leading the international community. We should become better at telling the world about our ideas, telling the world China's story, and working with people and the media. We should foster and retain talent—people who have strong theoretical backgrounds, political sense, professional skills, and global vision to help China on the world stage. This new round of modernization must deal with ups and downs and conflict. China should plan well to better manage the international order and prevent it from regressing.

References

Bull, Hedley. 2015. *The Anarchical Society: A Study of Order in World Politics.* Translated by Zhang Xiaoming. Shanghai: Shanghai People's Press.

Carmona, Michel. 1994. *Biography of Cardinal Richelieu (II).* Translated by Cao Songhao. Beijing: The Commercial Press.

CCTV. 1995. Central Compilation and Translation Bureau. *Lenin Selected Works*, vol. 2. Beijing: People's Press.

Chen, Yifeng. 2013. *Lundangdaiguojifashang de bugansheyuanze* (Principle of Non-Intervention in International Law). Beijing: Peking University Press.

Fu, Guangcun, Yu. Guihua, and Ma. Fenggang. 2009. *Jinxiandaiguojiguanxishilun gang (Essentials of Modern History of International Relations)*. Beijing: Social Sciences Academic Press.

Gaillard, Deniz, Bernadette Deschamps, J. Aldebert. 2000. *The History of Europe*. Translated by CaiHongbin, Guiyufang et al. Hainan: Hainan Press.

Goldin, Ian. 2013. *Divided Nations: Why Global Governance Is Failing, and What We Can Do about It* Oxford. Oxford University Press.

GTJ. 1994. *Guojitiaoyueji* (International Treaties: 1648–1871). Beijing: World Affairs Press.

He, Zhipeng. 2013. *Guojifazhexuedaolun* (Fundamentals on the Philosophy of International Law). Beijing: Social Sciences Academic Press.

Hsiung, James. C. 2001. *Anarchy and Order*. Translated by Yu Xunda and Zhang Tiejun. Hangzhou: Zhejiang People's Press.

Hsü, Immanuel Chung-Yueh. 2008. *Modern History of China: 1600–2000: The Rise of Modern China*. Translated by Ji Qiufeng et al., 6th ed. Beijing: World Publishing Corporation.

Ikenberry, G. John. 2008. *After Victory: Institutions, Strategic Restraint, and the Rebuilding of Order after Major Wars*. Translated by Men Honghua. Beijing: Peking University Press.

Kant, Immanuel. 2006. *Perpetual Peace*. Translated by He Zhaowu. Shanghai: Shanghai People's Press.

Kissinger, Henry. 2015. *World Order*, 27. Translated by Hu Liping, Lin Hua and Cao Aiju. Beijing: China CITIC Press.

Rao, Geping et al. 2013. *Guojizuzhiyuguojifashishijizhi de fazhan* (International Organizations and Implementation Mechanism of International Law), Beijing: Peking University Press.

Roach, Stephen S. 2016. *Global Growth–Still Made in China*, August 29, 2016. Accessed on October 20, 2016. https://www.project-syndicate.org/commentary/china-still-global-growth-engine-by-stephen-s–roach-2016-08.

Wang, Shengzu ed. 1995. *Guojiguanxishi* (History of International Relations), vol. 2. World Affairs Press.

Wang, Zhe. 1998. *Xifangzhengzhifalvxueshuoshi* (History of Western Politics and Law Theories). Beijing: Peking University Press.

Xu, Guangjian (ed.) 1998. *Lianheguoxianzhangquanshi* (Interpretations on 'UN Charter'). Taiyuan: Shanxi Education Press.

Yang, Zewei, 2006. *Zhuquanlun: guojifashang de zhuquanwentijiqifazhanqushiyanjiu* (On Sovereignty: Sovereignty and Its Development Tendency in International Law), 16. Beijing: Peking University Press, 2006.

Zhang, Naigen. 2010. Lunguojifazaiguojizhixuzhong de zuoyong (The Role of International Law in International Order). *Northern Legal Science* 3, 109–116.

Zhang, Youlun (ed.). 2002. *Meiguo tong shi* (A history of the United States of America). Beijing: People's Press.

Zi, Zhongjun. 1995. Daguobaozhengheping de yuanzeyudaxiaoguojiapingdeng de xinnian—lunlianheguo de chushishexiang (Principles of Great powers to keep peace and belief of equality of all states—Initial assumption of the founding of the United Nations). *Pacific Journal* 2.

Index

B.R. Deepak (ed.), *China's Global Rebalancing and the New Silk Road*,
https://doi.org/10.1007/978-981-10-5972-8

MIX
Papier | Fördert gute Waldnutzung
FSC® C083411

Kolibri 360 GmbH
Ferdinand-Jühlke-Straße 7
99095 Erfurt, Deutschland
produktsicherheit@kolibri360.de